SEX/GENDER OUTSIDERS, HATE SPEECH, AND FREEDOM OF EXPRESSION

Can They Say That About Me?

Martha T. Zingo

PRAEGER

Westport, Connecticut
London

Library of Congress Cataloging-in-Publication Data

Zingo, Martha T.
    Sex/gender outsiders, hate speech, and freedom of expression : can
they say that about me? / Martha T. Zingo.
        p.   cm.
    Includes bibliographical references and index.
    ISBN 0–275–95249–5 (alk. paper)
    1. Freedom of speech—United States.   2. Hate speech—United
States.   3. Gays—Legal status, laws, etc.—United States.
4. Lesbians—Legal status, laws, etc.—United States.   5. Bisexuals—
Legal status, laws, etc.—United States.   6. Transsexuals—Legal
status, laws, etc.—United States.   I. Title.
    KF4772.Z46   1998
    342.73′0853—dc21   97–33701

British Library Cataloguing in Publication Data is available.

Library of Congress Catalog Card Number: 97–33701
ISBN: 0–275–95249–5

First published in 1998

Praeger Publishers, 88 Post Road West, Westport, CT 06881
An imprint of Greenwood Publishing Group, Inc.

Printed in the United States of America

∞™

The paper used in this book complies with the
Permanent Paper Standard issued by the National
Information Standards Organization (Z39.48–1984).

10 9 8 7 6 5 4 3 2

For Susan Klimist and Pasquale A. Zingo
and
In memory of Elizabeth H. Zingo

*Some scared dogs
   cower*

*Some scared dogs
   bite*

—Cyddie

Contents

Acknowledgments

This book would not have been possible without the support and assistance of numerous individuals whose help was invaluable. Most notably, my thanks are extended to: William Macauley (Associate Dean, College of Arts and Sciences, Oakland University) and Vincent Khopoya (Chair, Department of Political Science, Oakland University), for the financial support they made available during the 1996 winter term; Barbara Somerville (librarian, Kresge Library, Oakland University) for processing numerous interlibrary loan requests and for persistently tracking down necessary materials; Zhanya Poske (editorial assistant); and Linda Luke (student researcher), Sean Kosfosky (student assistant), Kevin Coxe (research assistant), and Karen Meyers (secretary, Department of Political Science, Oakland University), for essential research and clerical work. Special thanks is also due to all of the staff at Praeger Publishers for making this project a reality, especially James T. Sabin, Leanne Jisonna, David Palmer, and Jason Azze.

On a more personal note, the following individuals were very important in ways only family can understand: Pasquale A. Zingo, Margaret Bachofen, Mary Emery, Michele Baray, Marie Gula, Marcie Bonsall, Michael Zingo, Nora Klimist, Saul Wineman, and Marilyn Wineman. Honor is also paid to the memory of Elizabeth H. Zingo and Ruth R. Zingo. A special debt of gratitude is owed Cyddie—for poetry, healing energy, and vision; Martha—for listening, believing, and helping me to stay focused and to remain calm in the face of adversity; and Leslie—a long-standing mentor, friend, and role-model, despite the distances of time, place, and circumstance. Heart-felt gratitude is also extended to Electa Arenal ("the force that through the green fuse drives the flower"—Dylan Thomas, 1934), Beatrix Gates, and Akasha Hull, each of whom in their own unique way provided strength, constancy, patience, and centering in the midst of "chaos." Finally, for unfailing support, and above all, for just being there, my love and appreciation is extended to my partner, Susan Klimist.

CHAPTER 1

Social and Legal Condition
of "Outsiders"

There is currently in law reviews a large literature debating hate speech restrictions. This debate centers on the necessity and sagacity of instituting legal sanctions on the use of certain words, gestures, graphic representations, or symbols. While the exact definition of hate speech is dependent on the specific policy under consideration,[1] a variety of speech forms may be prohibited, for example, speech which intimidates, stigmatizes, abuses, denigrates, or inflicts intentional emotional distress on individuals or groups[2] on the basis of race, color, national or ethnic origin, alienage, sex,[3] gender identity, religion, affectional orientation/preference,[4] disability, or other characteristics unrelated to individual merit.

In this literature, both acceptance and rejection of speech restrictions are defended in terms of the First Amendment,[5] either alone or in conjunction with some combination of the Equal Protection Clause of the Fourteenth Amendment[6] and Title VII of the Civil Rights Acts of 1964.[7] The centrality of the First Amendment to the speech controversy is obvious, since this amendment establishes the constitutionally recognized right to freedom of expression. The parameters of this right, however, are not firmly established. It is generally recognized that only some speech is fully protected by the Constitution and that line-drawing and balancing are intricate parts of all First Amendment analysis.[8] Indeed, numerous judicial decisions demonstrate that the precise scope of the First Amendment is not settled doctrine.[9] Thus, scholars and critics on both sides of the debate can (and do) utilize the

Supreme Court's holdings in cases arising under the Equal Protection Clause and/or Title VII for additional arguments to substantiate either unfettered or restricted speech[10]—if the target of the hate speech is a member of a class protected under these provisions.[11]

Race and sex, which are protected classifications under the Equal Protection Clause and Title VII, are the central points of departure in a major portion of the literature for analysis supporting or rejecting speech code restrictions.[12] Because victims of oppression due to race or sex are deemed by the courts to possess an immutable status—that is, they share an innate characteristic or genetic determinism that has resulted in their suffering a demonstrable pattern of discrimination resulting in substantial injury[13]—they have gained an amplified legal hearing from the courts under the Equal Protection Clause. By focusing the discussion on race or sex, scholars ensure that deliberations do not become quagmired in the moral judgments that usually attend considerations of gender identity and affectional orientation/preference.

The complex and violent nature of race and sex subordination in the U.S.A. has deep historical roots; the immediate and institutionalized sources that perpetuate this subordination have not been totally eradicated. Shrouded in myths, stereotypes, and half-truths created and cultivated within the dominant culture, race and gender remain primary social constructs through which at least some of society's subalterns are excluded from equal citizenship. When motivated by the dominant group's ignorance or fear, suppression of these "outsiders"[14] assumes an urgency and power which defies rational argument. Language is reduced to acculturated emotional discourse. Not surprisingly, this ignorance or fear frequently manifests itself through hate messages—which may include, but are not limited to, slurs, epithets, propaganda, threats, harassment, verbal terrorism,[15] and physical violence. The legal recourses available to the victims of these words and actions, either alone or in some combination, are to tolerate or ignore the messages, use existing laws to prosecute the perpetrator, create new laws to regulate hate speech, or counter hate speech with more speech and protest.

While some or all of these remedies may prove adequate for victims attacked on the basis of race or sex,[16] the same may not be true for members of other "outsider" groups. The complexities, problems, and contradictions inherent in the listed remedies have not been fully explored as they apply to individuals who are attacked for reasons other than race or sex. The question thus arises: what remedies are available to those who have been consistently denied legal protection, to those for whom prejudice and condemnation remain most harsh and most vile—lesbians, gay men, bisexuals, and transgenderists?[17] The compunctions that might stymie the impulse to deny social compassion and legal rights to individuals due to race or sex do not operate where affectional orientation/preference or "gender transgression" is concerned. It seems irrelevant that lesbians, gay men, bisexuals, and transgenderists "occupy every stratum of economic and social class, inhabit every construction of race or ethnicity; practice every religion, live and love in and around every sexual and familial structure the culture has to offer."[18] Unlike other "outsider" groups, *sex/gender outsiders*[19] are situated in a unique socio-legal position—federal laws, far from protecting *sex/gender outsiders* from discrimination, reinforce and institutionalize prejudices existing in both the private and public sectors of society with regard to gender identity or affectional orientation/preference. By excluding *sex/gender outsiders* from protection against bias while providing such protection to other minority groups, all branches of the government implicitly condone discrimination against and oppression of lesbians, gay men, bisexuals, and transgenderists in both the public and private sectors of society. Indeed, *sex/gender outsiders* are one of the few groups in U.S. society against whom it is (still) acceptable to engage in both *de jure* and *de facto* discrimination.[20]

Evidence of legally sanctioned discrimination based on gender identity and affectional orientation/preference is provided by official policies regarding security clearances, military service, criminal law, government employment, public benefits (i.e., social security and pension entitlements, workers compensation, taxes, standing to sue for wrongful death and other torts, property and inheritance rights, etc.), adoption, child custody laws, and marriage laws.[21] *De jure* discrimination takes a multitude of forms. One illustration is the 1990 and 1991 National Endowment for the Arts (NEA) funding restrictions,[22] which attempted to silence, censor, and render invisible positive images and representations of the lives and affectional orientation/preference of lesbians and gay men, while simultaneously using both public funds and legal sanctions to promote and depict (in a non-obscene manner) the lives and affectional orientation/preference of heterosexuals.[23] Another is a judicial decision wherein a federal court ruled that the decision of prison officials to administer replacement sex hormones (of testosterone instead of estrogen) to a transsexual prisoner who had performed a partial self-castration that required the complete removal of the testes by prison surgeons was not unconstitutional, since a total failure to provide medical attention did not occur.[24] A third illustration is the referenda placed on the ballots in both Colorado and Oregon effectively to strip lesbians, gay men, and bisexual women and men of a wide variety of civil rights.[25]

De facto discrimination includes verbal and/or physical assault, and denial of health and life insurance policies, private employment, and private housing.[26] A recent example of *de facto* discrimination, which targeted lesbians and gay men, is the Vatican Congregation for the Doctrine of Faith's June 1996 directive sent to U.S. bishops. It acknowledges that "homosexual persons, as human persons, have the same rights as all persons, including the right of not being treated in a manner which offends their personal dignity. . . . Among other rights, all persons have the right to work, to housing, etc."[27] This directive asserts however, that "these rights are not absolute."[28] Indeed, it specifically declares that "[t]here are areas in which it is not unjust discrimination to take sexual orientation/preference into account, for example, in the placement of children, for adoption or foster care, in employment, of teachers or athletic coaches, and in military recruitment."[29]

The rhetoric of "special rights" utilized by right-wing individuals conceals the fact that lesbians, gay men, bisexuals, and transgenderists are systematically denied rights enjoyed by most American citizens, in that their basic civil (and human)[30] rights are not guaranteed either socially, politically, or legally in this country. The physical and psychic tolls exacted by this denial include:[31] living in fear of public exposure,[32] being a potential victim of discrimination and harassment; being socially permissible targets for revulsion, scorn, ridicule, hatred, violence, and elimination;[33] living (symbolically, if not literally) outside the law in a hostile environment;[34] being denied legal and social justice; being in jeopardy as to professional or personal reputations and credentials; being perceived or treated as immoral, sick, perverted, or abnormal; being marginalized and suppressed in civil society; being defined exclusively or stereotypically in terms of one's real or perceived sexuality; being denied respect; being scapegoated; and being denied the constitutional rights of equality, due process, intimate association, privacy, freedom from cruel and unusual punishment, freedom of religion and conscience, freedom from arbitrary discrimination on the basis of gender identity or affectional orientation/preference, and freedom of speech.

While suffering from both blatant and subtle forms of discrimination in a manner similar to that experienced by other "outsider" groups, *sex/gender outsiders* are frequently and consistently perceived within "outsider" groups as lacking legitimacy when voicing their complaints. The expenditure of time, energy, and resources required to struggle against the daily onslaught to one's being is enormous, but battling the prejudices within one's own community becomes even more onerous when the government lends its weight to the hatred, prejudice, exclusion, and violence that one encounters. Laws are passed in an attempt to coerce *sex/gender outsiders* to conform to rigid, binary gender and affectional orientation/preference categories, by denying rights and privileges and by imposing stigma and punishment on lesbians, gay men, bisexuals, and transgenderists. Insofar as traditional legal theory operates from a heterosexual binary archetype of gender identity and affectional orientation/preference and institutionalizes the devaluation and rejection of those who differ from this prototype, *sex/gender outsiders* are not envisioned as fully human.[35]

Discrimination, of whatever type, encountered by lesbians, gay men, bisexuals, and transgenderists may have less to do with gender identity or affectional orientation/preference *per se* than with perceptions that *sex/gender outsiders* are "sex role deviants" who threaten the rigidity of sexual boundaries, "appropriate" gender behavior, and the privileged status of heterosexuality.[36] Since the gender identity and affectional orientation/preference of *sex/gender outsiders* is perceived as undermining the heterosexual community's lifestyle, both become pivotal in institutionalized and private discrimination. To the extent that the symbolic and ideological boundaries of gender identity and affectional preference/orientation are successfully challenged and disrupted by lesbians, gay men, bisexuals, and transgenderists, the underlying socio-political dimensions of gender identity and sexuality are exposed. Attempts to confine the concepts of "natural" and "normal" to the gender identity and affectional orientation/preference currently provided by the dominant discourse are then made problematic. Eventually, uncertainty seeps into the dominant culture regarding what exactly gender identity or affectional orientation/preference is: "a sensibility, an abnormality, a sexual act, a clandestine subculture, an overt subculture, the enemy within, the enemy without."[37]

The lack of certainty such reflections may elucidate can reinforce the sense of threat or insecurity experienced by many individuals when they encounter *sex/gender outsiders*. Socialized to believe that that which is different is automatically suspect, many people uncritically accept the idea that the gender identity or affectional orientation/preference of lesbians, gay men, bisexuals, and transgenderists defies normality; embodies psychic impairment; signals the end of decency and civility; necessitates corrective government action; and undermines the very stability of sex, gender identity, and affectional orientation/preference distinctions. These beliefs serve to reinforce and sustain the threat *sex/gender outsiders* represent to traditional gender roles—especially from the perspective of heterosexual males. For example, gay men and male-to-female transgenderists are seen as disputing the inherent superiority of males and as disloyal and stupid for forfeiting their privilege and position; lesbians are seen as questioning male privilege, insofar as "men fear . . . that [they] could be allowed sexual and emotional . . . access to women *only* on women's terms, otherwise [they will be] left on the periphery of the matrix;"[38] female-to-male transgenderists are viewed as encroaching on and usurping male privilege as well as undermining the authority and position of men within society.[39] Thus, the very existence of *sex/gender outsiders* and the accompanying condemnation of their gender identity or affectional orientation/preference reflects the hierarchy of men's and women's gender roles and the historic patriarchal[40] assumptions regarding male/female sex roles.[41] Traditional sex, gender, and affectional orientation/preference roles are elevated, as a matter of course, at the expense of *sex/gender outsiders.* Through the devaluation of lesbians, gay men, bisexuals, and transgenderists, all who deviate from or fail to conform to the stereotypical behaviors, attitudes, and expression decreed appropriate for men and women or males and females, become suspect and are penalized. Such individuals are perceived as threats to the fixity of sexual boundaries and to the privileging of the heterosexual viewpoint.[42] By contesting and making problematic the symbolic and ideological boundaries of gender identity and affectional orientation/preference, *sex/gender outsiders* expose the underlying socio-political dimensions of both. Attempts to confine such concepts as "normal" or "natural" to a single affectional orientation/preference, a binary expression of sex and gender, or to the definitions currently provided by the dominant discourse become much more difficult with the existence of lesbians, gay men, bisexuals, and transgenderists. As a consequence, *sex/gender outsiders* can be neither acknowledged nor legitimated without simultaneously challenging and disrupting the dominant culture.

This book seeks to explore the impact of hate speech laws through a lens that focuses predominantly on the experiences of lesbians, gay men, bisexuals, and transgenderists, in order to make evident the potential ramifications of hate speech restrictions, as a general policy, for *sex/gender outsiders.* The arguments on all sides of the hate speech debate (civil libertarians, civil rights adherents, and accomodationists) are critically examined in terms of the social and legal protection available to *sex/gender outsiders.* First, however, Chapter Two provides an historical overview of free speech jurisprudence and explains the importance of free expression to *sex/gender outsiders.* Chapter Three analyzes equality jurisprudence arising under the Equal Protection Clause and Title VII, and explores the interconnections between status based on religion and that based on gender identity or affectional orientation/preference. Chapter Four scrutinizes the National Endowment for the Arts controversy and the Hate Crimes Statistics Act, in the context of the harm lesbians, gay men, bisexuals, and transgenderists experience from hate speech in a polity shaped by both the First Amendment and discrimination against *sex/gender outsiders*—as characterized in the cases of *State of Ohio v. Phipps*[43] and *Bowers v. Hardwick*.[44] Chapter Five analyzes the judicial response to hate regulations in four cases: *Doe v. University of Michigan*,[45] *UWM Post v. University of Wisconsin*,[46] *R.A.V. v. St. Paul*,[47] and *Wisconsin v. Mitchell*.[48] Finally, Chapter Six concludes that *sex/gender outsiders* should be wary of hate speech restrictions, especially if those restrictions are not severely limited or are not linked to a comprehensive political, legal, and social agenda designed to eliminate discrimination on the basis of gender identity and affectional orientation/preference.

NOTES

1. For example: the St. Paul Bias-Motivated Crime Statute; ACLU-NC Policy Concerning Racist and Other Group-Based Harassment on College Campuses; University of California/Office of the President University-wide Student Conduct: Harassment Policy; Stanford University: Interpretation of Fundamental Standard; the University of Michigan Policy on Discrimination and Discriminatory Harassment; and the University of Wisconsin Design for Diversity.

2. Words exemplifying these characteristics will not appear in this book, as I assume that no one who lives in the U.S.A. has been shielded from such words or lacks knowledge of at least some of the vocabulary at issue. To repeat derogatory words for the mere sake of illustration would perpetuate the same lack of sensitivity and potential injury to the targeted class. The final reason these words will not appear here is, to paraphrase Audre Lorde's poem, "...a promise I made" myself to strive "never to leave [my pen] lying in either somebody else's [or my own] blood." For the complete version of the poem, see: Audre Lorde, "To the Poet . . ." at 40 [with a nod to Matsuda (1989) at 2329 fn.49, for the reminder].

3. Within law, "sex" and "gender" are generaly used interchangeably, thereby signifying that these terms are considered to be synonymous. As Mary C. Chase points out, however, "this interchangeability of the words 'sex' and 'gender' has contributed to some analytic confusion between the categories of male and female, on the one hand, and masculine and feminine, on the other" [at 10]. She observes that "[a]s most feminist theorists use the terminology, 'sex' refers to the anatomical and physiological distinctions between men and women [e.g., women typically can get pregnant; men cannot]; 'gender,' by contrast, is used to refer to the cultural overlay on those anatomical and physiological distinctions [e.g., females are conventionally deemed to be "emotional," "tentative," "passive," and "yielding"; males are traditionally deemed to be "rational," "firm," "aggressive," and "unyielding"]" [*Id.*; see also: *Id.* at 12–13; Bem (1974) at 155–157; Valdes (1995) at 56–71; Chase further notes that affectional orientation/preference is, in this society, primarily determined "by the sex the object(s) of one's desire bears to one's

own sex, i.e., whether the object(s) of one's desire are of the same or of a different sex than oneself" [*Id.* at 13; Valdes at 56–71]. Despite these differences between "sex" and "gender," Chase maintains, the "Courts toss around the words 'gender,' 'masculine,' 'feminine,' and 'sex stereotyping' fairly often in sex discrimination cases. But they do not always use these terms consistently or self-consciously, and they do not always recognize gender and sex and particularly [affectional] orientation[/preference], often without acknowledging and sometimes apparently without being aware that they are doing so" [Chase at 17]. One consequence of such judicial conflation, according to Chase is that "the concept of gender has been imperfectly disaggregated in the law from sex on the one hand and [affectional] orientation[/preference] on the other. . . . When individuals diverge from the gender expectations for their sex—when a women displays masculine characteristics or a man feminine ones—discrimination against her is now treated as sex discrimination, while his behavior is generally viewed as a marker for homosexual orientation[/preference] and may not receive protection from discrimination" [*Id.* at 2]. Consequently, the difference in social and legal treatment accorded feminine gender traits reinforces and perpetuates the devaluation of feminine qualities [*Id.* at 3]. Men who display qualities considered feminine are abhorred for surrendering the privileges of their gender; women who exhibit qualities considered masculine are considered more acceptable (up to a point), since masculine qualities are associated with success. As Chase astutely notes, feminine traits "will not be valued unless and until men can feel free to engage in them" [*Id.* at 3]. Unless and until traits characterized as feminine can be manifested by both men and women within society without negative judgments being attached to them, stereotypically feminine traits (e.g., wearing high heels and makeup, speaking softly, or being docile and graceful) may continue to be devalued by the judiciary regardless of who manifests them.

    4. The terms "affectional orientation/preference" and "sexuality" are used interchangeably throughout this book. The term "affectional orientation/preference" is adopted from the Internet posting of Curt Pavola. There are two main reasons why this term, used instead of either "sexual orientation" or "sexual preference," is used throughout this book. First, as Pavola points out, the phrase affectional orientation/preference "is a more accurate, descriptive phrase for human sexuality" [Internet: Pavola]. This phrase includes not only one's sexual activity with other individuals but also one's "feelings of caring, affection, and love" for them, regardless of how this attraction is manifested—whether same-gender (female-female or male-male), different-gender (female-male), or both. It should be noted, however, that rather than "affectional orientation/preference" Pavola deliberately uses the term "affectional orientation," because he believes that there is "no conscious, free-will 'decision'" involved in whom one chooses to love [*Id.*].

    The second reason for using the term "affectional orientation/preference" is exactly the reason for which the Committee on Lesbian and Gay Concerns of the American Psychological Association rejects the term "preference" in favor of "orientation" [*Id.*]. In contrast to the position of both Pavola and the Committee, I would contend that it is not definitely known, and for purposes of this book it is irrelevant, whether an individual's affectional orientation/preference is mutable. I will develop the argument (later in this book) that there exists no legal justification for discrimination, oppression, abuse, or opprobrium, regardless of whether one's affectional orientation/preference or sexuality is immutable or chosen.

Consequently, the dual construction of "affectional orientation/preference" used throughout this book resists the assumption, prevalent in many judicial decisions and scholarly articles, that if affectional orientation/preference is a matter of personal choice it is somehow less deserving of protection than if it is predetermined. Such thinking casts lesbians, gay men, bisexuals, and transgenderists into the roles of helpless victims who need protection, sick individuals who require help or pity, or criminals who deserve punishment. It erroneously suggests that through the act of choosing one's sexuality one has also chosen to accept not only society's construction of her/his sexuality but also the stigma and legal harms and consequences associated with society's judgement.

5. "Congress shall make no law . . . abridging the freedom of speech." This amendment is linked with the Fifth Amendment's due process clause to protect against federal action and with the Fourteenth Amendment's due process clause to protect against state action.

6. The Fourteenth Amendment states: "No State shall make or enforce any law which shall abridge the privileges or immunities of citizens of the United States; nor shall any State deprive any person of life, liberty, or property, without due process of law; nor deny any person within its jurisdiction the equal protection of the laws."

7. Title VII states: "It shall be unlawful employment practice for an employer . . . to discriminate against any individual with respect to his compensation, terms, conditions, or privileges of employment because of such individual's race, color, religion, sex, or national origin" [42 U.S.C. §2000e-2 (a) (1a)].

8. See for example: *Schenck* (1919); *Abrams* (1919); *Whitney* (1927); *Lovell* (1938); *Chaplinsky* (1942); *Dennis* (1951); *Beauharnais* (1952); *Yates* (1957); *Roth* (1957); *New York Times* (1964); *Paris Adult Theatre I* (1973); *Miller* (1973); *Broadrick* (1973); *Smith* (1974); *Virginia State Board of Pharmacy* (1976); *New York v. Ferber* [hereafter *Ferber*] (1982).

9. *Chaplinsky* (1942); See also: Matsuda (1989) at 2349 fn.151; Emerson (1983) at 15–16.

10. See for example: Baruch (1990); Battaglia (1991); Browne (1991); Brownstein (1991); Byrne (1991); Delgado (1991); Gale (1991); Hulschizer (1991); Karst (1990); Koepke (1990); Lawrence (1990); Linzer (1991); Massaro (1991); SeLegue (1991); Smolla (1990); Wolfson, "Free Speech Theory" (1991).

11. For example, race, sex, national origin, and religion.

12. Exceptions include Karst (1990); SeLegue (1991); Smolla (1990); Wolfson (1991).

13. Note that the legal definition of immutable status is under-inclusive with regard to gender identity and/or affectional orientation/preference. If one's gender identity and/or affectional expression *is not* chosen but, rather, is a result of genetic determinism, then it is immutable in a manner similar to race and sex; if one's gender identity or affectional orientation/preference *is* chosen, then it is mutable in a manner similar to religion. For a fuller discussion regarding the status differences and parallels between gender identity or affectional orientation/preference on the one hand, and religion on the other, see Chapter Three *infra*.

14. The term "outsider," as defined by Matsuda, emphasizes the powerlessness of those persons whom the term encompasses (regardless of their numeric size within society) and, more accurately, depicts the condition of those people it describes in relation to those within or privileged by the existing power structure. Matsuda identifies seven characteristics of "outsider" jurisprudence. It "is derived from considering the stories from the bottom"; is grounded in the particulars of the ["outsider's"] social reality and experience; "is consciously both historical and revisionist [insofar as it] attempts to know history from the bottom; rejects presentist, androcentrist, Eurocentric, and false-universalist descriptions of social phenomena; accepts the standard teaching of street wisdom: law is essentially political [and] accepts as well the pragmatic use of law as a tool of social change; recognizes, struggles within, and utilizes contradiction, dualism, and ambiguity; and focuses on effects." [Matsuda (1989) at 2322, 2323 fn.15, 2324, 2325].

15. This term is defined by Leslie F. Goldstein as ". . . not merely language that conveys hatred . . . but shows . . . an obvious attempt to intimidate, or terrorize or to provoke a fight" [Goldstein (1992) at 1].

16. The possibility that race or sex may specifically be protected from attack was called into doubt by the Supreme Court's ruling in *R.A.V. v. St. Paul* (1992), wherein the Court unanimously ruled that St. Paul's Motivated Crime Ordinance was unconstitutional. Justice Scalia, speaking for a five-judge majority, argued that the statute was unconstitutional on its face, because it constituted a content-based regulation that violated the First Amendment's free speech clause. Justices White, Blackmun, O'Connor, and Stevens, who joined for the minority concurrences, believed that the St. Paul statute was fatally over-broad. For a fuller discussion and analysis of *R.A.V. v. St. Paul*, see Chapter Five *infra*.

17. The term "transgenderist," first introduced by Virginia Prince in 1987 or 1988, was coined to name people like herself "who trans the gender barrier—meaning somebody who lives full time in the gender opposite to their anatomy" [Virginia Prince as quoted in Feinberg (1992), at x].

In this book, the term "transgenderist" is used to encompass all individuals who are transgendered, transsexuals (describe men and women "who transverse the boundary of the *sex* they were assigned at birth" [*Id.*]), and transvestites. It also includes intersexuals (a.k.a. hermaphrodites or "the third sex") and any other gender or sexual variants.

Transgender persons live in another gender identity; some choose to change cosmetically, chemically, or surgically, their bodies, but seldom their genitals. Feinberg states that "[t]rans*gender* people transverse, bridge, or blur the boundary of the *gender expression* they were assigned at birth" [*Id.*]. Transsexuals live full or part-time in the role of another gender; they do not always choose (or feel it is necessary) to cosmetically, chemically, or surgically change their bodies. Generally, only individuals who have had genital surgery are permitted by the government to change their official documents to reflect their changed sex identity. Neither transgender persons nor transsexuals are necessarily lesbian, gay, bisexual women or men, or heterosexual; their affectional orientation/preference might be better expressed by another point on the continuum of sexuality.

A Note on Pronouns: Throughout this book, a transsexual individual is referred to by the pronoun appropriate to her or his self-identified sex, notwithstanding how society classifies her or him. Regardless of whether genital surgery has occurred, a person whose birth sex is male but lives fully in the female gender role is referred to as she; one whose birth sex is female but who lives fully in the male gender role is referred to as he. A transgenderist, by contrast, is referred to by the pronoun "s/he," unless the individual designates a specific pronoun of choice.

These pronouns are used for several reasons. First, it feels presumptuous and inappropriate to use a pronoun designated by society to be anatomically or historically correct but deemed by the transgenderist to be inaccurate. Second, an exclusively male or female pronoun violates a transgenderist's self-perceived gender. Third, the pronoun "s/he" facilitates the elision of binary pronouns. Finally, the use of pronouns that accurately reflect a trangenderist's sex or gender identity, from his/her perspective, is meant to signify the complex realities that constitute transgendered and transsexual expression; symbolize the fluidity and diversity of sex and gender; and signal respect for those individuals who, by openly living their truth as transgenderists, are forced to endure multifaceted oppression and to fight for the strength necessary to survive countless physical, spiritual, psychic, intellectual, and emotional assaults, on a daily basis.

18. As Martha Minow aptly points out, "[w]e often describe a trait in language that seems to assign the trait to only one of the persons being compared. The choice of terms to describe an individual or group unavoidably reflects one perspective among others" [Minnow, *Making All the Difference*, at 22 fn.5. See also: Halley (1985) at 946: "The public status 'heterosexual' is an unmarked signifier, the category to which everyone is assumed to belong. Something has to *happen* to mark an individual with the identity 'homosexual.' "].

By marking only "others" with a signifier, the status quo's perspective becomes associated with that which is objective and neutral, while subjectivity and partiality are reserved for the "outsiders." Indeed, the political perspective of the status quo remains invisible and unacknowledged in our society. The charge that a perspective is political is reserved for those individuals who have been traditionally silenced or excluded but refuse to remain so. The charge that political correctness is "promoted by militants for political purposes" [Jeffrey at 3], is generally leveled by defenders of the status quo against those who challenge the status quo's marginalization of individuals and groups. Thus in our society heterosexuals, by virtue of their status quo membership, do not have an affectional orientation/preference; only lesbians, gay men, bisexuals, transvestites, transgenderists, and transsexuals do. This phenomenon is similar to the notion that only females, not males, have a sex; only women, not men, have a gender; only persons of color, not persons defined as Caucasian, have a race. While being marked with a signifier is detrimental to any "outsider" group, it is particularly problematic for those who do not conform to society's archetype of gender identity or affectional orientation/preference.

19. The term "*sex/gender outsiders*" is used inclusively to encompass lesbians, gay men, bisexual women and men, and transgender men and women, transsexuals, transvestites, and intersexuals. The "crime" of lesbians, gay men, and bisexual women and men is that their affectional orientation/preference does not match what society dictates; the "crime" of transgenderists is that their gender expression or genitals do not match what is dictated by society or what was assigned at birth; the "crime" of intersexuals is that their genitals do not conform to what society dictates. As a result, some intersexuals have been subjected to numerous surgeries, prior to the age of consent, in an attempt to have their bodies match their assigned gender expression.

20. Other groups against whom both *de jure* and *de facto* discrimination is still socially and legally acceptable include children, the elderly, and indigents [see: Forer (1991)]. Those who seek to perpetuate discrimination against *sex/gender outsiders* justify their position by appealing to myths, stereotypes, misinformation, and fears regarding lesbians, gay men, bisexuals, and transgenderists. While their assertions and arguments regarding *sex/gender outsiders* are frequently based on half-truths or total fabrications, it cannot be denied that many people in society and in the government believe the critics' statements to be true [for example: Dannemeyer (1989); Magnuson (1989)].

While it is obvious that *de jure* and *de facto* discrimination on the basis of race and sex still exists in this society, it can be argued that it is less socially and legally acceptable to target groups or individuals on the basis of race or sex than to target groups whose membership is deemed transient (i.e., children, the elderly, or indigents) or chosen (i.e., lesbians, gay men, bisexual women and men, transgenderists, transvestites, and transsexuals). Indeed, it is believed that (overt) racial or sexual discrimination is no longer condoned or tolerated in this society as a general rule. The courts have ruled that *de jure* racial and sexual discrimination is unconstitutional unless the government can demonstrate a compelling or important state interest for the discrimination, while *de facto* racial and sexual discrimination has become nominally less blatant. Unfortunately, this does not mean that race and sex are no longer problematic in U.S. society. For example, despite improvements in the social, political, and legal conditions of at least some non-Caucasian individuals and groups, the fact remains that racism and racial discrimination continue to exist and thrive in this country—a point which becomes obvious when Supreme Court decisions, which have had the effect of jeopardizing civil rights laws [see: *Adarand Constructors, Inc.* (1995) (Ginsberg, J., dissenting), *Croson* (1989), *Jetts* (1989), *Wards Cove Packing Co.* (1989), *Watson* (1988)] by reformulating rather than dismantling the institutionalized social, legal, and political elements of racism, legitimates racism that is expressed in a less blatant, more coded manner [see: Bell (1987); Bell (1992); Edsall and Edsall (1991); Ezorsky (1991); Hacker (1992); Jaynes and Williams (eds.) (1989)]. The same is true with regard to sexism and sexual discrimination in this country.

21. See: Achtenberg (1984, 1994); Baer (1983); Barrett (1990); Bornstein (1994); Colker (1996); Editors of the *Harvard Law Review* (1989, 1990); Ellis and Riggle (eds.) (1996); Faderman (1991); George (1993); Halley (1985); Mohr (1988); Pratt (1995); Robson (1992); Robson (1997).

22. The Helms Amendment reads, in significant part: "None of the funds authorized to be appropriated to the National Endowment for the Arts . . . may be used to promote, disseminate, or produce materials which in the judgment of the National Endowment for the Arts . . . may be considered obscene, including but not limited to, depictions of sado-masochism, homoeroticism, the sexual exploitation of children, or individuals engaged in sex acts and which, when taken as a whole, do not have serious literary, artistic, political, or scientific value."

23. Kate Bornstein, a transsexual, observes that "I'm not included in Senator Helms' amendment. We're not included in most legislation these days. But me and my people, we're the ones they'd *want* to legislate against, if they could even begin to conceive of us, because *we're* the ones who threaten their manhood" [Bornstein at 77].

24. *Supra* (1986).

25. Colorado's Amendment 2 repealed anti-discrimination laws which protected lesbians, gay men, and bisexuals. Titled "No Protection Status," Amendment 2 states:

Neither the State of Colorado, through any of its branches or departments, nor any of its agencies, political subdivisions, municipalities or school districts, shall enact, adopt or enforce any statute, regulation, ordinance or policy whereby homosexual, lesbian, or bisexual orientation, conduct, practices, or relationships shall constitute or otherwise be the basis of, or entitle any person or class of persons to have or claim any minority status, quota preferences, protected status or claim of discrimination. This Section of the Constitution shall be in all respects self-executing. [*The Washington Blade*, 9 October 1992, at 29]

Oregon's Measure 9 was considered more radical than Colorado's Amendment 2. In summary, Measure 9 mandated that

All governments in Oregon may not use their monies or property to promote, encourage, or facilitate homosexuality, pedophilia, sadism, or masochism. All levels of government, including the public education systems, must assist in setting the standard for Oregon youth that recognizes that these "behaviors" are "abnormal, wrong, unnatural, and perverse" and that they are to be discouraged and avoided. The State may not recognize this conduct under "sexual orientation" or "sexual preference" labels or through "quotas, minority status, affirmative action, or similar concepts." [*The Washington Blade*, 16 October 1992, at 21]

Colorado's Amendment 2 was passed on 3 November 1992; Oregon's Measure 9 was defeated. Activists opposed to Amendment 2 filed an action seeking to have it declared unconstitutional and obtained a preliminary court injunction to prohibit the amendment from becoming effective prior to court review. Oregon supporters of the defeated Measure 9 plan to introduce another initiative modeled on Colorado's Amendment 2 at the first opportunity [*The Washington Blade*, 16 October 1992 at 21].

On 19 July 1993, in *Evans* (1993), the Colorado Supreme Court ruled that Amendment 2 violated the Equal Protection Clause and infringed on the fundamental right of lesbians, bisexuals, and gay men to participate fully in the political process. On 14 December 1993 District Court Judge Bayless held Amendment 2 to be unconstitutional and ordered that the preliminary injunction be made permanent. The U.S. Supreme Court, in a 6–4 decision on 20 May 1996, ruled that Colorado's Amendment 2 was unconstitutional.

26. See: note 20 *supra.*

27. Navaro-Valls at 176. See also: Ratzinger; Seper.

28. Navaro-Valls at 176.

29. *Id.*

30. Wolfson states that "the first human right is the right to be considered and treated as a human." Lesbians, gay men, bisexuals, and transgenderists have systematically and consistently been denied this right each and every time they have been denied equal rights under the law. In every aspect of their life, *sex/genders outsiders* encounter the real or potential threat of discrimination, harassment, dehumanization, and violence. Virtually nothing can be taken for granted in a society where *sex/gender outsiders* are casually denied the basic civil rights and liberties guaranteed by the U.S. Constitution to every citizen, due to prejudices, stereotypes, and lies perpetrated within the dominant culture. Lesbians, gay men, bisexuals, and transgenderists have the same human needs, and ought to have the same legal rights and privileges, as every other person in this society. As Wolfson asserts, "[l]ike non-gay people, our human need is to be free to make choices that all recognize as undeniably fundamental to a human's life plan and self-conception, such as the choice of a lover or a life partner. We deserve protection so that we, too, can be free to lead our lives, share our hearts, and participate fully in community life. We deserve to have our relationships recognized [and respected] so that we can have the support and responsibility we want and now strive to build on our own. We deserve these inalienable civil and human rights, as equal citizens of a nation founded on freedom and esteeming equality, and as fully human beings" [Wolfson (1991) at 21, 37].

For information on the dehumanization of *sex/gender outsiders* throughout history, see: Boswell (1980); Bullough and Bullough (1993); Colker (1996); Feinberg (1996); George (1993); Heger (1980, 1994); Hutchins and Kaahumanu (1991); Katz (1976, 1992); Mackenzie (1994); Robson (1992); Shilts (1987).

31. See: Adam (1987); Baer (1983); Barrett (1990); Bem (1993); Blumenfeld and Raymond (1988); Bornstein (1994); Clausen (1997); Colker (1996); Editors of the *Harvard Law Review* (1989, 1990); Ellis and Riggle, (1996); Ettner (1996); Faderman (1991); Feinberg (1993); Feinberg (1992); Feinberg (1996); George (1993); Green (1992); Halley (1985); Hayes (1990); Hutchins and Kaahumanu (1991); Katz (1976, 1992); Law (1988); Mohr (1988); National Museum & Archive of Lesbian and Gay History, *The Gay Almanac* (1996); National Museum & Archive of Lesbian and Gay History, *The Lesbian Almanac* (1996); Pharr (1988); Polikoff (1990); Pratt (1991); Pratt (1990); Pratt, (1995); Rivera (1979); Robson (1992); Robson (1997).

32. As Ruthann Robson points out, "[l]esbians who are closeted face the public revelation as an identity that can be lawfully penalized in a variety of ways" [Robson (1992) at 151]. This observation is true for other *sex/gender outsiders*. Leslie Feinberg reports that the police in a small Nebraska town exposed the fact that a twenty-one-year-old transsexual male named Brandon Teena was a biological female. Shortly after the police exposed him, "Brandon was forcibly stripped at a Christmas party in front of a woman he had dated, and then was kidnapped, beaten, and gang raped." Although the two male attackers were identified for the police by Brandon, the police refused to arrest the men for their criminal actions. One week later, Brandon's body, which had been repeatedly stabbed, was discovered. His original attackers had shot and killed him [Feinberg (1996) at 132].

33. Historically, *sex/gender outsiders* have been executed by their governments for violating socially prescribed dress codes or behavioral norms regarding sex, gender, or orientation/preference [See: Feinberg (1996); Katz (1992)]. While it is true that as a general rule murder is forbidden and punished by law, judicial acceptance of the homosexual-advance defense implies (or has implied) that such an advance constitutes sufficient provocation to mitigate a murder charge to the lesser charge of manslaughter (or second-degree murder), due to the victim's alleged sexual orientation/preference. See: *State of Missouri v. Thornton* (1975) at 42 [hereafter *Thornton*] (court affirmed that whether a defendant had reasonable grounds for believing he was faced with real or apparent danger of sodomy is generally a question for the jury to decide); *Mills v. Shepherd* (1975) at 1232 (defendant convicted of voluntary manslaughter based on homosexual-advance defense); *Commonwealth v. Doucette* (Mass. 1984) at 1093 (judge instructed jury on homosexual-advance provocation); *Schick v. State* (1991) (jury instructed on involuntary manslaughter based on defense of homosexual-advance provocation); *State of Michigan v. Schmidt* (Mich. 1996) [hereafter *Schmidt*] (defendant found guilty of second-degree murder after being embarrassed on the Jenny Jones talk show by a male secret-admirer, Scott Amadour). Moreover, police officers have been responsible for harassing a transsexual male and for refusing to arrest his attackers—see note 32 *supra* regarding Brandon Teena.

34. Ruthann Robson has observed that *sex/gender outsiders* are forced outside the law because the law frequently fails to protect their constitutional rights. When the discrimination levied against lesbians, gay men, bisexuals, and transgenderists is based on gender identity or affectional orientation/preference, even the limited protection accorded other "outsiders" is denied to them [Robson (1992). See also: Baer (1983) at 249–252]. Although Robson confines her argument to lesbians throughout her work, it is applicable to *sex/gender outsiders* in general. In the words of Kate Bornstein, "[a]ll the categories of transgender find a common ground in that they each break one or more of the rules of gender: what we have in common is that we are gender outlaws" [Bornstein (1994) at 69].

35. Littleton (1989) at 26. Although Littleton confined her observation to lesbians and gay men, her conclusion is true for *sex/gender outsiders* in general.

36. See: Dollimore (1991).

37. *Id.,* at 30.

38. Rich (1980) at 643.

39. For a discussion of lesbians and gay men vis-a-vis heterosexual males, see: Comstock (1991).

40. Gerda Lerner defines patriarchy as "the manifestation of institutionalization of male dominance over women and children in the family and the extension of male dominance over women in general" [Lerner (1986) at 239].

41. Koppelman (1988) at 154–157, 159–160; Koppelman (1994) at 234–257; Law (1988) at 197–207, 218–221, 229.

42. Dollimore states that ". . . fears of the 'other' are found to involve fears of that which is potentially the 'same as'—not only in the psychic sense that the other is constructed from projected, internal fears, but also in the social sense that the other is often created from, and disavowed as, the proximate. The other is confirmed to be potentially a combination of (1) encountered difference, (2) constructed difference, (3) the object of displacement for fears within/of the 'same'" [Dollimore (1991) at 34].

43. 389 N.E.2d 1128 (1979) [hereafter *Phipps*].

44. 478 U.S. 186 (1986).

45. 721 F.Supp. 852 (E.D. Mich. 1989).

46. 774 F.Supp. 1163 (E.D. Wis. 1991).

47. 112 S.Ct. 2538 (1992).

48. 169 Wis.2d 153 (1992), 113 S.Ct. 2194 (1993).

CHAPTER 2

Free Speech and the
Hate Speech Controversy

FREE SPEECH JURISPRUDENCE: HISTORICAL
OVERVIEW

The First Amendment of the U.S. Constitution states, in part, that "Congress shall make no law . . . abridging the freedom of speech." This freedom is deemed a fundamental right, because it assures individual self-fulfillment or autonomy;[1] it is a means of advancing knowledge and searching for truth;[2] it gives all members of society an opportunity to participate in the political process of self-governance;[3] and it provides a safety valve for society.[4] This last factor is especially important, because suppression of discussion is injurious to society. According to Thomas Emerson, suppression makes "rational judgment impossible, substituting force for reason; [it] promotes inflexibility and stultification preventing society from adjusting to changing circumstances or developing new ideas; [and it] conceals the real problems confronting society by diverting public attention from critical issues."[5]

The fact that freedom of speech is fundamental,[6] however, does not render it an absolute right.[7] According to Chief Justice Vinson, freedom of speech "is not an unlimited, unqualified right[;] . . . the societal value of speech must, on occasion, be subordinated to other values and considerations."[8] Consequently, both the federal and the state governments are permitted to restrict an individual's or group's freedom of speech to some degree.[9] As Justice Oliver Wendell Holmes observed in *Schenck v. United*

States, which was the first time the Supreme Court ruled on a case challenging speech regulation,[10] "[t]he question in every case is whether the words used are used in such circumstances and are of such a nature as to create a clear and present danger that they will bring about the substantive evils that Congress has a right to prevent. It is a question of proximity and degree."[11]

Once Justice Holmes had articulated the "clear and present danger" test in 1919, he sharpened its parameters in his dissenting opinion in *Abrams v. United States*: "[i]t is only the present danger of immediate evil or an intent to bring it about that warrants Congress in setting a limit to the expression of opinion where private rights are not concerned."[12] In his view, the philosophical foundation of the First Amendment's freedom of speech provision is the test of truth "reached in the free trade in ideas."[13] Under the rubric of "the competition of the market," the government is forbidden to suppress ideas merely because the ideas are wrong or because the ideas are expressed through opinions that are thought to be "loathe [or believed] to be fraught with death,"[14] provided the ideas do not "imminently threaten immediate interference with the lawful and pressing purposes of the law."[15] If time for debate and discussion exists, legislative interference with speech is forbidden. Only in areas severed from First Amendment protection by the Court[16] is the legislature allowed discretion in determining what speech is harmful, nonvaluable, and unable to have its resulting harm cured through more speech.[17]

Justice Holmes's "clear and present danger" test was replaced by Justice Sanford's "bad tendency" test in 1925. In *Gitlow v. New York*, the Supreme Court ruled that "the general provisions of the statute may be constitutionally applied to the specific utterance of the defendant if its *natural tendency and probable effect* was to bring about the substantive evil which the legislative body might prevent."[18] The lax standard of the "bad tendency" test expanded the amount of speech the government could legitimately restrict. No longer was the danger required to be imminent; now it needed merely to be potential in order to run afoul of the government. Rather than requiring the government actually to prove that the speech challenged would produce a "substantive evil," in the form of riots or other forms of violence, as required under the "clear and present danger" test, the Supreme Court's use of the "bad tendency" standard allowed the government to suppress ideas. Any speech that might even remotely cause a social harm could be censored by the government. Thus, the focus of the free speech tests shifted from the effects of speech to the content of speech and its intended consequences. The "bad tendency" test dominated free speech cases for almost twenty years,[19] despite the fact that the "clear and present danger" test theoretically remained in effect. Just prior to World War II, however, the Supreme Court returned to a strengthened form of "clear and present danger" when Justice Rutledge noted in *Thomas v. Collins* that the "democratic freedoms secured by the First Amendment" are preferred freedoms.[20] Hence, any attempt on the part of the government to restrict freedom of speech could be justified by "[o]nly the gravest abuses, endangering paramount interests."[21] By articulating the test in this manner, the Supreme Court shifted the burden of proof from those who defended free speech to those who sought to restrict it. The range of permissible restrictions on speech was narrowed, such that "the rational connection between the remedy provided and the evil to be curbed"[22] had to be drawn more precisely by the government.

Some limits on the First Amendment's protection of free speech were identified by the Supreme Court in both *Cantwell v. Connecticut* and *Chaplinsky v. New Hampshire*: "the lewd and obscene, the profane, the libelous, and the insulting or 'fighting words' "—words "which by their very utterance inflict injury or tend to incite an immediate breach of the peace."[23] This definition of "fighting words" in effect censored hate speech, inasmuch as it ostensibly covered not only every offensive epithet that injured an individual's or a group's reputation, but also any provocative words that threatened to produce immediate violence. Such words were excluded from First Amendment protection for two reasons: they were not considered to be an essential part of any expression of ideas, and they were deemed to be of such slight social value that society's interest in morality outweighed any potential benefit that might be derived from them. As Justice Murphy noted in *Chaplinsky*, "[r]esort to epithets or personal abuse is not in any proper sense communication of information or opinion safeguarded by the Constitution."[24] The application of "fighting words" was confined in *Gooding v. Wilson* to those words that "have a *direct tendency* to cause acts of violence by the person to whom, individually, the remark is addressed."[25] But the test for determining whether the words constitute "fighting words" or are "insulting" has remained unchanged: "what men of common intelligence would understand . . . [as] words likely to cause an average addressee to fight."[26]

The Court's neat division in *Chaplinsky* of speech into protected and unprotected generated a dual consequence. First, the latter category was based on the court's judgment regarding its value and seemingly allowed a "heckler's veto" to silence a speaker.[27] Second, unprotected speech included hate speech—as evidenced by the Supreme Court's decision in *Beauharnais v. Illinois*. At issue in *Beauharnais* was whether the First Amendment prohibition against libel extended to states under the liberty protection of the Fourteenth Amendment's Due Process Clause.[28] Justice Frankfurter, writing for a sharply divided Court, answered in the affirmative. Speech that defamed racial groups could be constitutionally punished even if it was not directed at any specific member of the defamed group.

The unprotected category of libel was expanded in *Beauharnais* to include defamations "directed at designated collectivities and flagrantly disseminated."[29] In Justice Frankfurter's opinion there existed a clear distinction between libel of a creed or of a racial group and libel of a political party—"the rubric 'race, color, creed, or religion' which describes the type of [punishable] libel . . . has attained too fixed a meaning to permit political groups to be brought within it."[30] Justice Brennan warned in his dissent, however, that "the same kind of state law that makes Beauharnais a criminal for advocating segregation in Illinois can be utilized to send people to jail for advocating equality and nonsegregation."[31]

In 1969 the Supreme Court upheld an implicit narrowing of its protection against group defamation, in the Skokie controversy.[32] The state trial court accepted the Village of Skokie's argument that the wearing or displaying of the swastika in the predominately Jewish village amounted to an intentional infliction of emotional harm and constituted "fighting words" as defined in *Chaplinsky*. It further accepted the argument that materials "which incite or promote hatred against persons of Jewish faith or ancestry" constituted group libel under *Beauharnais*.[33] The District Court of Appeals, after initially affirming the injunction issued by the state trial court that had enjoined the Nazi march and then having the case remanded to it by the U.S. Supreme Court,[34] limited the ban to displaying the swastika, because it was "a personal affront to every member of the Jewish faith, in remembering the nearly consummated genocide of their people committed within memory by those who used the swastika as their symbol."[35] It ruled, however, that the village had failed to meet its burden of showing that an immediate harm would result from the Nazis marching, walking, or parading, distributing pamphlets or other materials, or from wearing the National Socialist Party uniform. Upon review, the Illinois Supreme Court ultimately held that the preliminary injunction that forbade the display of the swastika was also invalid, due to the presumptive unconstitutionality of prior restraint on speech. It ruled that the swastikas, however offensive to the Jewish citizens of Skokie, were symbolic speech intended to publicly exhibit the displayers' beliefs.[36]

When the District Court of Appeals, in *Collins v. Smith*, considered the legitimacy of a series of Skokie ordinances passed to block the Nazi march,[37] it weakened the segment of the "fighting words" definition articulated in *Chaplinsky* that referred to words which "by their very utterance inflict injury," but it left intact the prohibition on speech that "tend[s] to incite an immediate breach of the peace." In addition, it questioned the continued legitimacy of the *Beauharnais* statute. The appeals court concluded that

insofar as *Beauharnais* held that speech which defames racial and religious groups may be restricted in order to protect the reputation of such groups, it has been overruled, or at the very least has been so undermined that it should not be extended to new kinds of speech-inflicted damage to individuals, where such an extension would pose a substantial danger of inhibiting free speech and debate.

. . .

[I]f the court is wrong in concluding that *Beauharnais* has been overruled, at the very least it has been undermined so severely that it should be restricted to the facts.[38]

The United States Supreme Court refused to stay the Court of Appeals' ruling in *Smith v. Collins*; Justice Blackmun (joined by Justice Rehnquist) dissented from that decision. Justice Blackman specifically rejected the Court of Appeals' contention regarding *Beauharnais*, stating that "*Beauharnais* has never been overruled or formally limited in any way."[39] When the Supreme Court refused to review the Circuit Court's final decision, Justice Blackmun dissented again, this time joined by Justice White, and once more urged a reconsideration of *Beauharnais*.

Yet despite Justice Blackmun's protest, *Beauharnais* has been formally limited by the Supreme Court. In many ways the Court's "clear and present danger" test, becoming more stringent in *Brandenburg v. Ohio* through its demand that the nexus between action and advocacy be intimate, reduced the "fighting words" doctrine to an "incitement" test. The criterion was less the probability of injury and more the inciting language. Words which merely advocate the use of violence cannot be proscribed; words which directly incite violent resistance to the law can be proscribed. As Gerald Gunther has observed, in *Brandenburg* the Court combined "the most speech-protective ingredients . . . with the most useful elements of the clear and present danger heritage" to yield "the most speech-protective standard yet evolved by the Supreme Court."[40]

Brandenburg does not stand alone in its tacit restriction of both *Beauharnais* and *Chaplinsky*. Other cases might include: *Ashton v. Kentucky*, wherein the Court noted that Kentucky's criminal libel statute "involve[d] calculations as to the boiling point of a particular person or a particular group, not an appraisal of the nature of the comment *per se*;"[41] *Tinker v. Des Moines Independent Community School District*, wherein "[t]he Court repeatedly rejected attempts to ban certain kinds of language on the basis of an 'undifferentiated fear or apprehension of disturbance;' "[42] *Street v. New York*, wherein the Court maintained that the public burning of a personal flag while shouting "we don't need no damn flag" was not so inherently inflammatory as to constitute fighting words;[43] *Cohen v. California*, wherein the Court rejected "the state's position [which] amounted to an assertion that it could ban certain offensive epithets even without showing a possible breach, either because such epithets are inherently likely to cause violent reactions or in order to maintain a 'suitable level of discourse within the body politic;' "[44] *Gooding v. Wilson*, wherein "the Court struck down a Georgia statute punishing the use of 'opprobrious words or abusive language, tending to cause a breach of the peace,' language which would seem to conform with the definition of fighting words;"[45] *Lewis v. City of New Orleans*, wherein the Court held that words conveying or intending to convey disgrace are not "fighting words;"[46] *Hess v. Indiana*, wherein the Court ruled that the statement "we'll take the fucking streets later," shouted during an anti-Vietnam War demonstration, could not be punished by the state, since "there was no evidence, or rational inference from the import of the language, that [these] words were intended to produce, and likely to produce, *imminent* disorder;"[47] and *R.A.V. v. St. Paul*, wherein the Court asserted that "fighting words" were not a completely unprotected category under the First Amendment and seemed to flirt with the idea of overturning the fighting words doctrine in its entirety.[48]

In light of these decisions it seems apparent that for all intents and purposes, only the second half of the "fighting words" doctrine—words which "tend to incite an immediate breach of the peace"[49]—remains good law.[50] The Supreme Court's tacit restriction of both *Beauharnais* and *Chaplinsky* has eliminated protection against group defamation insofar as it has ruled unconstitutional prohibitions on speech which attacks a defined group.[51] In the eyes of the Court, antisocial attitudes and bigotry are protected by the First Amendment. As Justice Holmes observed in his dissenting opinion in *United States v. Schwimmer*, "if there is any principle of the Constitution that more imperatively calls for attachment than any other it is the principle of free thought—not free thought for those who agree with us but freedom for the thought that we hate."[52] The Seventh Circuit Court articulated a comparable sentiment in *American Booksellers Association Inc. v. Hudnut* when it observed that "[r]acial bigotry, anti-semitism, violence on television, reporters' biases—these and many more influence the culture and shape of our socialization. None is directly answerable by more speech, unless that speech too finds its place in the popular culture. Yet all is protected as speech, however insidious. Any other answer leaves the government in control of all of the institutions of culture, the great censor and dictator of which thoughts are good for us."[53]

THE HATE SPEECH CONTROVERSY

The validity of society's accommodation and toleration of hate speech has been and continues to be a hotly contested issue. The implications as well as the consequences of freely expressed hatred continue to be scrutinized from a multitude of perspectives, due to the fact that incidents of racial and sexual harassment (including violence) are escalating across the United States.[54] While the problems imputed to racist and sexist hate speech are well documented by legal scholars in their search for an adequate solution, it is important to recognize that race and sex are not the only traits singled out for malicious harassment. Persons whose affectional orientation/preference or gender identity is not, or is assumed not to be, "correct" or "normal" have been, and continue to be, assailed both on college campuses and in society at large. For example, the National Gay and Lesbian Task Force reported "7,031 hate-motivated incidents against gays in 1989, ranging from harassment to homicide."[55] Such victimization, however, is seldom reported by the mainstream media; the responsibility of chronicling the widespread hostility directed against *sex/gender outsiders* is left primarily to alternative outlets.[56]

Three opposing positions characterize the speech code controversy. In the first group are individuals, identified as civil libertarians, who place primary emphasis on the First Amendment's protection of an indiviudal's freedom of speech. The second group is composed of those who place primary emphasis on the Equal Protection Clause or Title VII equality arguments. These individuals are labeled civil rights adherents and include critical race scholars. The third group, referred to as accommodationists, is composed of individuals seeking to accommodate "the strong claims of civil discourse and the strong claims of untrammeled expression."[57]

Civil Libertarians

Individuals in the civil libertarian group[58] criticize various restrictive speech laws as tantamount to censorship. They regard such laws as illegal threats to freedom of expression and as violations of the fundamental principles inherent in the First Amendment. These principles are identified by Thomas Emerson as: self-fulfillment of the speaker; ascertainment of the truth; participation in democratic decision-making; and achievement of a balance between social stability and change.[59] According to civil libertarians, the ultimate danger in censoring speech arises from three sources: the inability of government to establish a principled basis for distinguishing between valuable and non-valuable speech; the impossibility of ensuring that implementation of a government criteria does not "become an expression of the political goals of the group that controls the censor's office;"[60] and the ability of government to stifle open debate and discussion of contentious social policies.

While free speech advocates tend to condemn hate speech in general, they defend the right of an individual to express her/his viewpoint in any terms that do not present a clear danger of an immediate outbreak of lawless behavior. Although many civil libertarians personally consider hate speech to be abhorrent and empathize with the listener, in their considered opinions, neither the content nor the form of a speaker's message can be limited or banned *per se*—regardless of how much it offends, demeans, insults, denigrates, or psychologically wounds the listener(s). Under First Amendment doctrine, as the Supreme Court made clear in *Gertz v. Robert Welch, Inc.*, "there is no such thing as a false idea. However pernicious an opinion may seem, . . . its correction [depends] not on the conscience of judges and juries but on the competititon of other ideas."[61]

Thus, however noxious or reprehensible the listener may find hate speech messages,[62] those messages (arguably) constitute a legitimate segment of public discourse insofar as they represent the speaker's socio-political viewpoint. It is the political nature of the communication which brings the speaker's expressions under the auspices of the First Amendment, but it is the autonomous element underlying the messages that makes the political possible. The political speech value which resides at the very center of First Amendment doctrine and marks it as one of *the* most important form of speech in a democracy presumes the existence of a rational being who possesses liberty of conscience—one who has a right to deliberate, critique, form opinions, reach conclusions, make decisions, and then to act on those thoughts and ideas provided no physical injury is caused to another. This liberty of conscience is premised on a distrust of both the majority and the government to protect those voices that challenge, reject, or deviate from the status quo. The costs associated with freedom of speech, as noted by Rodney Smolla, include "tolerance of even the speech of the intolerant," despite the fact that "[h]ate speech is an abomination, a rape of human dignity."[63] From the perspective of civil libertarians, "[t]olerating ugly, vicious speech is a small but necessary price to pay for the freedom to advocate social change and justice."[64]

Any government policy which regulates speech must satisfy two indispensable conditions in order to claim legitimacy. First and foremost, the speech limitations must focus exclusively on "verbal attacks directed at a particular individual in the sort of face-to-face confrontation that presents a clear and present danger of a violent physical reaction."[65] The scope of these restrictions must be narrowly drawn, so that they encompass no more speech than absolutely necessary to accommodate a compelling government interest. Second, the government's policy must be content and viewpoint-neutral with regard to the communicated message. It may not differentiate between or among ideas nor make privileged some viewpoints over others: as the Supreme Court warned in *Cohen v. California*, "we cannot indulge the facile assumption that one can forbid particular words without also running a substantial risk of suppressing ideas in the process. Indeed, government might soon seize upon the censorship of particular words as a convenient guise for banning the expression of unpopular views."[66] To eliminate or abridge public discourse under circumstances other than those covered by the two restrictions articulated by the Supreme Court would violate, according to Charles Fried, "the [central] idea of a fundamental right to liberty that no one should curtail (or ask the state to curtail), the liberty of another when the only reason is disagreement about another's conception of the good."[67]

Hate speech suppression, while perhaps cathartic for the victim, establishes dangerous precedent. History teaches that when government is the censor, those who express counter-cultural attitudes tend to be the victims.[68] Because the government has a monopoly on the coercive power of the state, it holds the authority to frame choices, mold normative judgments, and enforce the dominant culture's judgment regarding what is true or false, right or wrong, and dangerous or harmless within society. Once these concepts are defined, amnesia settles over the collective memory; the perspective of the dominant group becomes metamorphosed into a disembodied standard which is deemed to be natural, neutral, value-free, and objective. Since these concepts shape the moral, political, and social baseline within society and reflect its perception of reality, antithetical expressions are subject to censorship by the government. The voices and beliefs of "outsiders" are systematically devalued, silenced, punished, and eradicated by government laws designed to condemn "false" and "offensive" ideas and to deter expression of them in the future.

Civil libertarians embrace the classic position on free speech articulated by John Stewart Mill: "[i]f all of mankind minus one were of one opinion, mankind would be no more justified in silencing that one person than he, if had the power, would be justified in silencing mankind."[69] In their eyes, any law which expurgates the expression of dissidents in the name of free speech is ominous. Such laws equate individual or group beliefs with truth, thus circumventing the pragmatic element of the First Amendment, which requires that truth be tested in the "marketplace of ideas."[70] If truth develops over time, as opposed to being absolute, then discussion, debate, and the analysis of ideas becomes relevant and important. Everything can be questioned, for nothing is ever completely settled; nothing is static. Truth is found through the process of actively engaging and probing ideas. Those ideas capable of withstanding the test of time and open, unfettered scrutiny achieve consensus;[71] those which are not accepted as truth are rejected, at least temporarily. In either case, both the accepted and rejected ideas serve as reminders of human fallibility and the temporal condition of truth. From this clash of ideas answers arise—some affirming the status quo, some disputing it.

This outlook is implicit in Justice Holmes' dissenting opinion in *Abrams v. United States*, wherein he argues that

[p]ersecution for the expression of opinions seems to me perfectly logical. If you have no doubt of your premises or your power and want a certain result with all your heart you naturally express your wishes in law and sweep away all opposition. To allow opposition by speech seems to indicate that you think the speech impotent . . . or that you do not care whole-heartedly for the result, or that you doubt either your power or your premises. But when men have realized that time has upset many fighting faiths, they may come to believe the very foundations of their own conduct that the ultimate good desired is better reached through free trade in ideas—that the best test of truth is the power of thought to get itself accepted in the competition of the market, and that truth is the only ground upon which their wishes safely can be carried out. That at any rate is the theory of our Constitution. It is an experiment, as all of life is an experiment.[72]

Justice Holmes' position is reiterated by Justice Douglas in *Dennis v. United States*: "The airing of ideas releases pressures which otherwise might become destructive. When ideas compete in the market for acceptance, full and free discussion exposes the false and they gain few adherents. Full and free discussion even of ideas we hate encourages the testing of our own prejudices and preconceptions. Full and free discussion keeps a society from becoming stagnant and unprepared for the stresses and strains that work to tear all civilizations apart."[73] Full and free discussion ensures that no ideas are repressed, encompasses the possibility of growth and change, and recognizes that every individual within society is equal insofar as each has a right to determine the truth for her/himself. Anything less assumes an inequality between and among citizens, denies liberty of conscience to some individuals, and legitimizes the use of coercion to silence dissent and enforce the truth. Those individuals or groups who would obstruct or prohibit full and free discussion within society assume, in Mill's opinion, their own infallibility when they "think that some particular principle or doctrine should be forbidden to be questioned because it is *so certain*, that is, because *they are certain* that it is certain."[74] But as Justice Black cogently reminds us, "freedoms of speech, press, petition, and assembly guaranteed by the First Amendment must be accorded to the ideas we hate or sooner or later they will be denied to the ideas we cherish."[75]

Civil Rights Adherents

The civil rights adherents,[76] represented by critical race scholars Mari Matsuda, Richard Delgado, and Charles R. Lawrence III, adamantly disagree with the traditional civil libertarian approach to hate speech. They insist that it is inexcusably wrong for civil libertarians to conceptualize hate speech as equivalent to reasoned, political discourse of the kind that has been customarily protected by First Amendment jurisprudence.[77] In their eyes, those who spew hatred are conveying neither a political message nor any other type of idea. They maintain to the contrary that the sole purpose of hate speech is to debase, subordinate, and denigrate those targeted, and that therefore it is pernicious and totally without merit. In this view, hate speech is more akin to "spirit-murder"[78] than to political speech.

Scholars on this side of the hate speech controversy articulate a dual justification for excluding hate messages from speech that is properly entitled to First Amendment protection. On the one hand, they argue that hate speech conforms to the "fighting words" plus doctrine established by the Supreme Court in *Chaplinsky* insofar as "by their very utterance [the words] inflict injury or tend to incite . . . an immediate breach of the peace."[79] On the other hand, they contend that hate speech uniquely damages targeted individuals and denies them participation in society as full and equal citizens. Thus, the hate speaker's interest in freedom of speech directly conflicts with the listener's interest in freedom from harm. To grant First Amendment protection to the speaker simultaneously denies equality for the listener and perpetuates the listener's "outsider" status.[80] Moreover, civil rights advocates claim that by including hate messages under the First Amendment the government conveys the message that vituperative, dehumanizing, hateful speech is legitimate, acceptable, and supported by the law.[81]

By focusing on the victim's story, civil rights advocates attempt to expose the ways in which racist expression causes physical, emotional, and psychic harm to individuals who are targeted. These theorists, by descriptively portraying victims' responses to racist hate messages, expose some of the infinite ways in which hate messages methodically assault indiviudals. For example, Lawrence asserts that the experience of being called a derogatory name is analogous "to receiving a slap in the face,"[82] while Matsuda describes the psychological symptoms and emotional distress experienced by the victims of racist hate messages, which "[range] from fear in the gut to rapid pulse rate and difficulty in breathing, nightmares, post-tramatic stress disorder, hypertension, psychosis, and suicide."[83]

Civil rights theorists believe that freedom of speech is meaningless without equality; indeed, for them equality is an indispensible precondition to free speech,[84] because language reflects the power dynamics within society. Victims quickly learn that counterspeech is not a viable reaction to hate speech, due to the heightened possibility of physical violence. Rather than counterspeech, the victim's response is generally no speech; targeted individuals choke on words that cannot be uttered, thereby reinforcing the message that they are inferior to the attacker. Yet, unlike other forms of hate speech directed at "outsiders," civil rights theorists assert, racism is different from all other types of hate speech. Racist hate messages are *sui generis*, because only racist epithets, slurs, invectives, threats, insults, and the like present historically untenable ideas, are extremely dangerous, and are inseparable from the "perpetuation of violence and degredation of individuals who are least equipped to respond."[85] Absent true equality, racist language intrudes into the victims' psyche and projects a vision of the victims' self that is imposed by the dominating powers.[86] The strength of this self-image and its assaultive quality is derived from the legacy of racial interactions in this country. These racist utterances not only inflict severe injury on the victims by producing immediate mental or emotional distress, infringing on the targets' personal dignity, and inflicting psychological harm—facts well documented by the psychological, sociological, legal, and political effects of it[87]—they also seriously damage society as a whole by violating the egalitarian ideal expressed in the Declaration of Independence, thereby undermining the philosophical foundation of the U.S. moral and legal system.[88]

Because the U.S. remains deeply afflicted by racism, these civil rights adherents focus primarily on the role racism has played and continues to play in this country. They "present racism not as isolated instances of conscious bigoted decisionmaking or prejudiced practice, but as larger, systemic, structural, and cultural, as deeply psychologically and socially ingrained."[89] Tolerance of racist hate speech within this context forces targeted victims to bear the entire burden.[90] Racially subordinated individuals are compelled to figure out how to protect themselves without infringing on the dominant group's freedom of speech. By subjugating the equality rights of minorities to the speech rights of the majority, powerful, white dominant institutions within society benefit. Indeed, Delgado states that "[the highly educated, refined persons who operate the universities and major corporations] benefit, and on a subconscious level they know they benefit from a certain amount of low-level racism in the environment,"[91] because the existence of such racism "keeps non-white people on edge, a little off balance."[92] Delgado's argument is echoed by Lawrence in his assertion that "to engage in a debate about the first amendment and racist speech risks making the first amendment an instrument of domination rather than a vehicle of liberation."[93] Thus, in response to the numerous wrongs stemming from and caused by hate speech, civil rights advocates delineate three legal remedies designed to suppress racist hate messages.

Perhaps the most modest proposal is presented by Lawrence, who envisions a speech regulation that can "be defended within the confines of existing first amendment doctrine."[94] He argues that the speech regulation should be "narrowly drafted . . . [to] prohibit face-to-face vilification and protect captive audiences from verbal and written harassment."[95] This slight expansion of First Amendment protection to include captive audiences provides, in Lawrence's estimation, an essential link to a meaningful enforcement of the equality mandate contained in the Equal Protection Clause of the Fourteenth Amendment—the only amendment that specifically provides the requisite constitutional basis for restricting racist expression, per the Supreme Court's unanimous decision in *Brown v. Board of Education*.[96]

Delgado, unlike Lawrence, contends that an independent tort for racial insults needs to be created. Under his proposal, an individual who seeks to prevail in an action for racial insults must prove that "language was addressed to him or her by the defendant that was intended to demean through reference to race; that the plantiff understood as intended to demean through reference to race; and that a reasonable person would recognize as a racial insult."[97] This type of legal redress would achieve two objectives. First, it would safeguard the personality and equal citizenship interests valued within the United States; second, it would validate the right of all citizens to be free from vicious atacks on their dignity and psychological integrity.[98]

Matsuda's proposal is the most radical of those offered. Her model sharply curtails who can seek redress for racist speech. Athough Matsuda agrees that the victim's story ought to be heard and her/his perspective respected, she maintains that this does not include the story or perspective of individuals who are deemed to be, or who choose to align themselves with, members of the dominant group. She seeks to control only "the worst, paradigm example of racist hate messages."[99] Her approach, which is much more content-based than either Lawrence's or Delgado's, necessitates treating racist hate messages as *sui generis.* The three identifying characteristics that would distinguish such messages and make them qualitatively different from other forms of racist and nonracist speech, according to Matsuda, are: "1. The message is of racial inferiority; 2. [t]he message is directed against a historically oppressed group; and 3. [t]he message is persecutorial, hateful, and degrading."[100] All three of these elements must be present in order for someone to be prosecuted for hate speech under this standard. However, rather than suggesting an application of the Fourteenth Amendment in conjunction with the First, as Lawrence does, or supporting a specific type of legal intervention, as Delgado does, Matsuda includes both tort and criminal law as appropriate procedures for prosecuting speakers of racist hate messages, without indicating a preference. It should be noted, however, that although these scholars advocate different methods for eliminating racist insults, they collectively agree that a narrowly drafted regulation can be developed to protect against the most egregious forms of racist expression.

Accommodationists

Accommodationists[101] attempt to "walk the middle ground" between the civil libertarians and the civil rights advocates on the regulation of hate speech, although they are technically closer to the former than to the latter.[102] While in agreement with civil rights advocates that hate speech can be legitimately censored (but only under very limited and prescribed conditions), accommodationists also agree with civil libertarians that group libel would not be actionable. Thus, according to Toni J. Massaro, the proposals supported by accommodationists "share the common characteristics of being tightly worded, context-specific, and closely tied to the fighting words doctrine and/or the tort of intentional infliction of emotional distress. In essence, the proposals seek to regulate targeted, intentional vilification of a person or small group of persons in face-to-face encounters on the basis of a protected characteristic."[103]

Scholars who support the accommodationist position thus attempt to strike a balance "between strong individual expressive freedom and the prevention of human suffering."[104] They contend that the salient distinction between words that inflict harm on designated listeners (i.e., individuals possessing a protected characteristic) and words that merely wound listeners is the recognition that words in the first group embody the implicit threat of physical violence or force.[105] Thus, while they acknowledge that "discourse can influence thinking,"[106] accommodationists deliberately concentrate on the harms produced by words aimed at a designated individual and chosen to maximize direct visercal hatred or contempt, rather than on the destructive or prejudiced viewpoint espoused by a speaker to a general audience. In Massaro's judgement, "[t]he accommodationist proposals . . . seem to [be] fairminded attempts to deal with things as they are, without abandoning the more general aspiration of free and open discourse."[107]

Accommodationists, thus, confine the scope of regulatable speech to an interpretation of "fighting words," augmented by the common law tort of "intentional infliction of emotional distress."[108] Through such limitations the accommodationists seek to proscribe the subordinating and violent character of the hate speech without severely infringing an individual's freedom of speech. There is much disagreement among accommodationists, however, as exemplified by legal scholars such as David F. McGowan and Ragesh K. Tangri, Sean M. SeLegue, Kent Greenawalt, and Thomas Grey, regarding how best to achieve this objective.

McGowan and Tangri argue that the realm of unprotected speech needs to be narrowed in two ways. First, speech that is extraordinarily offensive to the listener should be prohibited even when nonconsequentialist justifications for protecting speech exist.[109] Second, the common law tort of "intentional infliction of emotional distress" should be modified to reach only private speech[110] that "eliminates the possibility of rational deliberation."[111] This modified limitation, in their opinion, preserves the integrity of the deliberative process while restricting any speech that curtails a listener's ability to rationally assess the speaker's message. Thus, their limitation places the primary focus on the form of the language (civility of discourse) rather than on the *content* of the message (viewpoint).

SeLegue's proposed speech regulation reflects that of McGowan and Tangri's to the extent that it also rests firmly on a specified interpretation of the "intentional infliction of emotional distress" tort. The approach SeLegue favors centers on "the susceptibility doctrine and the specific intent of the speaker . . . [in order] to define a narrow civility zone in which an individual's liberty interest in being left alone can be constitutionally enforced."[112] By concentrating on the known susceptibility of a victim to particular epithets or types of abuse, SeLegue rivets attention on the hearer's right to be left alone rather than on the social utility of the speaker's particular utterances. Under his speech restrictions, "[o]nly those utterances targeted at a particular individual or identified group of individuals, in a context creating an intimidating and hostile environment, which the speaker knew or should have known would greatly uspet the target, can be punished."[113]

Kent Greenwalt, unlike McGowan and Tangri or SeLegue, submits that group vilification in the form of racial and ethnic epithets and slurs should be made illegal through separate legal standards, despite the fact that fighting words are currently punishable and that the "intentional infliction of emotional distress" tort already exists. In his view, a "fighting words plus" standard—that is, a standard which incorporates both "fighting words" and a tort of extreme emotional distress—would "serve as [a] symbolic statement that such language [i.e., racial and ethnic epithets and slurs, is] particularly at odds with our constitutional values; and [it] could relieve prosecutors, or plantiffs, from having to establish all the requisites of a more general offense or tort."[114]

Finally, Thomas Grey proposes limiting speech regulations to speech or expression that intimidates by threat of violence, personally vilifies, or harasses individuals on the basis of sex, race, color, handicap, religion, sexual orientation/preference, or national and ehtnic origin.[115] In Grey's policy, designed for a university setting, speech or other expression constitutes harassment by personal vilification if it:

(a) is intended to insult or stigmatize an individual or a small number of individuals on the basis of [the aforementioned characteristics]; and

(b) is addressed directly to the individual or individuals whom it insults or stigmatizes; and

(c) makes use of insulting or "fighting" words or non-verbal symbols . . . which by their very utterance inflict injury or tend to incite to an immediate breach of the peace, and which are commonly understood to convey direct and visceral hatred or contempt for human beings on the basis of [the aforementioned characteristics].[116]

In his proposal, Grey strives to find an equilibrium between protecting freedom of expression and the discourse of ideas while minimizing or eliminating the use of slurs and epithets. He attempts to achieve this balance by remaining fairly close to the "fighting words" doctrine, insofar as he requires that hate messages be directly addressed to the speaker's target, while expanding the scope of the hate speech doctrine to cover words or symbols that inflict injury.

IMPORTANCE OF FREE SPEECH TO *SEX/GENDER OUTSIDERS*

Language and power are so intimately entwined that the values of the dominant culture are embedded in the very concepts of what constitutes "normal" or "natural." Yet a blind eye is cast upon the potential impact these embedded values may have on the lives of lesbians, gay men, bisexuals, and transgenderists by those who are apt to benefit from those values, either directly or indirectly. *Sex/gender outsiders* suffer the consequences of being labeled "perverted," "malefic," or "abnormal" for failing to adhere to socially permissible gender expressions or to the socially prescribed affectional orientation/preference. Through this labeling, individuals who transgress the socially acceptable boundaries of gender identity or affectional orientation/preference are, to varying degrees, ostracized and dehumanized.

The labeling of *sex/gender outsiders* in this manner serves two other societal purposes. First, these labels explicitly exclude lesbians, gay men, bisexuals, and transgenderists from full participation in the public domain. A cursory examination of U.S. history clearly illuminates the multitude of legal and political actions which have subordinated and oppressed lesbians, gay men, bisexuals, and transgenderists in society.[117] Through its denial of unabridged citizenship rights to *sex/gender outsiders*, society fortifies its view that *sex/gender outsiders* are aberrations of the "normal" manifestations of gender identity or affectional orientation/preference. It augments this view by deliberately omitting *sex/gender outsiders* from laws protecting the basic civil rights, civil liberties, and human rights of its citizens.

An intricate weaving of government and private actions reinforces and shapes the public's perception of individuals and groups labeled "other." Those who fail to conform (adequately) to the norms espoused by the dominant culture are penalized.[118] The price exacted frequently includes some or all of the following: insults, stereotypes, epithets, slurs, terroristic attacks, objectification, rejection, harassment, beatings, death; loss of life's necessities (i.e., jobs, licenses, housing, security); denial of personal benefits (i.e., marriage, child custody, adoption and visitation, medical care, security clearances, military careers); and loss or denial of insurance, tax advantages, or public benefits (i.e., workers compensation, social security and pension entitlements, standing to sue for wrongful death or other torts, property and inheritance rights).[119] The protests of *sex/gender outsiders* to these penalties are typically dismissed as ungrounded, self-serving, histrionic, insincere, flaunting, or inflammatory.

The second purpose effected by the labels used to characterize, and the messages communicated about, *sex/gender outsiders* is implicitly to silence not only that entire populace, but also members of society in general, through social constrictions placed on gender identity and affectional orientation/preference. Any individual who self-identifies as, or is perceived to be, a *sex/gender outsider* is marginalized within society and confronted by discrimination which is not only condoned, but rationalized and justified through a variety of religious, medical, legal, and moral arguments.

Little if any room exists in society for either ambiguity or difference; individuals are expected to fit cultural expectations. Natal genitals are believed to determine one's sex—if an individual is born with a penis, that person must be male. Clothes and mannerisms are believed to determine one's gender—if an individual wears make-up, dresses, and high heels, that person must be a woman. The sex of one's partner determine's one's affectional orientation/preference—if an individual displays affection for her/his partner in public, that person is deemed "normal" if such display occurs solely between partners of different sexes. When disagreement exists between what is seen (the external physical manifestation of sex, gender, or affectional orientation/preference) and what is known (the internalized acculturation of social convention regarding the "natural" or "authentic" representation of sex, gender, or affectional orientation/preference), cognitive dissonance arises. If a female possesses a penis or both a penis and a vulva; if a man wears dresses, high heels, and make-up; or if a person publicly displays affection with an individual of the same sex, cultural shock occurs—the visual cues directly conflict with the socialized internal belief system. Society dictates that when this happens, those who cause this dissonance must become physically and verbally invisible or suffer the consequences.

Indeed, even if the dissonance accurately reflects the lives and experiences of some individuals, *sex/gender outsiders* are expected to reinforce the majority's "reality" through self-denial. Lesbians, gay men, and bisexuals are expected to acquiesce to cross-sex affectional expression or remain celibate; transvestites, trangenderists, transsexuals, and intersexuals are expected to wear gender-appropriate clothes, behave in gender-appropriate ways, or possess sexually appropriate genitals as determined by society. Those who dare to name, embrace, or claim their difference become targets of the dominant culture's fear, distrust, and urge to punish the "other." If a *sex/gender outsider* engages, even briefly, in activities that render possible the self-congruence of external and internal cues—if s/he engages in intimacy with one of her/his own sex whether exclusively or not, dresses in clothes designated for the opposite gender, or attempts to alter or disguise her/his natal genitals or to retain her/his genital ambiguity—the dominant culture punishes the transgressor, while simultaneously making her/him feel guilty, ashamed, or responsible for her/his own punishment. By excluding and silencing *sex/gender outsiders*, society acts in unison to perpetuate the unabated subordination of lesbians, gay men, bisexuals, and transgenderists. Through laws and moral legislation, the government conveys the message that *sex/gender outsiders* are not entitled to the rights and privileges accorded full citizens, by denying lesbians, gay men, bisexuals, and transgenderists the freedom of openly expressing their gender identity or affectional orientation/preference without apprehension of persecution.

The message that *sex/gender outsiders* are second-class citizens is echoed in the private sphere.[120] Through the technique of labeling and silencing *sex/gender outsiders*, society reinforces the internal repression and external suppression not only of lesbians, gay men, bisexuals, and transgenderists but also of individuals who ostensibly conform to the social constructs of sex, gender, and affectional orientation/preference. One of the primary ways this is accomplished is through actual and symbolic speech. Members of the dominant group who criticize or protest against the discrimination or violence levied against society's subalterns, according to Arthur J. Deikman, endanger themselves by their transgression: "We can feel secure in the protection provided by a group, but that protection has its price. Compliance with the group often extends further than acceptance of the group's views to include participation in the attack on deviants by subtle (or not so subtle) disapproval, punishment, or rejection of any member who voices criticism of the consensus. . . . [The] dissident is criticized as disloyal, lacking commitment, interfering with the important work of the group."[121]

The dissident's criticism of the majority view, either alone or in unison with *sex/gender outsiders*, may cause at least some in the dominant group to feel threatened. As Kenneth Schneyer notes, "[s]ince sexuality is neither an externally visible physical characteristic, such as race or sex, nor normally perceived to follow parentage, such as ethnic identity, the viewer has difficulty excluding the possibility that she herself may partake of it. How do you know you're straight if that's what you claim to be?"[122] While self-reflection can provide a personal answer, the superficial means by which viewers can protect themselves from perceived threats to their gender identity or affectional orientation/preference is through the perpetuation and practice of discrimination and hatred. Stereotypes, verbal harassment, insults, epithets, and innuendos enable those who feel threatened by *sex/gender outsiders* to distance themselves from those who transgress the established norms in order to prove to themselves and others that they are in fact "normal." These speech acts simply mirror the injustice perpetrated by those institutionalized structures within society that assault the dignity of lesbians, gay men, bisexuals, or transgenderists and spread the message that *sex/gender outsiders* are morally inferior to "normal" individuals and thus are undeserving of respect.[123] By legitimating the fears and animosities of non-*sex/gender outsiders*, both explicitly and implicitly, through its laws and social mores, society's judgment that lesbians, gay men, bisexuals, and transgenderists are "outsiders" is effectively transmitted, while the identity anxieties of "real" males, females, men, women, and heterosexuals are assuaged.

Unfortunately, neither the speech acts nor the messages delivered by the majority may be directly or immediately answerable by more speech. As a result, *sex/gender outsiders* may, as Richard Mohr observes, "[be] left with only the equally unjust alternatives of the resignation of the impotent or the rage of man in a state of nature."[124] While such options are acutely unsatisfactory, attempts to silence legally the denigrators of *sex/gender outsiders* would violate one of the core principles of the First Amendment, which holds that even despicable speech acts are protected under the Constitution. As the Seventh Circuit Court of Appeals correctly noted in *American Booksellers Association Inc. v. Hudnut,* "[a]ny other answer leaves the government in control of all of the institutions of culture, the great censor and dictator to which thoughts are good for us."[125]

Acceptance of this core principle is not intended as a denial of the pain or injury imposed by expressions of disrespect, hatred, abuse, dehumanization, or vehement anti-lesbian/gay/bisexual/transgendered sentiments. Rather, it is merely a recognition of the fact that it is inherently dangerous, if not outright self-destructive, for *sex/gender outsiders* to embrace restrictions on speech. Laws that outlaw or eradicate hate speech will not obliterate the fundamental sense of threat, fear, insecurity, or enmity felt by "normal" individuals within society. They may, however, provide the dominant culture with yet another means by which it can continue to silence or further restrict the permissible range of speech for lesbians, gay men, bisexuals, and transgenderists. Minnie Bruce Pratt provides an excellent example of just such an occurrence. In her essay "Poetry in the Time of War,"[126] Pratt reveals how an attempt to censor *sex/gender outsiders* was translated into a statute placing limits on what information could be provided by federally funded projects: "[The] Helms amendment on AIDS-specific funding during the 101st Congress directed that 'no educational material that promotes homosexuality' could be financed with federal money. The legislation originally was written by Helms and Rep. William Dannemeyer in response to a safe-sex comic book produced by a gay men's health clinic; the depiction of two men demonstrating life-saving safe sex techniques was declared by Dannemeyer to be 'pornographic,' by Helms to be 'obscene.' "127

Another example is provided by the National Endowment of the Arts legislation passed in the late 1980s whereby any art funded with public money was required to be "sensitive to the general standards of decency . . . of the American public."128 While the phrase "general standards of decency" sounds innocuous when defined from a heterocentric or heterosexist perspective, this standard readily translates into the dictum that "art about gay and lesbian life, 'homoerotic' art, . . . [is] obscene by definition."129 The reason, as Pratt acerbically notes, lies in the fact that "hatred . . . hides behind the word *decent* in this country, hundreds of years of hatred."130 It takes little or no imagination to deduce that artistic expressions or representations of the gender identity or affectional lives of *sex/gender outsiders* would have extreme difficulty meeting a decency standard interpreted through the "traditional values" pontificated by such individuals as the Reverend Donald Wildmon, Senator Jesse Helms, Representative William Dannemeyer, Patrick Bucannan, or Senator Trent Lott, to name but a few. Since "traditional values" exclude the very existence of lesbians, gay men, bisexuals, and transgenderists, positive characterizations of *sex/gender outsiders* would be banned by individuals such as these—in clear violation of the principles underlying the First Amendment.

One of the premier reasons why freedom of speech is deemed fundamental in this country is that it secures the right to personal self-expression. As Thomas Emerson observes, "freedom of expression is essential to a means of assuring individual self-fulfillment."131 Whether one finds that self-fulfillment through expression such as wearing insignias; announcing one's gender identity or affectional orientation/preference; advocating for rights; writing letters, editorials, or scholarly papers; dancing, kissing, embracing, or holding hands; holding membership in political or social organizations; or in taking one of the other infinitely expressive avenues available to humans, First Amendment speech is involved. In Emerson's words, "[t]he proper end of man is the realization of his character and potentialities as a human being. . . . Hence, suppression of belief, opinion, or other expression is an affront to the dignity of man, a negation of man's essential nature."132

Society's denial of an individual's right to speak is tantamount to repudiating an essential aspect of one's being. The degree to which lesbians, gay men, bisexuals, and transgenderists are coerced into concealing their self-identity and living a public lie through omission, commission, or ambiguity, due to the prevalence of social and political discrimination and to the numerous obstacles to legal redress, is proportionate to the First Amendment protection denied *sex/gender outsiders.* The Supreme Court has clearly ruled in *Woodley v. Maynard* that the state can not use persons as instruments to foster a point of view that the individuals themselves may find to be morally, religiously, or politically objectionable.[133] But if the state offers *sex/gender outsiders* a Hobson's choice between self-renunciation and the threat of retaliation, then in effect it is circumventing the proscription of the Supreme Court and destroying the essence of the First Amendment. By silencing individuals about their lives and rendering them invisible, the state denies *sex/gender outsiders* the opportunity to participate in the human experience of building a new community or becoming part of an existing community, since community membership necessarily involves identification and communication.[134] As long as the government refuses to ameliorate and eradicate the legal infirmities based on gender identity and affectional orientation/preference and the courts fail to protect vigilantly the literal and symbolic speech of *sex/gender outsiders*, lesbians, gay men, bisexuals, and transgenderists can neither safely nor completely afford to shed the masks that conceal their identification or overcome the silences that deny community.

Yet even if one is unwilling to recognize self-expression as the most significant reason for protecting freedom of speech, accepting instead Alexander Meiklejohn's judgment that political speech is the most important type of speech to protect,[135] censoring the speech of *sex/gender outsiders* still violates an essential First Amendment principle. Meiklejohn's conception of political speech includes deliberation on all public matters with which government policy is concerned. In his view, speech is part of one's social obligation; through it society's thought process is engaged and stirred by allowing the expression of "everything worth saying."[136] Thus, no speaker who is addressing a political matter can be summarily dismissed or silenced merely because the majority regards what the speaker has to say as disagreeable, critical, worthless, unreasonable, wrong, challenging, or offensive. This is especially true for *sex/gender outsiders.* As David Richards notes, "[h]omosexuality is today essentially a form of political, social, and moral dissent, on par with the best American traditions of dissent and even subversive advocacy."[137]

Attempts by the state to regulate speech it labels "offensive" and "abhorrent" may have the effect of stifling the advocacy of lesbians, gay men, bisexuals, or transgenderists,[138] or of censoring the messages, ideas, content, or subject matter of *sex/gender outsiders*' speech. Historical evidence abounds. For example, when the government sought to control both information and ideas through censorship in the 1920s:

The Well of Loneliness [a novel by Radcliff Hall] and . . . *Captive* [a Broadway play] were declared obscene. . . . Radcliff Hall's appeal overturned the decision of publishers, but New York state outlawed overt references to homosexuality on the stage. Controversial plays such as Lillian Hellman's *The Children's Hour* were tolerated as long as the word "lesbian" was not mentioned. In Hollywood, a film version of Oscar Wilde's *Salome* was produced with a purportedly all gay cast. But the censorship forces eventually prevailed. In 1935, the Motion Picture Code banned all references to homosexuality.[139]

Over seventy years later, according to the National Lesbian and Gay Task Force,

U.S. Customs officials . . . seized two separate shipments of books and other literature en route to Boston's Glad Day Bookstore, a gay and lesbian bookseller. Agents first seized a shipment from Barcelona on 6 April [1992] and then a shipment from Italy on 21 May [1992]. Glad Day reports that customs officials say the literature was in violation of an obscenity provision of the U.S. Code. Among the many titles seized was *Guía Gay*, a gay guide to Spain, and a periodical called the *Gay Book*.[140]

When the state engages in such behavior, the question that immediately arises is: will the courts uphold the First Amendment rights of *sex/gender outsiders*, or will they side with the state? In general, the courts have been most rigorous and consistent in protecting the speech of lesbians, gay men, bisexuals, and transgenderists in traditionally protected settings, such as universities[141] and public forums.[142] Judicial recognition of the fact that the speech rights claimed by *sex/gender outsiders* are significantly comparable to the speech rights the courts have been protecting for non-*sex/gender outsiders* lies at the core of the majority of First Amendment victories. In nontraditional settings, however, the courts have not been as willing to protect the expression of *sex/gender outsiders*. When free speech claims have been raised in the context of federal tax-exempt status,[143] in circumstances regarding the denial, suspension, or revocation of liquor licenses,[144] and in defense of sexual expression,[145] for example, *sex/gender outsiders* have historically encountered insensitive or hostile judiciaries. The courts have also shown themselves to be less than sympathetic to the speech rights of *sex/gender outsiders* when organizations have attempted to incorporate. For example, in *State ex. rel. Grant v. Brown*, the Ohio Supreme Court held that the state's denial of the Greater Cincinnati Gay Society's request to incorporate did not violate the organization's rights to freedom of speech, assembly, or association. In the Court's words, "although homosexual acts between consenting adults are no longer statutory offenses, we agree with the Secretary of State that the promotion of homosexuality as a valid life style is contrary to the public policy of the state."[146]

Perhaps the most egregious infringement of the First Amendment rights of *sex/gender outsiders* occurs in the area of employment. In this context, lesbians, gay men, bisexuals, and transgenderists have experienced difficulty convincing the courts that the expression of gender identity and affectional orientation/preference ought to be fully protected speech.[147] The courts seem more intent on focusing on the employer's reaction to the information disclosed or discovered rather than on the ability of lesbians, gay men, bisexuals, and transgenderists to perform the requisite job or on the interests of *sex/gender outsiders* in keeping their jobs. Overall, the judiciary appears reluctant to pronounce without qualification that *sex/gender outsiders* possess a constitutional right to self-identify through speech or association. This is illustrated by two judicial decisions—*Shahar v. Bowers* and *Rowland v. Mad River Local School District.*

In the first case, *Shahar v. Bowers,*[148] the plaintiff, Robin Joy Brown, was offered a permanent job by Attorney General Michael J. Bowers in the Georgia Law Department, which she accepted. When she finished law school and passed the bar, she contacted the Deputy District Attorney for Administration to "touch base" and to notify him that she was changing her last name from Brown to Shahar. She also informed him that she was getting married that summer. Prior to the wedding, however, Bowers withdrew the job offer because of information he had received that the intended marriage was between Shahar and another woman. A lawsuit was filed by Shahar maintaining that Bowers had violated her constitutional rights to freedom of speech, free expression of religion, freedom of association, equal protection, and substantive due process. In its decision, the district court asserted that Shahar's lesbian marriage constituted an intimate association that was constitutionally protected under the First Amendment. After recognizing this, however, the court proceeded to hold that Attorney General Bowers could legitimately withdraw his offer of employment to Shahar, because her lesbian relationship necessarily violated Georgia's sodomy law—despite the fact that Shahar had never been legally indicted, arrested, or convicted of violating this law—and interfered with the efficient operation of the state's law-enforcement department.[149] As Bowers asserted in the Defendant's Reply, "[r]egardless of whether plaintiff has actually committed sodomy, plaintiff's Amended Complaint admits that she has purportedly 'married' her female companion, and that she made such 'marriage' public knowledge. On these facts alone, the Attorney General is justified in withdrawing the offer of employment in order to ensure public perception (and the reality) that his department is enforcing and will continue to enforce the laws of the State."[150]

In the second case, *Rowland v. Mad River Local School District*, a nontenured high school guidance counselor, Marjorie Rowland, was fired from her job after informing several individuals at the school that she was bisexual. Chief Judge Lively relied heavily on the Supreme Court's decision in *Connick v. Myers*, wherein the Court had held that a federal court is not the appropriate forum to review personnel decisions when "a public employee speaks not as a citizen upon matters of public concern, but instead as an employee upon matters only of personal interest."[151] Based on this holding, Chief Judge Lively stated that Rowland's statements regarding her bisexuality—made to the secretary, the vice principal, and several teachers who were personal friends—were not protected speech under the First Amendment. In his view "[t]here was absolutely no evidence of any public concern in the community or at Stebbins High with the issue of bisexuality among school personnel when she began speaking to others about her sexual preference."[152] Chief Justice Lively argued that Rowland's requests for confidentiality were evidence that her statements were not made as a citizen on matters of public concern. Moreover, her additional disclosures to other staff members were merely efforts on her part to avoid an unfavorable action by her employer.[153]

Justice Edwards began his dissent by asserting that the U.S. Constitution does not deny its protection to citizens based on their sexuality. Similar to all other citizens, Edwards argues, "bisexuals and homosexuals are protected [by the First and Fourteenth Amendments], . . . certainly to the extent of being homosexual and stating their sexual preference in a factual manner where there is no invasion of any other person's rights."[154] Although he recognized the Supreme Court's decision in *Connick*, he was not persuaded that that precedent was applicable to Rowland's situation. In his view, while Rowland's initial disclosures regarding her bisexuality "may not have had its origin in an overt attempt to exercise freedom of speech,"[155] they became such when "her statements about her status resulted in 'public concern'—both pro and con."[156] By adhering to "her right to be what she was and to state that fact,"[157] Rowland found herself in the center of a public controversy. While Judge Edwards acknowledged that the incident was not a matter of national attention, "in southern Ohio it was an important matter of public concern. It thus became a part of the nationwide debate on homosexuality and the rights or lack thereof of homosexuals—a debate of far greater significance than the majority opinion recognizes."[158]

Contrary to what the majority in *Rowland* or the district court in *Shahar* would prefer, sexuality stays neither in the bedroom nor hidden. Heterosexuals visibly "flaunt" their affectional orientation/preference at work, in public, and in the media. It is so much a part of the dominant culture that, according to José Gomez, "[t]he public expression of heterosexual personhood is . . . favored socially and legally by tacitly being seen neither as sexual nor as speech. This occurs because it is dominant in both arenas."[159] Because heterosexuality is so prevalent within society, the speech and conduct of *sex/gender outsiders* is frequently characterized as extreme and is pushed outside the boundaries of constitutional protection. In numerous cases concerning the First Amendment rights of *sex/gender outsiders*,[160] the courts have adopted the term "flaunting" to deny constitutional protection to a wide range of expressive conduct and gestures that the courts have ruled to be within the scope of the First Amendment when engaged in by heterosexuals. By this dual standard, the judiciary virtually eclipses the speech of *sex/gender outsiders* and marks it as subordinate to that of heterosexuals. The social, political, and legal silencing and exclusion of lesbians, gay men, bisexuals, and transgenderists thus persists.

As Mohr accurately states, "it is the recriminations that descend upon gays who are publicly gay that effectively deny them first amendment rights."[161] This observation is true with regard to all *sex/gender outsiders*. Only the official elimination of the multitudinous conditions which perpetuate the existence of the "closet" will make possible a meaningful claim of First Amendment rights for lesbians, gay men, bisexuals, and transgenderists. But *sex/gender outsiders* can ill afford to try and obtain these rights at the expense of suppressing the First Amendment speech of others. Despite the fact that the judiciary generally appears to be on opposite sides from *sex/gender outsiders* on free speech issues which arise in non-traditional settings, it is hazardous to attempt to beat the dominant culture at its own game. By supporting laws that censor speech, even if they are directed against one's enemies with the intention of stopping their hateful words and messages, *sex/gender outsiders* leave themselves open to having those laws applied to their own words, expressions, and images. As a distinct minority within society, Karst warns, *sex/gender outsiders* cannot afford to forget a corollary to Murphy's Law: "Suppressions that *can* happen *will* happen."[162]

NOTES

1. See: Emerson (1970) at 6–7; Gressman (1990) at 390–391; Richards (1974) at 74; Scanlon (1972) at 213–214; *Palko* at 326–327; *Procunier* at 427.

2. Emerson (1970) at 6–7; Mill (1975), Chapter 2; *Abrams* at 630 (Holmes, J., dissenting); *Whitney* (Brandeis, J., concurring).

3. Emerson (1970) at 6–7; Meiklejohn (1961) at 255–257; *Time, Inc.* at 388. See also: *Whitney* (Brandeis, J., concurring); Bork (1971); *Olleman* (1984); Karst (1975).

4. Emerson (1970) at 6–7. See also: *Whitney* (Brandeis, J., concurring); *Masses Publishing Co.* (1917); Black (1960).

5. Emerson (1970) at 6–7. See also: *Whitney* (Brandeis, J., concurring).

6. *Gitlow* at 666; *Near* at 707; *Palko* at 327. See also: *Abrams* (Holmes, J., dissenting); *Whitney* (Brandeis, J., concurring); *West Virginia State Board of Education* (1934); *United States v. Carolene Products Co.* (1938) [hereafter *Carolene Products*] at fn.4; *Cantwell* (1940); *New York Times Co.* (1964); Mill (1975); McKay (1959).

7. Chief Justice Vinson noted in *Dennis* (1951) that "the majority of the Court . . . have recognized that [freedom of speech] is not an unlimited, unqualified right, but that the societal value of speech must, on occasion, be subordinated to other values and considerations." See also: *Konigberg* (1961); *Elrod* (1976) at 360; McKay (1959).

8. *Dennis* at 503.

9. For example: *Schenck* (1919); *Schneider* (1939); *Cox* (1941); *Chaplinsky* (1942); *Valentine* (1942); *Dennis* (1951); *Beauharnais* (1952); *Yates* (1957); *Roth* (1957); *Bates* (1960); *Police Dept. v. Mosley* (1972) [hereafter *Mosley*]; *R.A.V.* (1992); *State v. Talley* (1993) [hereafter *Talley*]; *People v. Steven S.* (1994) [hereafter *Steven S.*]; *State v. Vawter et al.* (1994) [hereafter *Vawter*]. See also: Goldstein (1978).

10. According to Justice Vinson in *Dennis*, "[n]o important case involving free speech was decided by [the] Court prior to *Schenck*." [*Dennis* at 503].

11. *Schenck* at 52.

12. *Abrams* at 628.

13. *Id.* at 630.

14. *Id.*

15. *Id.*

16. See Scalia's comments (and the concurrences' counter-comments) regarding unprotected speech in *R.A.V.* (1992), Chapter Five *infra*.

17. For example: obscenity, fraudulent misrepresentation, advocacy of imminent lawless behavior, defamation, "fighting words," etc. Whether this is still true, however, is now open to debate in light of the Supreme Court's decision in *R.A.V.* (1992).

18. *Gitlow* at 671 [emphasis added].

19. See: Chafee (1941); Rabban (1981); Tribe (1985).

20. *Thomas* at 516.

21. *Id.*

22. *Id.*

23. *Chaplinsky* at 571–572.

24. *Id.* at 571–572, quoting *Cantwell* at 310.

25. *Gooding* at 523–524 [emphasis added]. In addition to the speech boundaries created by the "clear and present danger" test, "bad tendency" test, and "fighting words," the Supreme Court has historically limited the scope of free speech through other tests and devices. Such limitations include overbreadth, vagueness, ad hoc balancing, incitement, prior restraint, reasonableness, content-based regulation, imminent danger, chilling effect, obscenity, offensive speech, national security, public order, commercial speech, and time, place, and manner. At the core of each of these limitations is the idea that the potential harm resulting from the regulation of speech in these areas is considerably outweighed by the potential harm of allowing speech in these areas to be completely unfettered. In each instance the restrictions are required to be narrowly tailored to serve a significant government interest. The further removed the speech under consideration is considered to be from political discourse, the less First Amendment protection it is given; the closer the restriction is to being viewpoint and content-neutral, the less infringement on the free speech ideal is judged to have occurred. See: Emerson (1983) at 303, 305–312; Gunther (1937, 1980), chapters 12 and 13; Ducat (1974, 1996), chapter 11.

26. *Gooding* at 523.

27. The Court defined this term in *Terminiello v. Chicago*: the "heckler's veto" permits the arrest or conviction of a speaker if the listeners are stirred to anger, invited to publicly dispute, or brought to a condition of unrest by the speaker [at 5]. See: *Feiner* (1951); *Forsyth County, Georgia v. Nationalist Movement* (1992) [hereafter *Nationalist Movement*].

28. *Beauharnais* at 250, 255–258.

29. *Id.* at 250. The Court asserted that "we are precluded from saying that speech concededly punishable when immediately directed at individuals can not be outlawed if directed at groups with whose position and esteem in society the affiliated individual may be inextricably involved" [*Id.* at 263]. The Court further observed that libelous utterances were not within the area of constitutionally protected speech [*Id.* at 266].

30. *Id.* at 252 fn.18.

31. *Id.* at 274.

32. *National Socialist Party v. Skokie* (1977); *Village of Skokie v. National Socialist Party of America* (1977); *Smith v. Collins* (1978).

33. *Village of Skokie* at 352.

34. *Village of Skokie* at 349.

35. *Village of Skokie* at 357.

36. *Collins* at 695.

37. Ordinance #995 prohibited the "dissemination of any material which promotes and incites racial or religious hatred, with intent to incite such hatred;" Ordi-

nance #996 prohibited "public demonstrations by members of political parties while wearing military-style uniforms" [*Collins* at 681].

38. *Collins* at 697, 698. Judge Decker noted, "The analysis of *Beauharnais* is also obsolete in that the Court seemed to assume that its only options were to permit the state to ban racial defamation completely or to require a showing of clear and present danger of violence in every case. At the time of *Beauharnais* the concept of clear and present danger was still developing, and it was unclear whether it applied at all to unprotected speech cases. . . . *Brandenburg* and *Cohen* have since made clear the distinction between speech that causes a danger of imminent violence and that which is used in a personally abusive manner [*Collins* at 698 fn.16].

39. *Smith* at 953 (Blackmun, J., dissenting).

40. Gunther (1975) at 754, 755.

41. *Ashton* at 200.

42. As quoted in *Smith* at 693.

43. *Street* at 576.

44. As quoted in *Smith* at 691.

45. As quoted in *Smith* at 692.

46. *Lewis* at 972.

47. *Hess* at 329.

48. *R.A.V.* at 2543–2545. For a detailed discussion of this case, see Chapter Five *infra*.

49. *Chaplinsky* at 572.

50. See: *UWM Post* at 1170.

51. See: *R.A.V.* at 2538.

52. *Schwimmer* at 644, 654–655 (1929).

53. *American Booksellers Association, Inc.* at 330.

54. See for example: Gale at 123; Lange (1990); Linzer (1991) at 188; Massaro (1991); SeLegue at 920; Smolla (1990).

55. Herscher (1990) at A4, col. 4.; National Gay and Lesbian Task Force Policy Institute (1989). See also: Fernandez (1991).

56. See: Brownworth (1991) at 52; Robson (1992) at chapter 12. See also: Berrill, "Anti-Gay Violence . . ." (1990); Berrill, "Primary and Secondary Victimization . . ." (1990); Comstock (1991); "Student Discriminatory Harassment" (1989).

57. Massaro (1991).

58. Baruch (1990); Hein (1983); Hentoff (1992) at 50–58; Karst (1990); Linzer (1991); Rosenberg (1991).

59. Emerson (1963) at 878–879.

60. Bryne (1991) at 403.

61. *Gertz* at 339–340.

62. In *Collins* at 686, the court stated that "defendants have no power to prevent plantiffs from stating their political philosophy, including their opinions of black and Jewish people, however noxious and reprehensible that philosophy may be."

63. Smolla (1992) at 169.

64. Heins at 592 fn.39.

65. Smolla (1990) at 198.

66. *Cohen* at 26.

67. Fried at 236.

68. See: Rabban (1981); *Abrams* (1919); *Debs* (1919); *Frohwerk* (1919); *Schenck* (1919); *Whitney* (1927); *Adderley* (1966); *Walker* (1967); *O'Brien* (1968); *Flower* (1972); *Greer* (1976).

69. Mill at 18.

70. See: *Abrams* (1919) at 630 (Holmes, J., dissenting).

71. Posner (1990) at 466.

72. *Abrams* (1919) at 630 (Holmes, J., dissenting).

73. *Dennis* (1950) at 585.

74. Mill at 22.

75. *Communist Party of the United States* (1961) at 137 (Black, J., dissenting).

76. Delgado (1982); Lawrence (1990); Matsuda (1989).

77. Matsuda *et al.* (1993) at 1–15; Matsuda (1989) at 2355–2356.

78. Williams (1985) at 129, 151, 155. For Williams, "spirit-murder" is "no less than the equivalent of body murder." It is "an offense [which is] deeply painful and assaultive"; a "cultural obliteration . . . or disregard for others whose lives qualitatively depend on our regard [;] a cultural cancer . . . [; a] spiritual genocide [; and a] numbing pathology." See also: Matsuda (1989) at 2337.

79. *Chaplinsky* at 568.

80. Matsuda (1989) at 2323, 2338.

81. *Id.* at 2323, 2378–2379.

82. Lawrence at 452. Lawrence's point is reiterated by Leslie F. Goldstein—who does not advocate the position articulated by the civil rights adherents—insofar as she observes that "extremely abusive personal insults . . . are a verbal version of spitting in someone's face, an act which the law treats as an assault even though all Americans understand it as an act of symbolic expression" [Goldstein (1992) at 1].

83. Matsuda (1989) at 2336.

84. Lawrence at 467.

85. Matsuda (1989) at 2357.

86. Williams (1987) at 141.

87. See: Matsuda *et al.* (1993); Delgado (1982); Williams (1987) at 141; Matsuda (1989); Lawrence (1990).

88. Delgado (1982) at 140–145.

89. Matsuda *et al.* (1993) at 5.

90. Lawrence at 472.

91. Address by Richard Delgado, State Historical Society, Madison, Wisconsin (24 April 1989), as quoted by Lawrence at 475.

92. *Id.*
93. Lawrence at 459.
94. *Id.* at 457.
95. *Id.* 457.
96. *Brown* (1954).
97. Delgado (1982) at 179.
98. *Id.* at 180.
99. Matsuda (1989) at 2357.
100. *Id.*
101. Battaglia (1990); Brownstein (1991); D'Amato (1991); Gale (1991); Greenwalt (1990); Grey (1991); McGowan and Tangri (1991); Massaro (1991); Minow (1990); SeLegue (1991); Smolla (1990).
102. Massaro (1991) at 251.
103. *Id.* at 249.
104. *Id.* at 255.
105. *Id.*
106. *Id.* at 253.
107. *Id.* at 265.
108. The standard for such torts is that "one who by extreme and outrageous conduct intentionally or recklessly causes severe emotional distress to another is subject to liability for such emotional distress" [Restatement (Second) of Torts §46 (1965)]. The constitutionality of this standard was upheld in *Ledsinger* (1982) at 18–19 and in *Hustler Magazine, Inc.* (1988).
109. According to McGowan and Tangri, "[t]he nonconsequentionalist rationales for protecting speech necessarily view speech as good *per se*" [at 844]. Under this rationale, speech which offends without inciting a listener to violence is protected speech [at 854]. In their estimation, however, the nonconsequentionalist rationales are flawed and must be contricted to exclude that speech which does not incite violence—thereby preventing the state from invoking the public safety rationale to regulate it—merely because the listener is incapable of an immediate response. An example of speech McGowan and Tangri would not protect is that of a speaker who screams vile invectives into the face of a recipient who cannot fight (due to infirmity or to being physically locked in a cell), who will not fight (due to religious or philosophical beliefs, socialization, prevailing circumstances, or fear), or who is deprived of a chance to respond or process the speech (because the listener experiences the speech as the verbal equivalent of an assault) [at 854–855].
110. According to McGowan and Tangri, private speech focuses on topics outside the realm of normatively or descriptively public issues that are intended for private consideration. Thus, personal invectives, by definition, would be deemed private rather than public speech [*Id.* at 857]. Public speech, on the other hand, concerns "topics of normative public interest or speech that the speaker intends to be heard by a group rather than merely by the immediate object of the speech" [at 862]. Moreover, the assessment of whether the speech is public or private hinges

on the speaker's motive—"whether [the speech is intended] to be publicly, rather than privately, considered" [*Id.* at 857].

111. *Id.* at 860.

112. SeLegue at 955.

113. *Id.*

114. Greenwalt (1990) at 306.

115. "Stanford University Interpretation of Fundamental Standard," drafted by Thomas Grey, as quoted in Battaglia (1991) at 389–390.

116. *Id.* at 390.

117. See: Bornstein (1994); Bullough and Bullough (1993); Feinberg (1996); Feinberg (1992); Green (1992); Hutchins and Kaahumanu (1991); Leyland (1993); Miller (1995); Pratt (1995); Robson (1992); Rubenstein (1993); Snitow (1990).

118. See generally: Achtenberg (1984, 1994); Colker (1996); Editors of the *Harvard Law Review* (1989, 1990); Rubenstein (1993); Sr. Mary Elizabeth, *Legal Aspects of Transsexualism* (1988); Sr. Mary Elizabeth, "Transsexual Civil Rights" (1988).

119. See Chapter One *supra.*

120. See generally: Achtenberg (1984, 1994); Editors of the *Harvard Law Review* (1989, 1990); Rubenstein (1993).

121. Deikman (1990) as quoted by Bornstein (1994) at 78.

122. Schneyer (1994) at 1323–1324.

123. See: *Bonanno* (1964) at 1123–1124, quoted in *Linsey* (1975) at 91; *Stokes* (1968); *McConnell* (1971) at 196; *Silva* (1974) at 739; *Coffeeville Consolidated School District* (1975) at 251; *People v. Rodriquez* (1976) at 766; *Ratchford* (1978) at 1084 (Rehnquist, J., dissenting from *cert. denied*).

124. Mohr (1988) at 168.

125. *American Booksellers Association, Inc.* (1985) at 330.

126. Pratt (1991) at 227–246.

127. *Id.* at 237.

128. For a detailed analysis of the NEA controversy, see Chapter Four *infra.*

129. Pratt (1991) at 230.

130. *Id.* at 241.

131. Emerson (1970) at 6.

132. *Id.*

133. *Woodley* at 707.

134. Schneyer (1994) at 1365.

135. Meiklejohn (1965).

136. *Id.* at 26.

137. Richards, "Constitutional Legitimacy" at 905.

138. See: *Gay Alliance* (1976), wherein Chief Justice Markey maintained that "the ideas advocated by an association may to some or most of us be abhorrent, even sickening. The stifling of advocacy is even more abhorrent, even more sickening" [*Id.* at 168 (Markey, C.J., concurring)].

139. "Before Stonewall" (a documentary).

140. National Gay and Lesbian Task Force, "Activist Alert" at 2. See also: *Lesbian/Gay Freedom Day Committee* (1982); *Hill* (1983).

141. *Gay Student Organization* (1974); *Gay Alliance of Students* (1974); *Gay Lib* (1977); *Gay Student Services* (1980); *Fricke* (1980); *Gay & Lesbian Students Ass'n* (1988).

142. *Toward a Gayer Bicentennial Committee* (1976); *Alaska Gay Coalition* (1978); *Gay Activists Alliance* (1979); *New York County Board of Ancient Hiberians* (1993).

143. See: Rivera (1981) at 342.

144. *Paddock Bar, Inc.* (1957); *Kottenman* (1957); *Vallerga* (1959); *One Eleven Wines and Liquors, Inc.* (1967).

145. *Phipps* (1979).

146. *State ex. rel. Grant* (1974) at 848.

147. See Chapter Three *supra*.

148. As drawn from *Shahar* (1992) and *Shahar* (1993).

149. *Shahar* (1993).

150. *Shahar* (1992) at 671.

151. *Connick* (1983) as quoted in *Rowland* (1984) at 449.

152. *Rowland* at 449.

153. *Id.*

154. *Id.* at 452 (Edwards, J., dissenting).

155. *Id.* at 453 (Edwards, J., dissenting).

156. *Id.*

157. *Id.*

158. *Id.*

159. Gomez (1983) at 128.

160. See: *McConnell* (1971); *In re J.S. & C* (1974); *Acanfora* (1974); *Gish* (1977); *Singer* (1976); *Childers* (1981).

161. Mohr.

162. Karst (1990) at 142.

CHAPTER 3

Equality Jurisprudence and Suspect Classifications

EQUALITY JURISPRUDENCE

While arguments based on the First Amendment emphasize freedom of expression and focus on process, arguments based on the Equal Protection Clause of the Fourteenth Amendment and Title VII of the Civil Rights Act of 1964 emphasize equality and focus on effect. In fact, the Fourteenth Amendment is the only section of the U.S. Constitution that explicitly mentions equality.[1] Yet, full equality has never been and is not currently guaranteed to members of society who are disadvantaged by race, sex, gender identity, affectional orientation/preference, religion, ethnicity, age, class, or other characteristics that deviate from the "mythical norm."[2]

By definition, "equality" cannot exist independently of a standard or unit of measure; it is a subjective and relational concept. To understand the concept of equality requires an identification of the standard being used. As Kent Greenwalt has observed, "in the absence of substantive criteria indicating which people are equal for particular purposes and what constitutes equal treatment, the formal principle of equality provides no guidance of how people should be treated."[3] But the unit of measure is not a natural phenomenon; it is a socio-political-legal construct, which is determined by the dominant society. Thus, the meaning of equality is relative to the perspective of whomever demarcates the applicable standard. The definer's values determine what aspect is focused on in ascertaining whether two things or persons are equal. Consequently, only those things or persons which can be measured by the *same* unit or standard can be deemed equal; otherwise the comparison becomes unintelligible.[4] For example, horses can be judged equal due to their speed, bloodline, or strength. But what unit of measure would render meaningful an equality statement about a nasturtium and a human? Quite possibly there is no meaningful one. But the examples illustrate Elizabeth Wolgast's point that "[t]aking any pair of things at random, [there is] no guarantee that there is an answer to the question are they equal or not?"[5] The answer is contingent upon the selected criterion of the specified relevant and identical attributes possessed by members of both groups.

While this seems evident in instances when the objects under consideration do not appear to be measurable by the same standard—a nasturtium and a human, an orangutan and a nidus—it becomes less obvious when the compared categories are *presumed* to be measurable by the same standard—males and females,[6] men and women, or heterosexuals and *sex/gender outsiders*.[7] It is seldom noticed when comparing members in these three categories, however, that the unit of measure used is inherently male, man, and heterocentric. As Iris Marion Young makes clear, ignoring the differences in experiences, culture, and socialized capacities that exist between individuals based on sex, gender, or sexuality allows the privileged group (males, men, heterosexuals) to define the standard according to which all others (females, *sex/gender outsiders*) will be measured, without acknowledging that the unit of measure is culturally or experientially specific. Moreover, as Young points out, this standard serves to masquerade the definers' norms as an "unsituated, group-neutral" and universal point of view, as opposed to identifying it as group specific. The resulting denigration of those who deviate from the standard, according to Young, often produces a devaluation of those delegated to the position of "other," both externally and internally, as a consequence of their inability to "measure up" to the (male, man, heterosexual) standard.[8]

If equality statements about sex, gender, or sexuality are confined to the realm of legal equality, they can be approached in one of three ways.[9] The first approach identifies the characteristic(s) deemed relevant by the prevailing social order and then judges how well each group meets that standard. The second approach asserts that the concept of equality is "empty of content"[10] and seeks to ground the equal protection claim substantively. The third approach maintains that equality statements place groups in "binary opposition" that precludes the possibility of equality between them. While the third approach offers the possibility of rethinking the existing conceptual framework of legal equality, all three approaches can be utilized to reinforce and legitimate existing normative standards. In general, the first approach has dominated the Supreme Court's equal protection decisions, insofar as the Court maintains that the Fourteenth Amendment "merely requires that all persons [who are subjects of a law or regulation] . . . shall be treated alike, under like circumstances, and conditions."[11]

Fourteenth Amendment

The Equal Protection Clause states: "nor [shall any state] deny any person within its jurisdiction the equal protection of the laws."[12] Interpreting this amendment, the Supreme Court has ruled that the state is under an affirmative obligation to ensure that individuals are not denied equal protection of the law through state action, but the State is not similarly obligated to protect individuals from private discrimination.[13] Indeed, the Court has specifically held that the Fourteenth Amendment does not prohibit private discrimination "unless to some significant extent the State in any of its manifestations has been found to become involved with it."[14] Thus, even though state inaction may be a form of state action, it does not automatically follow that the state has violated its equal protection duties to the affected individuals. The determining factor is the intent, as opposed to the effect, of the policy in question.

Three questions tend to guide the Supreme Court's decisions: (a) whether the policy is facially neutral; (b) whether the policy is invidiously motivated; and (c) whether the state conduct is undertaken "because of," not merely "in spite of," the adverse effect.[15] But when one group is clearly the majority and another the minority (either numerically or in terms of social or political power), rules which are ostensibly neutral may be inconsistent with the principle of equality.[16] Under such conditions, according to Toni M. Massaro, "[e]quality is not merely a matter of identical social and legal treatment of individuals, but it must take into account inequalities in legal and social outcomes and the historical maldistributions of social goods and political power."[17]

Under equal protection analysis, the Supreme Court adheres to a three-tier structure[18] to determine whether laws or regulations that classify groups violate an individual's or group's constitutional rights. The first tier is occupied by the traditional or rationality standard of review and is used by the Court predominantly for state tax and economic regulations.[19] Under this standard, which is not very rigorous, violations of the law receive, at best, minimal review. The Court accords extreme deference to the legislative statute, presuming the challenged statute to be constitutional. When this traditional standard is used, the Court merely requires that the classifications be reasonable, that the classifications have a rational relationship to a legitimate state interest, and that the law treat all persons within a class equally.[20] Whomever challenges the classification bears the burden of proving that the statutory classification does not rest upon some reasonable basis, but rather is patently arbitrary, capricious, or irrational. As the Court stated in *Lindsley v. Natural Carbonic Gas Co.*, "[w]hen a classification [which in practice results in some inequality] is called into question, if any state of facts reasonably can be conceived that would sustain it, the existence of that state of facts at the time the law was enacted must be assumed."[21]

Rejecting the inadequacy of a bifurcate test of equal protection, Justice Marshall argued for an approach which could address variable degrees of scrutiny depending on factors such as "the constitutional and social importance of the interests adversely affected" and the "invidiousness of the basis upon which the particular classification is drawn."[22] The second tier, which is the intermediate or heightened standard of review, applies to classifications based on sex, birth status, or alienage. It requires that a substantial relationship exist between the classification and an important government objective in order to be permissible.[23] While stricter than mere rationality, the intermediate standard of review is not the strictest equal protection standard utilized by the Court. Although classifications scrutinized under this heightened standard are less likely to be upheld by the Court than those reviewed under the rationality standard, they are more likely to be upheld than those reviewed under the last equal protection test.

The third tier, known as the strict scrutiny standard of review, is triggered if a suspect class (i.e., against which a state discriminating on the basis of race or national origin) is encompassed, or if a fundamental right or interest (i.e., one guaranteed explicitly or implicitly by the Constitution) is abridged, by a legislative statute. A statute assessed under this level of review is generally presumed to be unconstitutional by the Court, and the classification is frequently rejected.[24] Moreover, under strict scrutiny, the state bears the burden of proving not only that the classification is necessary to achieve a compelling or paramount government interest but also that the challenged classification is the least intrusive alternative available for meeting the government's interest.[25]

In 1938, the Court signaled its concern about the rights of traditionally disadvantaged minorities. Justice Harlan Stone, in the now famous footnote 4 of *United States v. Carolene Products Company*, observed that "prejudice against discrete and insular minorities may be a special condition, which tends seriously to curtail the operation of those political processes ordinarily to be relied upon to protect minorities and . . . may call for a more searching judicial scrutiny."26 However, it was not until six years later that the Court finally declared race a suspect category. In *Korematsu v. United States*, the Court declared that "all legal restrictions which curtail the civil rights of a single racial group are immediately suspect."27 More importantly, the Court asserted that such restrictions "must be subjected to the most rigid scrutiny."28 Twenty-three years later, in 1967, the Supreme Court ruled that all racial classifications were "inherently suspect."29

Two years prior to the Court ruling that race was a suspect class, however, in *Skinner v. Oklahoma*, Justice Douglas focused on the constitutional protection of fundamental rights or basic personal liberties. According to Justice Douglas, "marriage and procreation are fundamental to the very existence and survival of the race. The power to sterilize . . . can cause races or types which are inimical to the dominant group to wither and disappear. . . . [S]trict scrutiny of the classification which a state makes in a sterilization law is essential."30 Over the course of time, the Court has recognized as fundamental the rights enumerated in the Bill of Rights, as well as the right to vote,31 to marry (if heterosexual),32 to travel between states,33 to use contraception,34 to procreate,35 to possess pornography,36 and to have an abortion.37

According to the Court, a right can justifiably be deemed fundamental if it is explicitly stated in the Constitution, if it is "implicit in the concept of ordered liberty,"38 or if it is "deeply rooted in this Nation's history and tradition."39 Very few claims have fulfilled this criteria to the Court's satisfaction since 1969. Justice Harlan explained his reluctance to expand the doctrine of fundamental rights in *Shapiro v. Thompson*: "when a statute affects only matters not mentioned in the Federal Constitution and is not arbitrary or irrational . . . [there is] nothing which entitles this Court to pick out particular human activities, characterize them as 'fundamental,' and give them added protection under an unusually stringent equal protection test."40 His sentiments were echoed four years later in *San Antonio Independent School District v. Rodriguez*, wherein the majority noted that it is "not the province of this Court to create substantive constitutional rights in the name of guaranteeing equal protection of the laws.41

Based on this line of reasoning, the Supreme Court formally proclaimed that individuals possess a fundamental, substantive right to privacy—which includes procreation, contraception, possession of pornography, and (heterosexual) marriage. Yet it refuses to extend this privacy right to include the right of *sex/gender outsiders* to engage in private, consensual, sexual intimacy.42 As Senior Circuit Judge Bryan, speaking for the majority, observes in *Doe v.*

Commonwealth's Attorney for Richmond, prior Supreme Court decisions rest on the precept that "the Constitution condemns State legislation that trespasses upon the privacy of the incidents of marriage, upon the sanctity of the home, or upon the nurture of family life. . . . [However,] homosexuality . . . is obviously no portion of marriage, home, or family life. . . . If a State determines that punishment [for adults engaging in consensual and private acts of same-sex sodomy] therefore, is appropriate in the promotion of morality and decency, it is not for the courts to say that the State is not free to do so."[43] Judge Merhige resolutely disagreed with the majority's decision, because "the legal viability of a marital-nonmarital distinction in private sexual acts if not eliminated, was at the very least seriously impaired [by virtue of *Eisenstadt v. Baird*]."[44] By curtailing the significance of this distinction, he argues, "the Court to a great extent vitiated any implications that the state can . . . forbid extra-marital sexuality."[45] In *Eisenstadt* the Supreme Court expanded the right of privacy beyond marital relationships, according to Judge Merhige. Indeed, he declares that "[b]oth *Roe* [*v. Wade*] . . . and *Eisenstadt* . . . cogently demonstrate that intimate personal decisions or private matters of substantial importance to the well-being of the individuals involved are protected by the Due Process Clause. The right to select consenting adult sexual partners must be considered within this category. The exercise of that right, whether heterosexual or homosexual, should not be proscribed by state regulation absent a compelling justification"[46]—which he claims the state did not present. Judge Merhige asserts that "the sole basis of the proscription of homosexuality was what the majority refers to as the promotion of morality and decency . . . [therefore] I can find no authority for intrusion by the state into the private dwelling of a citizen."[47]

Judge Jones reiterated Judge Merhige's position in *People v. Onofre,*[48] when the court held that §130.38 of the New York Penal Law making consensual sodomy a crime violates the federal Constitution. Under the challenged statute, "a person is guilty of consensual sodomy when he engages in deviate sexual intercourse with another person. . . . Deviate sexual intercourse means sexual conduct between persons not married to each other consisting of contact between the penis and the anus, the mouth and the penis, or the mouth and the vulva."[49] Judge Jones ruled that the right to privacy does encompass private sexual conduct between consenting adults and therefore the statute was unconstitutional, "because the statutes are broad enough to reach noncommercial, cloistered personal sexual conduct of consenting adults and because it permits the same conduct between persons married to each other without sanction."[50]

The basis for his decision was the Supreme Court's ruling in *Eisenstadt* which stated that the right to privacy applied to individuals, married or single, to be free from unwanted governmental intrusions into decisions of whether to bear or beget a child.[51] He also noted that in *Stanley v. Georgia* the Supreme Court ruled that individuals possessed as well a fundamental right "to be free, except in very limited circumstances, from unwanted governmental intrusions into one's privacy,"[52] and that in *Olmstead v. United States* Justice Brandeis articulated the principle that the right to be let alone is "the most comprehensive and the right most valued by civilized man."[53] By putting these decisions together, Judge Jones concluded that

protecting under the cloak of the right of privacy individual decisions as to indulgence in acts of sexual intimacy by unmarried persons and as to satisfaction of sexual desires by resort to material condemned as obscene by community standards when done in a cloistered setting, no rational basis appears for excluding from the same protection decisions . . . to seek sexual gratification from what at least once was commonly regarded as "deviant" conduct, so long as the decisions are voluntarily made by adults in a noncommercial, private setting.[54]

A similar result was reached by the U.S. District Court in *Baker v. Wade*. Before reaching the constitutional questions raised in this case, the court took notice of the fact that the Supreme Court had refused to answer questions such as whether the right to privacy includes private sexual behavior between consenting adults and whether an individual can be prosecuted for engaging in same-sex sexual activity with a consenting adult.[55] It further noted that the Supreme Court summarily affirmed the court of appeals decision in *Doe* and denied certiorari in *Onofre*. As a result, the lower-court decisions in *Doe* and *Onofre* are inconsistent insofar as "the constitutional right of privacy extends to private sexual conduct between consenting adults in New York, but it does not in Virginia. And there is no Supreme Court opinion that determines which approach is constitutionally correct [regarding] whether and to what extent the Constitution prohibits state statutes regulating private consensual sexual behavior among adults."[56]

At issue in *Baker* was the constitutionality of §21.06 of the Texas Penal Code (and the related definitions in §§1.05 and 21.01) which provides that "a person commits an offense if he (or she) engages in deviate sexual intercourse with another individual of the same sex. 'Deviate sexual intercourse' means any contact between any part of the genitals of one person and the mouth or anus of another person."[57] Judge Buchmeyer, in his memorandum opinion, announced that he agreed with Judge Merhige's dissenting opinion in *Doe* and the majority opinion in *Onofre*. He then proceeded to state that "[t]he right of two individuals to choose what type of sexual conduct they will enjoy in private is just as personal, just as important, just as sensitive—indeed, even more so—than the decision by the same couple to engage in sex using a contraceptive to prevent unwanted pregnancy."[58] In addition, Judge Buchmeyer pointed out that it was absurd to differentiate between an individual's right to seek sexual satisfaction by viewing pornographic materials and his/her right to seek sexual satisfaction privately with another consenting adult.[59] Therefore, it follows that "homosexual conduct in private between consenting adults is protected by a fundamental right of privacy. Any state restriction upon that right must be justified by some compelling state interest"[60]—which the state of Texas had failed to do during the initial trial.

His reasoning failed to convince Judge Reavley of the Fifth Circuit Court of Appeals. As a result, Judge Reavley reversed the ruling of the District Court for the Northern District of Texas due to the fact that the Supreme Court had summarily affirmed the lower court's decision in *Doe.* Contrary to Judge Buchmeyer's opinion, Judge Reavley held that he considered the Supreme Court's affirmance of the *Doe* decision to be binding until such time as the Supreme Court issues an "unequivocal statement that [it] no longer controls."[61]

In a similar fashion, Judge Bork held in *Dronenburg v. Zech* that "the Supreme Court has never defined the right [to privacy] so broadly as to encompass homosexual conduct."[62] As evidence for this position, he cited the Court's summary affirmance of *Doe* and posited that if homosexual conduct could be proscribed in a civilian context it could surely be proscribed in a military context. Moreover, Judge Bork suggested that even if he did not accept the Supreme Court's action in *Doe* as binding, an analysis of the Court's development of the constitutional right to privacy would still prevent him from extending that right to include same-sex sodomy.[63] In his opinion, while the Supreme Court "has listed as illustrative of the right to privacy such matters as activities relating to marriage, procreation, contraception, family relationships, and child rearing and education[, i]t need hardly be said that none of these covers a right to homosexual conduct."[64] Based on his analysis of previous Supreme Court privacy rulings, Judge Bork deemed it impossible to conclude either that same-sex sodomy is "a 'fundamental' [right] or 'implicit in the concept of ordered liberty' unless any and all sexual behavior falls within those categories."[65]

Judge Bork's ruling, that same-sex sexual behavior is not protected by the right to privacy and that such conduct is neither a fundamental right nor implicit in the concept of ordered liberty, was confirmed by the U.S. Supreme Court in 1986. *Bowers v. Hardwick* [66] stands as the only Supreme Court case to directly confront the issue of whether the federal constitutional right to privacy prohibits the government from criminalizing private consensual intimacy between same-sex adults.[67] The plurality ruling in *Hardwick* can be understood as essentially declaring that the sexual expression of one's affectional orientation/preference, free from unwanted governmental intrusion, is not guaranteed to *sex/gender outsiders* under the constitutional right to privacy—a perception that continues to prevail at the federal court level.

At the state court level, however, a somewhat greater protection for the privacy rights of *sex/gender outsiders* has managed to emerge. Prior to *Hardwick*, for example, the New Jersey Supreme Court held that the state's fornication statute violated the privacy rights of consenting adults.[68] In the court's opinion,

the conduct statutorily defined as fornication involves, by its very nature, a fundamental right to personal choice. Although persons may differ as to the propriety and morality of such conduct and while we certainly do not condone its particular manifestation in this case, such a decision is necessarily encompassed in the concept of personal autonomy which our Constitution seeks to safeguard.

. . . [Prior Supreme Court decisions have] underscored the inherently private nature of a person's decision to bear or beget children. It would be rather anomalous if such a decision as to whether to engage in the conduct which is a necessary prerequisite to child-bearing could be constitutionally prohibited. Surely such a choice involves considerations which are at least as intimate and personal as those which are involved in choosing whether to use contraceptives. We therefore join with other courts which have held that such sexual activities between consenting adults are protected by the right to privacy.[69]

Similar rulings have been issued by other state courts. Indeed, the willingness of state courts to render a more accurate reading of the Supreme Court's privacy doctrine than even the highest federal court itself is exemplified in cases such as *Commonwealth v. Wasson, Michigan Organization for Human Rights v. Kelley*, and *City of Dallas v. England*. In each of these cases, the state courts have ruled that statutes infringing on the private sexual intimacy of consenting adults violate the right to privacy guaranteed by their respective state constitutions. But these judicial acknowledgments that the right to privacy existing in the states' governing instruments includes *sex/gender outsiders* are neither appealable to the U.S. Supreme Court nor applicable across state borders. As a result, *sex/gender outsiders* are second-class citizens under the federal constitution and will remain so according to Hunter, "[u]nless or until [the Supreme Court] narrow[s] or overrule[s *Hardwick*, so that it no longer] dominate[s] the law concerning government regulation of [affectional orientation/preference]."[70] To date the Court has shown no indication of a willingness to reconsider its decision in *Hardwick* or to extend the federally guaranteed right of privacy to *sex/gender outsiders.*

The Court also steadfastly refuses to enlarge the category of suspect or quasi-suspect classifications to include gender identity or affectional orientation/preference. In general, the Supreme Court evaluates three factors when analyzing a suspect classification argument: (a) whether the members of a group have suffered a history of purposeful discrimination such that the classification stigmatizes them as inferior,[71] or they suffer arbitrary or invidious discrimination due to prejudice and stereotypes regarding their abilities;[72] (b) whether the members of a group constitute a distinct and insular minority who have been excluded from full participation in the political process;[73] and (c) whether members of a group bear an immutable characteristic upon which the classification rests.[74] The Court has never clearly indicated, however, if all three of these factors are necessary for a classification to be labeled suspect or if only some of them are necessary.[75] For example, in his plurality decision in *Frontiero v. Richardson,* Justice Brennan states that "since sex, like race and national origin, is an immutable characteristic determined solely by the accident of birth, the imposition of special disabilities upon the members of a particular sex because of their sex would seem to violate 'the basic concept of our system that legal burdens should bear some relationship to individual responsibility.' And what differentiates sex from such nonsuspect statutes as intelligence or physical disability, and aligns it with the recognized suspect criteria, is that the sex characteristic frequently bears no relation to ability to perform or contribute to society."[76] He implies in this argument that immutability is not a necessary and sufficient requirement for determining suspect classifications. Justice Brennan indicates, as well, that it is not merely the immutability of sex that is relevant; it is that the characteristic "frequently bears no relation to ability to perform or contribute in society" that is significant.[77]

An appeal to the existence of a relationship between individual ability and the legislative classification is relied upon once more by the Court in *City of Cleburne v. Cleburne Living Center.* Although Justice White, in the majority opinion, agrees that "those who are mentally retarded . . . [are] different, immutably so, in relevant respects from [others],"[78] he contends that "[t]he lesson of [*Massachusetts v.*] *Murgia* is that where individuals in the group affected by a law have distinguishing characteristics *relevant to interests the state has the authority to implement,* the courts have been very reluctant . . . to closely scrutinize legislative choices as to whether, how, and to what extent those interests should be pursued."[79] As he clearly states, it is important to establish the relevance of the immutable characteristic to the legislatively imposed discrimination, not simply establish that the characteristic is immutable.

The significance of immutability in the determination of suspect classifications by the Supreme Court is particularly relevant to *sex/gender outsiders*. Although lesbians, gay men, bisexuals, and transgenderists meet the first two criteria of a suspect class, whether the criterion of immutability can be satisfied is questionable.[80] Although various scientific studies purport to prove the immutability of gender identity or affectional orientation/preference,[81] the validity of these studies is contested.[82] Ultimately what can be derived from these studies is the conclusion that sexual and affectional feelings are a basic part of one's psyche and are established in early childhood. They are deeply ingrained, very difficult to change, and an important part of one's core identity.

These studies, by and large, do not suggest, however, that gender identity or affectional orientation/preference can be totally explained by science. The extent to which environment is involved in the development of gender identity or affectional orientation/preference is still unknown. Also unknown is the degree of choice an individual has in determining her or his gender identity or affectional orientation/preference. At present, there is no definitive answer to the question of what causes gender identity or affectional orientation/preference.

Since the Court itself has suggested that immutability is not a necessary and sufficient condition for determining whether the evaluation of a classification requires heightened judicial scrutiny, the essential component seems to be the relevant relationship of gender identity or affectional orientation/preference to a legitimate compelling state purpose. Under this conceptualization of the strict scrutiny test, discrimination against *sex/gender outsiders* should be subjected to the Court's most exacting standard of analysis, since *sex/gender outsiders* are routinely the targets of invidious discrimination and hostility, which in turn compounds their political powerlessness.

It is well documented that discrimination against lesbians, gay men, bisexuals, and transgenderists has existed in the world since biblical times[83] and that it persists to the present day.[84] At the federal level, all three branches of the government actively participate in perpetuating the legal disabilities of *sex/gender outsiders*. One need only consider President Clinton's "Don't Ask, Don't Tell" military policy;[85] Congress' passage of, and the president's support for, the "Defense of Marriage Act;"[86] and the Supreme Court's Equal Protection decision in *Romer v. Evans*.[87] At both the federal and state levels, lesbians, gay men, bisexuals, and transgenderists experience discrimination on a daily basis. A sampling of the intolerance encountered might include the facts that sixteen states criminalize non-commercial same-sex solicitation;[88] consensual adult same-sex sodomy is still criminalized in approximately twenty to twenty-four states;[89] same-sex marriage is prohibited in all fifty states and is not legally recognized by the federal government;[90] *sex/gender outsiders* are banned from military service; widespread prejudice continues to permeate housing, employment, child custody, adoption, insurance, and taxation; and that threats, harassment, and violence based on one's gender identity or affectional orientation/preference remain a constant threat, one which all too frequently becomes real.[91]

This discrimination contributes to the political powerlessness of *sex/gender outsiders*. Although strides have been made, the vicious "Catch-22" identified by Donald Webster Cory[92] over forty-five years ago still persists:

to acknowledge one's gender identity or affectional orientation/preference is to become a potential target of discrimination, abuse, and violence; but to conceal it is to relinquish one's ability to break down the barriers [of discrimination]. Until the world is able to accept us on an equal basis as human beings entitled to the full rights of life, we are unlikely to have any great numbers willing to become martyrs. . . . But until we are willing to speak out openly and frankly in defense of our activities [and identities], and to identify ourselves with the millions pursuing these activities [and identities], we are unlikely to find the attitudes of the world undergoing any significant change.[93]

While silence and invisibility may be the safer option, visibility is essential if *sex/gender outsiders* are to acquire "the full rights of life"[94] through the political process. By remaining concealed, lesbians, gay men, bisexuals, and transgenderists risk political disempowerment through paralytic reactions that prevent them from engaging in any activity supportive of *sex/gender outsiders*. Individuals "in the closet," fearing "guilt by association," attempt to keep the door firmly shut and remain silent. As the level of intimidation, discrimination, and violence experienced by *sex/gender outsiders* increases, the number of lesbians, gay men, bisexuals, and transgenderists who are vocal and visible may shrink even further. Society's lack of respect for *sex/gender outsiders* and its toleration of opprobrious treatment of lesbians, gay men, bisexuals, and transgenderists reinforces the disinclination of individuals to self-identify as members of a targeted group. It also serves as a disincentive for individuals in other groups to join in coalitions with *sex/gender outsiders*, since they may be mistaken for lesbians, gay men, bisexuals, or transgenderists and subjected to mistreatment.

Despite these obstacles, lesbians, gay men, bisexuals, and transgenderists have managed to convince lawmakers to pass some anti-discrimination legislation. Unfortunately, the reality is that overall very little legislation exists which protects *sex/gender outsiders* from discrimination in either the public or private sphere. There is no federal statute barring discrimination by private citizens or organizations on the basis of gender identity or affectional orientation/preference. Nor is much protection provided at the state level, as evidenced by the fact that in 1993, only eight states[95] had comprehensive statutes preventing employers from discriminating on the basis of gender identity or affectional orientation/preference.[96] Yet the judiciary has been less than forthcoming in recognizing the degree to which such discrimination impinges on the ability of lesbians, gay men, bisexuals, and transgenderists to participate fully in the political arena.

Notwithstanding the ability of lesbians, gay men, bisexuals, and transgenderists to document the existence of invidious discrimination against them and their lack of political power, and despite their ability to make a good argument regarding immutability (if necessary), the federal judiciary, with few exceptions,[97] refuses to include gender identity and affectional orientation/preference as a suspect or even a quasi-suspect classification.[98] As a consequence, the constitutional promise of equality contained in the Equal Protection Clause continues to elude *sex/gender outsiders*.

Title VII

The antidiscrimination principle embedded in the Equal Protection Clause also exists in Title VII of the Civil Rights Act of 1964.[99] In essence, this statute, as amended, prohibits employment discrimination on the basis of race, color, sex, religion, and national origin by most federal employers, by all other public employers, by labor organizations, and by most private employers who have fifteen or more employees. While the term "harassment" is not explicitly mentioned in Title VII, lower federal courts[100] and the U.S. Supreme Court[101] have recognized that sexual harassment is prohibited under Title VII.[102] Neither the U.S. Equal Employment Opportunity Commission (EEOC)[103] nor these courts,[104] however, have accepted the argument that employment discrimination or harassment based on gender identity or affectional orientation/preference constitutes a form of sex discrimination.

According to the EEOC, Title VII does not prohibit affectional orientation/preference discrimination.[105] As a consequence, it consistently rejected such claims at a time when it was assumed that filing a claim with the EEOC was a jurisdictional prerequisite to filing a Title VII suit.[106] Indeed, the

EEOC completely relinquished any claim it might have had to jurisdiction over affectional orientation/preference discrimination through its interpretation of the terms "sex" and "homosexuality" in Title VII. Insofar as the EEOC is concerned, "sex . . . [refers to] a person's gender, an immutable characteristic with which a person is born."[107] "Homosexuality," on the other hand, refers to "a condition which relates to a person's sexual practices or proclivities, not to his or her gender. . . . [I]n enacting Title VII Congress [did not intend] to include a person's sexual practices within the meaning of the term sex."[108] Transsexualism, transvestitism, and transgenderism are not discussed at all in the EEOC's definitions. Thus, according to the EEOC, sex and gender are synonymous under Title VII; sex and affectional orientation/preference are not.

The EEOC's sentiments were echoed by the Ninth Circuit Court of Appeal in *Holloway v. Arthur Anderson and Co.* In the court's estimation, "the sole issue . . . is whether an employee may be discharged, consistent with Title VII, for initiating the process of sex transformation."[109] Although Holloway argued that the term "sex" as used in Title VII is synonymous with "gender" and as such encompasses transsexuals, the court disagreed. According to Judge Nielsen, who wrote the court's opinion, Congress had the traditional notion of sex in mind when it passed Title VII. Consequently, Title VII does not embrace transsexual discrimination.

The Ninth Circuit Court reached a similar decision with regard to the concept of "sex" in *DeSantis v. Pacific Telephone & Telegraph Co., Inc.*[110] At issue in *DeSantis* were three major claims. First, the appellants argued that the congressional intent in prohibiting "sex discrimination" in Title VII was "to include discrimination on the basis of sexual orientation."[111] Second, the appellants contended that "discrimination against homosexuals disproportionately affects men and that this disproportionate impact and correlation between discrimination on the basis of sexual preference and discrimination on the basis of 'sex' requires that sexual preference be considered a subcategory of the 'sex' category of Title VII."[112] Third, the appellants asserted that "discrimination against an employee because of the race of the employee's friends may constitute discrimination based on race in violation of Title VII. . . . [A]nalogously, discrimination because of sex of the employees' sexual partner should constitute discrimination based on sex."[113]

In his repudiation of each of these claims, Judge Choy allowed the use of heterosexual preference to deny lesbians and gay men of employment opportunities. He ruled, with regard to the congressional intent of the "sex" category of Title VII, that in accordance with *Holloway* the prohibition "on 'sex' discrimination applies only to discrimination on the basis of gender and should not be judicially extended to include sexual preference such as homosexuality."[114] As support for the interpretation that Congress had only the traditional notion of "sex" in mind, Judge Choy quoted the *Holloway* decision, wherein the court ruled that a narrow definition of "sex" was justified by legislative activity, insofar as "several bills have been introduced to amend the Civil Rights Act to prohibit discrimination against 'sexual preference.' None have been enacted into law."[115]

In addition to rejecting the appellants' assertion that affectional orientation/preference discrimination was prohibited under Title VII, Judge Choy rejected their argument regarding disproportionate impact. According to Judge Choy, disproportionate impact theory, which was articulated by the Supreme Court in *Griggs v. Duke Power Co.*,[116] may not be applied to extend Title VII protection to lesbians and gay men, because "[i]t would achieve by judicial 'construction' what Congress did not do and has consistently refused to do on many occasions."[117] He argued that providing Title VII protection for lesbians and gay men would have the effect "of employing the disproportionate impact decisions as an artifice to 'bootstrap' Title VII protection for homosexuals under the guise of protecting men generally."[118] Such a rule, in the his view, would violate the legislative intent and will of Congress[119]—something the court majority was unwilling to facilitate.

The Ninth Circuit Court also rejected the appellants' arguments with regard to differences in employment criteria and interference with association. The appellants maintained that an employer's policy involving different decisional criteria for the sexes, whereby male employees who prefer males as sexual partners are treated differently from female employees who prefer males as sexual partners, violated the Supreme Court's ruling in *Phillips v. Martin-Marietta Corp.*[120] Judge Choy disagreed. In his opinion, the employers used the exact same employment policy for men and women; the employers would not hire or promote anyone who preferred same-sex partners. Moreover, since the appellants were not alleging that their employers would fire anyone with a male or female friend, but rather that their employers discriminated against employees who had a certain type of relationship—homosexual—with certain friends, Title VII was not violated, because "that relationship is not covered by Title VII."[121]

Finally, the court rejected the claim articulated by one of the appellants[122] that termination due to his employer's reliance on stereotypes regarding the appropriate appearance of men constituted a violation of Title VII. Judge Choy noted that this issue had been addressed and answered both by the Ninth Circuit Court[123] and by the Fifth Circuit Court.[124] Discrimination because of affectional orientation/preference, transsexualism, or effeminacy did not violate Title VII. As the court observed in *Smith v. Liberty Mutual Insurance Co.*, failure to hire a male "because he was classified as effeminate by the company . . . is not forbidden by Title VII."[125]

By the 1980s, *sex/gender outsiders*, for the most part, had stopped filing Title VII discrimination claims based on gender identity or affectional orientation/preference, due to the judiciaries's denial of recovery[126] and to the federal legislature's failure to amend Title VII and include affectional orientation/preference as a protected characteristic.[127] However, one more defeat awaited lesbians, gay men, bisexuals, and transsexuals, in the 1984 case of *Ulane v. Eastern Airlines, Inc.* The district court held that Ulane was discriminated against as a transsexual, in violation of Title VII, but the Seventh Circuit Court of Appeals reversed the judgement.

Judge Wood, writing for the court, stated that "although we do not condone discrimination in any form, we are constrained to hold that Title VII does not protect transsexuals."[128] He noted that while the district court had correctly determined that the term "sex" as used in Title VII covered neither "homosexuals or transvestites,"[129] it had erred in so liberally construing the term "sex" as to consider that it literally and scientifically applied to transsexuals. According to Judge Wood, "[t]he words of Title VII do not outlaw discrimination against a person who has a sexual identity disorder . . .; a prohibition against discrimination based on an individual's sex is not synonymous with a prohibition against discrimination based on an individual's sexual identity disorder or discontent with the sex into which they were born. The dearth of legislative history on section 2000e-2(a)(1) strongly reinforces the view that that section means nothing more than its plain language implies."[130] It should, that is, be given no more than a narrow, traditional interpretation, thereby excluding lesbians, gay men, bisexuals, and transgenderists. Relying on the only two circuit court cases to address the issue of transsexuality in relation to Title VII,[131] Judge Wood concluded that "Ulane is entitled to any personal belief about her sexual identity she desires."[132] But in his estimation she was "a biological male who takes female hormones, cross-dresses, and has surgically altered parts of her body to make it appear to be female."[133] Furthermore, "even if one believes that a woman can so easily be created from what remains of a man, that does not decide this case,"[134] for transsexuals have no protection from discrimination under Title VII.

Toward the end of the decade, however, judicial tolerance of normative stereotyping—deemed acceptable in both *DeSantis* and *Smith* under Title VII—was limited by the Supreme Court. In *Price Waterhouse v. Hopkins*, the Court was asked to decide whether an employer who gives conscious credence and effect to the sex stereotyping of a female employee has acted on the basis of sex in violation of Title VII. Justice Brennan, who delivered the plurality decision, asserted that with regard to the legal relevance of sex stereotyping "we are beyond the day when an employer could evaluate employees by assuming or insisting that they match the stereotype associated with their group, for 'in forbidding employers to discriminate against individuals because of their sex, Congress intended to strike at the entire spectrum of disparate treatment of men and women resulting from sex stereotypes.' "[135]

Although the Court refrained from determining what specific facts, standing alone, would establish that sex stereotyping discrimination had been employed in reaching an employment decision,[136] its decision in *Price Waterhouse* seems to have narrowed considerably—perhaps even implicitly overruled—its holdings in *DeSantis* and *Smith*. By ruling that impermissible sexual stereotyping violates Title VII, without precisely defining the evidentiary parameters needed adequately to establish sex stereotyping discrimination, the Supreme Court effectively passed on to the lower courts responsibility for making the determination on a case-by-case basis.

The Court's determination that impermissible sexual stereotyping violates Title VII, however, does not require the lower courts to find that affectional orientation/preference is, by extension, prohibited by Title VII. In the 1990s the lower courts made it clear that sexual stereotyping was not equivalent to sex discrimination under Title VII. For example, in *Dillon v. Frank*, the Sixth Circuit Court of Appeals rejected the Title VII claim of Dillon, a male postal worker who was verbally and physically harassed because his coworkers assumed he was gay, that he had been treated differently from other male employees on the basis of sex stereotyping. The court differentiated Dillon's plight from that of the plaintiff in *Price Waterhouse* by noting that Dillon had not been placed "in an intolerable and impermissible Catch-22."[137] While the "aggressiveness" for which Hopkins had been penalized was required by her job, the alleged sexual activities and characteristics ascribed to Dillon were not job related.[138] Despite the court's concession that the harassment Dillon was subjected to was "sexual," it noted that his harassment was based on his actual or perceived affectional orientation/preference and thus was not in violation of Title VII. The court pointed out, however, that if Dillon could demonstrate that he had been treated differently than lesbian employees, his claim might be actionable under Title VII, insofar as he would have been singled out based on his sex as a male rather than on his affectional orientation/preference.[139]

In *Barbour v. Department of Social Services*, the Michigan Court of Appeals echoed the Sixth Circuit's decision in *Dillon*. It ruled that harassment of a male believed by coworkers to be gay does not raise an actionable claim under Title VII's prohibition on sex discrimination—a position reiterated by the courts in *Vandeventer v. Wabash National Corporation* and in *Fox v. Sierra Development Corporation.* In both cases the courts repeated that only discrimination based on being male or female, not discrimination based on one's actual or perceived affectional orientation/preference, was proscribed by Title VII. Since evidence had been presented in neither case that the harassment of which Vandeventer and Fox complained was against men or masculinity or that it created a sex-biased work environment, Title VII had not been violated.

In keeping with the heterocentric perspective of society, every circuit court that has heard cases regarding discrimination based on an individual's known or presumed affectional orientation/preference has ruled that such discrimination is not sex discrimination and, thus, is not prohibited by Title VII. Despite the fact that some *sex/gender outsiders* are perceived as deviating from the normative gender identifications or affectional orientation/preference of society, the judicial system consistently refuses to regard harassment based on affectional orientation/preference as severe enough to create an abusive working environment in violation of Title VII.

This is not to suggest that neither the EEOC nor at least some federal courts do not recognize same-sex sexual harassment as actionable under Title VII. The EEOC's Compliance Manual specifically states:

The victim does not have to be of the opposite sex from the harasser. Since sexual harassment is a form of sex discrimination, the crucial inquiry is whether the harasser treats a member or members of one sex differently from members of the other sex. The victim and the harasser may be of the same sex where, for instance, the sexual harassment is based on the victim's sex (not on the victim's sexual preference) and the harasser does not treat employees of the opposite sex the same way.[140]

Moreover, the first example provided by the EEOC is that of a male supervisor of both male and female employees who makes unwelcome sexual advances toward a male employee because the employee is male but does not make similar advances toward the female employees. Under this set of circumstances, the EEOC suggests that the male supervisor's conduct may constitute sexual harassment, since the disparate treatment is based on the male employee's sex.[141]

Following the guidelines of the EEOC, some federal courts appear somewhat willing to accept that same-sex harassment violates Title VII—particularly if the harassed employee's supervisor is lesbian or a gay male.[142] For example, a federal district court observed that "[t]o deny a claim of same gender harassment allows a homosexual supervisor to sexually harass his or her subordinates either on a *quid pro quo* basis or by creating a hostile work environment, when a heterosexual supervisor may be sued under Title VII for similar conduct."[143] In a similar vein, a federal appeals court ruled, upon reviewing the complaint of a female employee that she was sexually harassed by both her female supervisor and a female consultant, that "[i]t is clear . . . from the plain language of Title VII, that same-sex harassment is an unlawful employment practice. . . . Defendant's gender is irrelevant."[144]

In the Fourth Circuit, the federal court has held that while a Title VII cause of action for hostile work environment sexual harassment does not exist when both the perpetrator and the target of the harassment are heterosexuals of the same sex,[145] "a Title VII claim for same-sex 'hostile work environment' harassment may lie where the perpetrator of the sexual harassment is homosexual."[146] Other circuit courts have also indicated that same-sex claims might fall within Title VII's purview. The District of Columbia Circuit Court granted the possibility that where "a subordinate of either gender" is harassed "by a homosexual superior of the same gender" the subordinate might have an actionable sexual harassment claim under Title VII.[147] In the Second Circuit Court, Judge Van Graafeiland noted in his concurrence that "harassment is harassment regardless of whether it is caused by a member of the same or opposite sex,"[148] while in the Seventh Circuit the court commented that while "[s]exual harassment of women by men is the most common kind,. . . we do not mean to exclude the possibility that sexual harassment of men by women, of men by other men, or women by other women would not be actionable in appropriate cases."[149]

Based on the courts various rulings, it becomes evident that a dual standard exists under Title VII with regard to *sex/gender outsiders*. On the one hand, discrimination based on an individual's known or presumed affectional orientation/preference does not constitute sex discrimination in violation of Title VII. But same-sex harassment may be actionable under Title VII if, and only if, an individual can prove that "because of" one's sex s/he was treated differently than employees of a different sex. Interestingly enough, it is much more likely that employees who are harassed by lesbian or gay male supervisors will have an actionable claim under Title VII than employees who are harassed by heterosexual supervisors of their own sex.

The question thus arises: if *sex/gender outsiders* are not adequately protected under the antidiscrimination principle contained within the Equal Protection Clause or Title VII, are there any laws or policies that provide the necessary protection? The answer is no. It is true that the federal government has codified in its personnel procedures a policy that prohibits discrimination based on affectional orientation/preference, provided an individual's affectional orientation/preference does not interfere with the agency's public reputation or efficient functioning. In pertinent part, this federal policy states: "[a]ny employee who has authority to take, recommend, or approve any personnel action, shall not, with respect to such authority . . . discriminate for or against any employee or applicant for employment on the basis of conduct which does not adversely affect the performance of the employee or applicant or the performance of others; except that nothing in this paragraph shall prohibit an agency from taking into account in determining suitability or fitness any conviction . . . for a crime." Unfortunately, the phrase "adversely affect" is ambiguous enough to permit *sex/gender outsiders* to lose their jobs.[150] Moreover, the "Employment Non-Discrimination Act"—which would have provided full protection against employment discrimination based on affectional orientation/preference, while providing exemptions to certain employment-related claims permitted by Title VII—was defeated by both the 103rd and the 104th Congresses. Whether it will pass the 105th Congress remains to be seen.

DIFFERENCES AND PARALLELS: RELIGIOUS CONVICTION VERSUS GENDER IDENTITY OR AFFECTIONAL ORIENTATION/PREFERENCE

Legally, religion is an abstract concept which the Court has struggled to define.[151] Lawrence Tribe observes that "[a]t least through the nineteenth century, religion was given a fairly narrow reading. . . . '[R]eligion' referred to theistic notions respecting divinity, morality, and worship."[152] Gradually, however, the Court has moved away from the idea that a necessary and sufficient condition of religion is belief in a supernational power. For example, in *United States v. Kauten*, the Court held that "[c]onscientious objection may justly be regarded as a response of the individual to the inward mentor, call it conscience or God, that is for many persons at the present time the equivalent of what has always been thought of as a religious impulse."[153] Eighteen years later, in *Torcaso v. Watkins*, the Court ruled that "freedom of religious belief . . . embraces the right to maintain *theories of life and of death and of the here-after* which are rank heresy to the followers of the orthodox faith. . . . [T]he fact that [religious experiences] may be beyond the ken of mortals does not mean that they can be made suspect before the law."[154] In 1965 the Court went even further by announcing that "where [a belief that is sincere and meaningful occupies a place in the life of its possessor parallel to that filled by the orthodox belief in God, the government] cannot say that one is 'in relation to a Supreme Being' and the other is not."[155] In this same vein, five years later in *Welsh v. United States*, the Court maintained that "[i]f an individual deeply and sincerely holds beliefs that are purely ethical or moral in source and content but that nevertheless impose upon him a duty of con-science . . . those beliefs certainly occupy in the life of that individual 'a place parallel to that filled by God' in traditionally religious persons. . . . [H]is beliefs function as a religion in his life."[156]

These decisions illustrate that the concept of religious liberty, protected by the First Amendment, has evolved slowly into a more inclusive concept that encompasses multiple forms of conscience, rather than being confined to only theistic forms. The concept of religion, from a constitutional per-spective, encompasses any belief system or philosophy which forms and shapes an individual's sense of moral identity and ethics, and from which principles and standards of right and wrong are derived.[157] Thus, a universal definition of religion embodies, at a minimum, a sincerely and deeply held belief or philosophy that imposes a duty of conscience upon an individual to adhere faithfully to its tenets in thought, word, and deed. If the belief system or philosophy consistently reflects the moral values of the majority within the community, or of those with sufficient political power to influence or dictate the content of law, it becomes the basis of state regulations for public morality—commonly referred to as the general welfare—of the community. If it does not, it is deemed to be outside mainstream thought or practice and may be viewed as a fundamental challenge or threat to the dominant per-spective of conventional morality. A clear example of a religious belief fal-ling outside accepted majoritarian views and being subjected to state regulation is the legal treatment of Mormons within this society.

In 1878, the U.S. Supreme Court refused to invalidate the government's repression of Mormons due to their religious belief in, and advocacy and practice of, polygamy. In *Reynolds v. United States*, the Supreme Court up-held a federal prohibition of polygamy holding that it did not violate the free exercise clause of the First Amendment. Chief Justice Waite justified this conclusion by noting that "polygamy has always been odious among the northern and western nations of Europe, and, until the establishment of the Mormon Church, was almost exclusively a feature of the life of Asiatic and of African people."[158] Twelve years later, the Supreme Court once more re-lied upon the affront to conventional morality posed by the Mormon Chur ch's endorsement and practice of polygamy to rationalize discrimination against its members. Justice Frankfurter, speaking for the majority in *Davis v. Beason*, held that an Idaho statute was non-violative of the Constitution's establishment clause, despite the fact that the right to vote at any election, or to hold any position or office of honor, trust, or profit within the territory of Idaho was denied to any "person who is a bigamist or polygamist or who teaches, advises, counsels, or encourages any person or persons to become bigamists or polygamists . . . either as a rite or ceremony of such order, organization, or association, or otherwise."[159] He dismissed the idea of a religious tenet advocating bigamy or polygamy as offensive to common sense. Drawing on a western Christian tradition, Justice Frankfurter postulated that it has probably never been seriously contended in U.S. history "that the whole punitive power of the Government for acts, recognized by the general consent of the Christian world in modern times as proper matters for prohibitory legislation, must be suspended in order that the tenets of a religious sect encouraging crime may be carried out without hinderance."[160]

That same year, 1890, the Court legitimated the cultural reprobation of polygamy by allowing the Mormon Church's charter to be annulled and most of its property to be seized under the Anti-Polygamy Act and the Act of March 3, 1887. In *Late Corporation of the Church of Jesus Christ of Latter-Day Saints v. United States*, as a result of its acknowledged prejudice the Court gave a negative answer to the question of "whether the promotion of such a nefarious system and practice, so repugnant to our laws and to the principles of our civilization, is to be allowed to continue by the sanction of government itself; and whether the funds accumulated for that purpose shall be restored to the same unlawful uses as heretofore, to the detriment of the true interests of civil society."[161] Finally, in 1892, the Court identified the reason why the Mormons' efforts to legalize polygamy were consistently rejected. In *Church of the Holy Trinity v. United States*, Justice Brewer asserted that "[o]ur civilization and our institutions are emphatically Christian. . . . From the discovery of this continent to the present hour, there is a single voice making this affirmation . . . that this is a Christian nation."[162]

By placing the imprimatur of the state on the Judeo-Christian[163] moral tradition, the Court clearly demonstrates that that tradition legitimately prescribes and shapes conventional morality.[164] In addition to configuring public attitudes towards acceptable religious beliefs and practices, the Judeo-Christian tradition has historically formed society's perspective of *sex/gender outsiders* in this country. In fact, the primacy of these values has long been used in the United States to justify pernicious discrimination based on sex, gender identity, and affectional orientation/preference. More specifically, Christianity—a religious tradition that historically has branded *sex/gender outsiders* "as abominable, perverse beings"[165]—underpins many government policies.

The importance of the Judeo-Christian "biblical condemnation of homosexual behavior suffused American culture from its origins," according to John D'Emilio.[166] He observes that "[a] society hostile to homosexual expression shaped the contours of gay identity and the gay subculture [in this country]. In Judeo-Christian tradition, homosexual behavior was excoriated as a heinous sin, the law branded it a serious crime, and the medical profession diagnosed homosexuals and lesbians as diseased. Together, they marked gay people as inferior—less moral, less respectable, and less healthy than their fellows."[167]

D'Emilio notes that Kinsey was convinced, based on information obtained from numerous interviews, that twentieth-century U.S. views regarding sexuality and sexual behavior still reflect seventeenth-century religious teachings. In Kinsey's estimation, "nothing in American society [has] 'more influence upon present-day patterns of sexual behavior than the religious backgrounds of that culture. . . . Ancient religious codes are still the prime source of the attitudes, the ideas, the ideals, and the rationalizations by which most individuals pattern their sexual lives.' "[168] The veracity of Kinsey's observation is echoed in Leslie Feinberg's account of Christianity's negative stance towards transgenderists.[169] S/he states that the Christian church, in its attempt to eliminate the ancient religious rituals of the peasants, systematically banned and suppressed cross-dressing, cross-gender behavior, and trans expression and practices.[170] The attacks on transgenderists were also connected to the Church's economic interests in preserving its feudal role and in strengthening "patriarchal inheritance and rule."[171] As Feinberg notes, "[t]rans people, women charged with lesbianism, gay men, Muslims, Jews, herbalists, healers—anyone who challenged feudal rule was considered a threat and faced extermination."[172]

The social and legal antipathy against *sex/gender outsiders*, which has been incorporated into the major social, political, cultural, and legal institutions, reflects a perspective that leans heavily both on the (alleged) biblical condemnation of homosexuality and sodomy[173] and on English precedents intimately entwined with the attitudes of the Anglican Church, that banned "crimes against nature," "deviant sexual conduct," "unnatural acts," and "buggery."[174] In fact, the supposedly uniform opposition in Western Christianity to same-sex affectional orientation/preference and cross-dressing and its condemnation of lesbians, gay men, bisexuals, and transgenderists as sinful moral reprobates continues as the last decade of the twentieth century draws to a close—as does the consequent legal disabilities still suffered by *sex/gender outsiders* throughout the United States.

Yet, despite the fact that Christian religions are not unanimous in regarding either same-sex affectional orientation/preference[175] or cross-dressing as immoral, religious grounds are frequently employed to justify heterocentric and heterosexist statutes, ballot initiatives, and judicial rulings which discriminate against *sex/gender outsiders.* Prime examples might include: (a) *Bowers v. Hardwick*, in which the Supreme Court "invoked prior discrimination and intolerance against lesbians and gay men as a justification for continued discrimination and criminal sanctions;"[176] and (b) Colorado's Amendment 2,[177] the purpose of which was "to promote free exercise values" and to protect "core religious values," which included the right of persons "who have sincere and profound religious objections to homosexuality" to discriminate on the basis of sexual orientation/preference.[178]

A strategy utilized by the Christian radical right, for example, is to have their particular religious beliefs regarding gender identity and affectional orientation/preference codified to the detriment of opponents who hold equally sincere and profound contrary beliefs (of religion and conscience) regarding these issues. This tactic, when successful, preempts rational public discourse by elevating one theological perspective above all other perspectives. In so doing, it makes the state actively complicit in violating the religion clauses of the First Amendment through the passage of laws which translate Judeo-Christian values, regarding what constitutes right or wrong expressions of gender identity and affectional orientation/preference, into official codes.[179] Insofar as the law operates as the government's official pronouncement on the issue, it conveys the messages that "a [particular] religion or a particular religious belief is *favored or preferred*"[180]—because the machinery of state and its monopoly on force is employed to enforce a religious orthodoxy regarding expressions of gender identity and affectional orientation/preference.

Such state action transgresses the Free Exercise Clause and the Establishment Clause of the U.S. Constitution.[181] In effect, the state facilitates the ability of religious objectors to non-traditional expressions of sex, gender identity, and affectional orientation/preference to legally enforce their own religious beliefs, by lending its weight, power, money, voice, and legitimacy to the furtherance of discrimination. Although numerous judicial rulings maintain that laws prohibiting non-traditional expressions of affectional orientation/preference are valid,[182] David B. Cruz notes that "no state court of last resort has directly addressed the problem of how to evaluate challenges to laws prohibiting [affectional] orientation discrimination brought on the ground that such laws infringe the free exercise of religion."[183]

Through a systematic undervaluing of "non-orthodox" religious beliefs and conscience with regard to gender identity and/or affectional expression or conduct, a state establishes a morality that formally condemns both non-traditional gender or sex identifications and non-heterosexual affectional orientation/preference,[184] and grants official approval for discrimination. Through coercive laws, which perpetuate social and lexical subordination and which stigmatize and punish individuals (both singularly and as a class) who are perceived as not conforming to permissible forms of gender identity and/or affectional expression or conduct, the state repudiates the dignity and autonomy of a percentage of its own population. The state thus denies lesbians, gay men, bisexuals, and transgenderists the right to be regarded as equal citizens. This in turn places substantial pressure on the "non-orthodox" to modify their expression or behavior and thereby violate their own beliefs, or to find a more tolerant community.[185]

As religious orthodoxy becomes the status quo position of the state, the state itself gradually becomes culturally ossified by systematically repressing or extinguishing, through legislative statutes, unconventional perspectives and behaviors from the public arena. While *sex/gender outsiders* wage a desperate battle to defend existing civil and human rights in an attempt to prevent this ossification from being completed, the religious right fights to eradicate the social, political, and legal gains made by *sex/gender outsiders*. The clash between these two factions has achieved the frenetic intensity of "a culture war."[186] As James Hunter observes, "few issues in the contemporary culture war generate more raw emotion than the issue of [*sex/gender outsiders*]. The reason is plain: few other issues challenge the traditional assumptions of what nature will allow, the boundaries of the moral order, and finally the ideals of middle-class family life more radically."[187]

This "culture war" is perceived by many as a zero-sum game—gains in status for one side signify loss in status for the other. To the extent that this view is based on "different moral visions" at the "war's" nucleus,[188] compromise is a feasible option for neither *sex/gender outsiders* nor their religious opponents. The equal citizenship rights of lesbians, gay men, bisexuals, and transgenderists can neither be guaranteed nor actualized as long as stigmatizing laws exist—regardless of whether those laws are actually enforced. Religious adherents of the Judeo-Christian moral tradition, on the other hand, see legal approval of non-traditional gender or sex identifications and non-heterosexual affectional orientation/preference as exceedingly dangerous, because of the potentially damaging effects on marriage, family life, young people, heterosexuality, social morality, and society at large.[189]

In essence the "culture war" is, according to Hunter, "ultimately a struggle over national identity—*over the meaning of America*;"[190] it is a "comprehensive and momentous struggle to define . . . how and on what terms . . . Americans will live together."[191] But while Hunter contends that the resolution of this "culture war" requires a principled pluralism and a principled toleration, he acknowledges that the requisite conditions for establishing an adequate public discourse and/or a common understanding of *sex/gender outsiders* do not yet exist. Nor will they exist, in Hunter's opinion, unless all factions involved in the "culture war" agree to establish and maintain four civic practices. These would include a commitment to: (a) change the environment of public discourse to make it conducive to principled deliberation;[192] (b) accept the necessity for discovering a public vision of the common good;[193] (c) recognize the non-negotiable limits within different moral communities;[194] and (d) acknowledge the inherent flaws in their own moral commitments.[195] While Hunter believes this commitment is necessary, he expresses a qualified pessimism regarding the possibility that a public discourse could occur even if these conditions were to come into being.

Whether the public discourse he envisions can be achieved is unknown. Chris Bull and John Gallagher suggest that such a public discussion can occur if *sex/gender outsiders* are willing to settle for tolerance rather than demanding acceptance from the religious right, and if the religious right is willing to acknowledge that lesbians, gay men, bisexuals, and transgenderists deserve equal rights and privileges within this country despite their personal beliefs that *sex/gender outsiders* are sinners.[196] While such a compromise might alleviate tensions regarding the social and political standing of *sex/gender outsiders* in this country, it is unknown whether such a compromise is even possible, given the rhetorical dehumanization of *sex/gender outsiders* by the religious right. As Bull and Gallagher concede, "[h]owever mutually demeaning the two groups, gay activists do not go nearly as far as the leaders of the religious right in defaming an entire group of people and creating an atmosphere that contributes to harassment or worse. While both sides mischaracterize the other, the religious right goes beyond distortions to promulgating outright lies about [*sex/gender outsiders*]."[197] An interim solution might be to recognize the existing parallels between gender identity and affectional orientation/preference (hereafter GI/AOP) on the one hand, and religion on the other—parallels that are neither factious nor fatuous—to facilitate a better understanding of why discrimination against lesbians, gay men, bisexuals, and transgenderists ought to be subjected to the most exacting judicial review of strict scrutiny.

Evan Wolfson reports that historically Jews, like *sex/gender outsiders*, have suffered from dehumanization and persecution due to their difference. He points out that

[c]lassic charges leveled against minorities by the intolerant, including spreading disease, molesting children, sexual depravity, and selfishness, have all been made against the Jews. For example, a . . . law in England, promulgated as all Jews were expelled from that country, condemned to death "arsonists, sorcerers, those who abandoned the Christian faith, those who dared sleep with the wife of their feudal lord (or even the nurse of his children), and *those who had intercourse with Jews, animals, or persons of their own gender.*"[198]

Wolfson further notes that according to Isaiah Shachar, the sub-motif present in all representations of Jews is that they "belong to another and abominable category of beings."[199] Wolfson points out that of particular relevance to *sex/gender outsiders* is Shachar's observation that the persistence of the totally alien quality attributed to the Jews could not have survived "had it not been stereotyped at various cultural levels, including verbal abuse, proverbs, and jokes [and with] forceful image[s] which kept imprinting itself on the mind, conditioning, indeed stereotyping, an attitude toward Jews . . . help[ing] in fixing the idea of Jews being absolutely not 'of us. ' "[200]

The link between discrimination based on GI/AOP and religion, suggested by Wolfson, is echoed by Richard Posner. In his discussion of judicial discrimination against *sex/gender outsiders*, Posner includes the observation that "statutes which criminalize homosexual behavior express an irrational fear and loathing of a group that has been subjected to discrimination, much like that directed against the Jews, with whom indeed [*sex/gender outsiders*]—who, like the Jews, are despised more for what they are than for what they do—were frequently bracketed in medieval persecutions."[201]

The parallels between GI/AOP and religion are deeper, however, than a shared history of intolerance and abuse. Indeed, David Salmons suggests that "the proponents of a more vibrant Free Exercise Clause should take notice of recent developments in ['identity speech' in the area of affectional orientation/preference legal] theory."[202] In his opinion, "similar arguments in the religious context might provide a basis for a fuller vision of what religious exercise entails and hence greater protection of religious freedom."[203] While Salmons cautions that important legal differences exist between GI/AOP and religion—most notably, that the latter is specifically protected within the scope of the First Amendment while the former is not mentioned in the Constitution—he contends that the analogy he draws will reveal the importance of "adapting identity speech arguments to the free exercise realm."[204]

The first parallel Salmons discerns is "the fundamental rule that both [GI/AOP and religion] appear to play in shaping an individual's concept of identity and personhood."[205] While these elements are not the sole components of an individual's identity and personhood, and indeed their degree of importance may vary between and among individuals, both are intimate parts of one's core experiences.[206] Both reflect, to some degree, a person's interior sense of self, insofar as GI/AOP and religion deeply impact such issues as autonomy, privacy, intimacy, and family. They also reflect a person's relationship to society in general and the roles played or performed in public spheres. The strength with which claims regarding GI/AOP and religion are held by the individual concerned often renders rational discourse on these subjects almost impossible—and for good reason. GI/AOP and religion represent constructs that help individuals explain themselves to themselves or others, or place themselves in relation to others. Through their claims of GI/AOP and religious identity, individuals are able to authenticate themselves, communicate their true and complete selves, articulate their beliefs, recognize others who similarly identify themselves, and reveal an inner sensibility that transforms them into a community. Ultimately, claims of GI/AOP and religious identity, according to David Richards, rest "on the most fundamental principles of human rights in our tradition, in particular, the right to conscience, a right central to any sound understanding and conservation of the enduring values of American constitutionalism."[207]

The second parallel between GI/AOP and religion, according to Salmons, centers on the fact that both contain a significant behavioral component.[208] Because of the law's inadequate recognition of the behavioral component of GI/AOP and religion, there has been a "creation of artificial dichotomies between status or belief on the one side and behavior on the other—with the former considered inviolate and the latter receiving little or no protection."[209] Such dichotomies presume that status or belief and conduct can be completely separated from one another, a presumption which is inaccurate and obfuscates the fact that status or belief "are so intimately connected with human behavior that they cannot be disentangled."[210] To eradicate one is to render the other incomprehensible. Status or belief and conduct are integral parts of each person's lifestyle and identity, inasmuch as "the ability to express openly one's membership in the group is essential to the group's continued vitality."[211] Together they make possible the development of individual dignity, autonomy, and developmental interests; together they render visible that which society, because of custom and unexamined assumptions, would rather did not exist; together they give shape and substance to the full spectrum of self-representation and expression; and together they define the individual. If one's status or beliefs are severed from conduct, then the influence of GI/AOP and religion can be excluded from the public debate. The full range of human experiences is thus muted in order to protect the status quo and prevent necessary amplification of its world view.

The third parallel recognized by Salmons is that both GI/AOP and religion are deemed intensely personal, and thus private, matters.[212] As such, neither is considered appropriate for public discourse. Silence and invisibility are the operative modes; what is not discussed or (symbolically) displayed does not exist. Only public declarations of a GI/AOP or religion which differs from that of the majority causes alarm. For this reason the ability of GI/AOP or religious "outsiders" to develop or express their ideas is fettered by state manipulation. Identities are expected to be kept submerged rather than "blatantly" affirmed. Indeed, whether the trait is GI/AOP or religion, the nonconforming "offenders" are expected to obliterate their difference and "pass" as members of the dominant culture. Yet, as Salmons points out, "[p]ublicly declaring one's status or membership in a group that is central to one's identity, even if that expression takes the form of openly engaging in the activities that define group membership, is at the core of free speech."[213] Free speech, however, is not absolute. The legislatures and the courts define the parameters of words, ideas, and expressions which are valued and protected in our society.

As a result, revelations spoken or acted out, pertaining to one's GI/AOP or religion potentially entail danger for those courageous enough to live their truth openly. In the case of *sex/gender outsiders*, for example, Jonathan Katz records that for over four centuries lesbians and gay men in the U.S. have been "condemned to death by choking, burning, and drowning; they were executed; jailed; pilloried; fined; court-martialed; prostituted; fired; framed; blackmailed; disinherited; declared insane; driven to insanity, to suicide, murder, and self-hate; witch hunted; entrapped; stereotyped; mocked; insulted; isolated; pitied; castigated; and despised . . .[;] castrated, lobotomized; shock-treated; and psychoanalyzed."[214]

The treatment of *sex/gender outsiders* chronicled by Katz, reinforces Salmon's final parallel between GI/AOP and religion. They share similar group characteristics: a history of discrimination, an invisible criteria of membership, and lack of political power.[215] While the specifics may vary, the histories are similar with regard to both GI/AOP and religion: persecutions, hatred, violence, and unjust treatment. Identification of one's GI/AOP or religion may, if classified as wrong or dangerous by the state, serve as the foundation upon which discrimination rests. Scholars attest to the historic treatment of individuals who claim (or are perceived as belonging to) the "wrong" GI/AOP or religion.[216] Whether the offending trait is GI/AOP or religion, those who bear its label are treated as undesirables, branded as scapegoats, and frequently dehumanized. These individuals find themselves kin to witches[217]—truth may be of little interest to those who condemn or persecute them.

Since outside signifiers seldom betray one's GI/AOP or religion, as no discernable traits or markings indicate either, those targeted must either identify themselves or be identified by another. Rumor and (mis)perception play important roles in targeting members of "condemned fellowships," which renders all vulnerable to accusation and innuendo. Yet individuals in the minority due to GI/AOP or religion seldom find the political branches of the government sympathetic to their plight. It is not uncommon to find themselves on the receiving end of legislated discrimination, which effectively legitimates social practices that treat GI/AOP and religious "outsiders" as second-class citizens before the law. If the social opprobrium manifested on the basis of GI/AOP or religion is severe and immediate enough, members of the designated groups become particularly powerless to pursue their rights openly in the political arena, due to fear of reprisals.

A parallel between GI/AOP and religion that Salmons does not fully explore is the question of immutability. Neither GI/AOP nor religion are immutable in the same way as race. Although racial categories are socio-political-legal constructs, the biological component of race is indisputable.[218] This is not the case, however, for either GI/AOP or religion. To assert that GI/AOP is biologically determined is highly controversial,[219] while no one even argues that there exists a biological cause for religion. GI/AOP and religion are immutable, however, insofar as either may be so central to an individual's or group's identity that to change it would be abhorrent, regardless of the physical ease of the change. To the degree that GI/AOP or religion are an essential aspect of one's personal identity—even to those who keep their identity secret—it is untenable to require an individual or group to alter either in order to conform to societal norms or to stave off irrational prejudice and discrimination. Acquiescence to such a demand would entail an arduous reorientation process that would be psychologically, psychically, intellectually, or physically wrenching and painful to at least some of the individuals or groups affected.[220] Yet, even if one ignores the suffering endured by GI/AOP or religious "outsiders" who participate (either willingly or under duress) in some form of reparative therapy, there is no guarantee that the "cure" will be effective.[221]

Perhaps the strongest parallel between GI/AOP and religion is that both deserve protected status under the Equal Protection Clause as a constitutionally protected, fundamental right. Religious freedom, which is explicitly protected by the Bill of Rights, is, according to David Richards, "the oldest suspect classification under American public law,"[222] because "the identifications central to one's self-respect as a person of conscience are not to be subject to sectarian impositions through public law that unreasonably burden the exercise of one's conscientious convictions (the free exercise principle) or encourage change of such convictions to sectarian orthodoxy (the antiestablishment principle)."[223] The legal enforcement of sectarian views undermines the foundation of human rights, inasmuch as such laws enforce a sectarian interpretation of the facts and foreclose rational discussion and debate—as evidenced by the dehumanization and persecution of Jews in the Christian West,[224] and of Native Americans,[225] African slaves,[226] and Mormons,[227] in the U.S.

The imposition of sectarian views in the realms of race and religion to the detriment of human rights is mirrored with regard to *sex/gender outsiders* in this country. Richards asserts that

[n]ormative claims by [*sex/gender outsiders*] today have exactly the same ethical and constitutional force [as the constitutional protection of religion]: they are in their nature claims to a self-respecting personal and moral identity in public and private life through which they may reasonably express and realize their ethical convictions of the moral powers of love and friendship in a good, fulfilled, and responsible life against the background of an unjust and now quite conspicuously sectarian tradition of moral subjugation.[228]

Laws embodying sectarian religious truths with regard to gender identity or affectional orientation/preference have no more constitutional validity than similar laws affecting other manifestations of conscientious convictions designated by the courts as suspect classifications. Even on the most traditional and conservative reading of constitutional principles, Richards argues, GI/AOP ought to be a suspect classification "on the ground that it has been and is the object of unjust sectarian religious intolerance against the essential and inalienable human rights of conscience. [*Sex/gender outsiders*] have as much right to make claims on the basis of such principles as any persons and citizens in America."[229] For the government to legitimately discriminate against *sex/gender outsiders* on the basis of disputed religious beliefs[230] cannot be defended in a pluralistic society.[231] Whether lesbians, gay men, bisexuals, and transgenderists can convert to the dominant expression of GI/AOP is irrelevant, just as it is irrelevant whether Jews can convert to Christianity. It is immaterial, as well, whether *sex/gender outsiders*, Jews, or other non-Christian religious sects can be secretive and silent about their identities. Of primary importance is the fact that individuals and groups in this country are constitutionally protected from persecution on the basis of conscience.

Even if one concedes that the state possesses the right to legislate morally, as the Supreme Court maintained in *Hardwick*,[232] the moral convictions of the state's populous cannot trump the moral conviction inherent in the Fourteenth Amendment that individuals deserve to be and ought to be treated equally. Stigmatization and discrimination are neither condoned nor allowed under the Equal Protection Clause. In those instances where the Supreme Court has permitted the state to disadvantage a group of individuals, due to the state's desire to promote certain moral principles, its decisions were wrong,[233] despite later legislative or judicial attempts to rectify the government action.[234] Obviously, not all injustices in society have found remedies, but a judicial recourse is available for the legal discrimination encountered by *sex/gender outsiders*. The courts need to rule that lesbians, gay men, bisexuals, and transgenderists have a constitutional right to be free of arbitrary and invidious discrimination based on the moral claims held by a segment of individuals ascribing to the Judeo-Christian tradition. To do less is equivalent to a violation of both the Establishment and Free Exercise clauses of the First Amendment, for it would unduly burden the conscientious convictions of *sex/gender outsiders* and their allies regarding GI/AOP and pressure these individuals to conform to conventional orthodoxy. Moreover, as David Richards points out, "it deprive[s lesbians, gay men, bisexuals, and transgenderists] of the very foundation of human rights, freedom of conscience in knowing and acting on one's moral rights and duties."[235] If the Judeo-Christian tradition, as interpreted by the Christian right, is accepted as the measure of what constitutes permissible ethical and conscientious beliefs and actions, the judiciary thereby grants to the states the right to enforce a conception of religious truth—in violation of the First Amendment[236] and the principle of equal respect.

NOTES

1. Indeed, prior to the Civil War amendments, the U.S. Constitution explicitly recognized inequality as valid law. For example, Article I, section 2, clause 3 stipulated that a slave counted as three-fifths of a person for purposes of direct taxes and congressional representation; Article I, section 9, clause 1 and Article V prohibited any federal restrictions on the importation of slaves prior to 1801; and

Article IV, section 2, clause 3 prohibited runaway slaves from becoming free, requiring them to be returned to their "owners."

2. Audre Lorde states that "[i]n america, this norm is usually defined as white, thin, male, young, heterosexual, christian, and financially secure. It is with this mythical norm that the trappings of power reside in this society. Those of us who stand outside that power often identify one way in which we are different, and we assume that to be the primary cause of all oppression, forgetting other distortions around difference, some of which we ourselves may be practicing" [Lorde, "Age, Race, Class, and Sex" at 116].

3. Greenwalt (1983) at 1169.

4. Wolgast (1980) at 37–39.

5. *Id.* at 39.

6. *Id.* Perhaps the best articulation of this phenomenon is provided by Catherine MacKinnon, who has observed that in cases focusing on gender inequality women have been and continue to be measured in relation to men [MacKinnon (1991) at 1286, 1287, 1324]. She accurately states that "women's merits are recognized if and only if they meet the male standard; but no one notices that this standard is a male one" [*Id.* at 1292].

7. According to Rosemary Tong, "society continues to ignore, trivialize, and even ridicule gay people's problems. Unless a gay rights bill is passed, the gay men and gay women will remain the law's stepchildren" [Tong (1984) at 190]. Ruthann Robson makes a similar point in her observation that the Equal Protection Clause fails to protect "lesbians as lesbians" [Robson (1992) at 81]. Indeed, both public and private entities discriminate on the basis of affectional orientation/preference in the U.S.A. See also Baer (1983) at 21; Brown & Rounsley (1996); Docter (1988); Ekins & King (1996); Feinberg (1996); Weinberg, Williams, & Pryor (1994); Wilkinson and White (1977).

8. Young (1990) at 164–165.

9. For an in-depth analysis of these three approaches, see: Zingo and Early (1994), Chapter 3.

10. See: Western (1982).

11. *Hayes* (1887) at 71.

12. Constitution of the United States, Amendment XIV, section 1 (ratified on 9 July 1868). Although there is no explicit constitutional provision requiring that the federal government provide equal protection of the law, the Supreme Court suggested in *Korematsu* (1944) that the Fourteenth Amendment's Equal Protection Clause applied to federal action via the Fifth Amendment's Due Process clause. This position was reiterated by the Supreme Court in *Bolling* (1954) [at 499], wherein Chief Justice Earl Warren stated: "The Fifth Amendment [does] not contain an equal protection clause. But, the concepts of equal protection and due process, both stemming from our American ideal of fairness, are not mutually exclusive. The 'equal protection of the law' is a more explicit safeguard of prohibited unfairness than 'due process of law,' and therefore, we do not imply that the two

are always interchangeable phrases. But, as this Court has recognized, discrimination may be so unjustifiable as to be violative of due process. In view of our decision that the Constitution prohibits the state from maintaining racially segregated public schools, it would be unthinkable that the same Constitution would impose a lesser duty on the Federal Government." The Court reaffirmed that the Constitution requires the federal government to guarantee equal protection of laws from arbitrary discrimination in *Wiesenfeld* (1975) at 638 n.2; *Buckley* (1976) at 93; *Hampton* (1976) at 100.

13. *DeShaney* (1989) at 197; *McLaurin* (1949). While private discrimination does not violate the Equal Protection Clause of the Fourteenth Amendment, Congress or the states may legislate protection against private discrimination. See: *The Civil Rights Cases* (1883) (Harlan, J., dissenting); *Jones* (1968); *Runyon* (1976); *Mahone* (1977) at 1028–1029; *Patterson* (1989).

14. *Blum* (1982) (Brennan, J., dissenting). See also: *Burton* (1961); *Moose Lodge No. 107* (1965).

15. *McKeey* (1989) at 416; *Personnel Administrator of Massachusetts* (1979) at 279; *Washington* (1976).

16. Catherine MacKinnon makes this point quite forcefully in her argument regarding sex inequality [MacKinnon (1991) at 1297, 1299]. See also: Delgado (1982) at 140–141; Matsuda (1989).

17. Massaro (1991) at 241.

18. It should be noted that the Supreme Court's use of this three-tiered approach has not been consistent. Justice Marshall states that the Court's equal protection tests lack the "precision of mathematical formulas" [*Dunn* (1972) (Marshall, J., dissenting)], while Justice Stevens points out that the Court uses a continuum of standards rather than the three generally identified with equal protection analysis [in *Cleburne Living Center* (1985) (Stevens, J., concurring)].

19. *Lindsley* (1911); *City of New Orleans v. Duke* [hereafter *Duke*] (1976).

20. See: *Gulf, Colorado, & Santa Fe Railway Company* (1897); *F.S. Royster Guano Co.* (1920); *McDonald* (1969); *McGinnis* (1973); *US Railroad Retirement Board* (1980); *Logan* (1982).

21. *Lindsley* (1911) at 78–79. See also: *McGowen* (1961); *McLaughlin* (1964) at 191; *Duke* (1976).

22. *San Antonio Independent School District* (1973) at 98 (Marshall, J., dissenting).

23. *Craig* (1976) at 197; *Trimble* (1977); *Plyler* (1982).

24. The Court has upheld classifications under strict scrutiny only twice: in *Korematsu* (1944), wherein the Court upheld an executive order excluding people of Japanese ancestry from military areas in California; and *Hirabayashi* (1945), wherein the Court upheld a curfew imposed on persons of Japanese ancestry.

25. *Cleburne Living Center* (1985) at 440. See also: *Carolene Products* (1938) at 152 fn.4; *Hernandez* (1954); *Harper* (1966); *Shapiro* (1969).

26. *Carolene Products Company* (1938) at 152 fn.4.

27. *Korematsu* (1944) at 216. The Court went on to note, however, that while such restrictions are suspects, they are not necessarily unconstitutional—"[p]ressing public necessity may sometimes justify the existence of such restrictions; racial antagonism never can" [*Ibid*].

28. *Id.*

29. *Loving* (1967).

30. *Skinner* (1942) at 541.

31. *Harper* (1966); *Kramer* (1969); *Dunn* (1972).

32. See for example: *Maynard* (1888); *Skinner* (1942); *Loving* (1967); *Cleveland Board of Education* (1974); *Zablocki* (1978); *Turner* (1987).

33. *Shapiro* (1969); *Dunn* (1972); *Memorial Hospital* (1974).

34. See for example: *Griswold* (1965); *Eisenstadt* (1972); *Roe* (1973); *Carey* (1977).

35. See for example: *Skinner* (1942) at 541; *Griswold* (1965); *Eisenstadt* (1972).

36. *Stanley* (1969).

37. *Roe* (1973); *Harris v. McRae* (1980); Thornburgh (1986); Planned Parenthood of Southeastern Pennsylvania (1992).

38. *Hardwick* (1986) at 2844.

39. *Id.*

40. *Shapiro* (1969) at 662.

41. *San Antonio Independent School District* (1973) at 33.

42. *Doe* (1975); *Enslin* (1975); *Hardwick* (1986). It should be noted that *Hardwick* is not an equal protection case; it was decided under the Due Process Clause. However, because *Hardwick* focuses on the question of a substantive fundamental right, the Supreme Court's reasoning has been considered applicable to equal protection arguments regarding consensual sexual relationships. Justice Blackmun discussed the potential impact of *Hardwick* on equal protection principles at 2848 fn.2. Moreover, lower courts have relied on *Hardwick* as precedent for their denial of the equal protection claims of lesbians and gay men. See: *Padula* (1987); *Woodward* (1989); *Ben-Shalom* (1989).

43. *Doe* (1975) at 1200, 1202.

44. *Id.* at 1204 (Merhinge, J., dissenting).

45. *Id.*

46. *Eisenstadt* (1972).

47. *Id.* at 1205.

48. The New York Court of Appeals consolidated three cases, all of which challenged the constitutionality of Penal Law §130.38, which criminalized consensual sodomy or deviate sexual intercourse between persons not married to each other [*Onofre* at 947]. In *People of New York v. Onofre*, Onofre was convicted of committing acts of deviate sexual intercourse with a 17–year-old male at defendant's home; in *Peoples v. People of New York*, defendants Peoples and Goss were convicted of engaging in an act of oral sodomy in an automobile parked in the City

of Buffalo in the early hours; and in *People of New York v. Sweat,* Sweat was convicted of a similar act with a male in a truck parked on the street in a residential area of the city about 1:30 a.m. Neither of the two incidents occurring in the motor vehicles were considered to have taken place "in public" [*Id.* at 948].

49. *Onofre* at 949.

50. *Id.*

51. *Id.* at 950.

52. *Id.*

53. *Id.* at 949.

54. *Id.* at 951.

55. *Baker* (1983) at 1135.

56. *Id.* at 1139.

57. *Id.* at 1124.

58. *Id.* at 1140.

59. *Id.* at 1141.

60. *Id.*

61. *Baker* (1985) at 292.

62. *Dronenburg* (1984) at 1391.

63. *Id.* at 1392.

64. *Id.* at 1395–1396.

65. *Id.* at 1396.

66. For a detailed discussion of this case, see Chapter Four *infra.*

67. The Supreme Court vacated the judgment in *Buchanan v. Batchelor* (1970) on procedural grounds, without reaching the merits of the federal district court's ruling (which held that the Texas sodomy statute, which prohibited all oral or anal intercourse—regardless of the affectional orientation/preference of the participants—was unconstitutional because it violated the right of privacy of marital couples). In *Doe v. Commonwealth's Attorney* (1975) it summarily affirmed the judgment of the federal district court without issuing an opinion. Finally, the Supreme Court denied *certiorari* in *People v. Onofre* (1980).

68. *Saunders* (1977).

69. *Id.* at 339–340.

70. Hunter, "Life After Hardwick" at 531.

71. See: *Bowen v. Gillard* (1987) at 602–603; *Frontiero* (1973) at 684–686; *Lyng* (1986) at 683; *Massachusetts Board of Retirement* (1976) at 313; *San Antonio Independent School District* (1973) at 28; Note, "The Constitutional Status. . . " (1985) at 1299, 1301.

72. See: *Bowen* (1987) at 602–603; *Cleburne Living Center* (1985) at 442; *Frontiero* (1973) at 686; *Massachusetts Board of Retirement* (1976) at 313; *Mathews* (1976) at 505; *Weber* (1972) at 175.

73. See: *Bowen* (1987) at 602–603; *Carolene Products* (1938) at 152 n.4; *Cleburne Living Center* (1985) at 445; *Plyler* (1982) at 216 n.14; *Rowland* (1985) at 1014 (Brennan, J., dissenting from denial of cert.); *Watkins* (1988) at 1348.

74. See: *Bowen* (1987) at 602–603; *Frontiero* (1973) at 686; *Lyng* (1986) at 638; *Mathews* (1976) at 505–506; *Plyler* (1982) at 216 n.14, 220; *Watkins* (1988) at 1346–1348; Karst (1977) at 23.

75. See: "The Constitutional Status. . . " (1985) at 1298.

76. *Frontiero* at 686 (quoting *Weber* at 175).

77. *Id.*

78. *Cleburne Living Center* at 448.

79. *Id.* at 441–442 [emphasis added].

80. For an in-depth analysis of the problems associated with legal arguments regarding immutability for *sex/gender outsiders*, see: Halley (1994).

81. Bailey and Pillard (1991); Hammer *et al.* (1993); and LeVay (1991).

82. See: Halley (1994).

83. See: Boswell (1980); Feinberg (1996); Ide (1985).

84. See: Achtenberg (1984, 1994); Bornstein (1994); Colker (1996); D'Emilio (1983); Editors of the *Harvard Law Review* (1989, 1990); Heger (1980, 1994); Herdt (1993); Katz (1976, 1992); MacKenzie (1994); Rubenstein (1993); Sr. Mary Elizabeth, *Legal Aspects. . .* (1988).

85. See: "Don't Ask, Don't Tell. National Defense Authorization Act for Fiscal Year 1994."

86. U.S. Senate, 104th Congress (1996).

87. Although the U.S. Supreme Court affirmed the judgment of the Colorado Supreme Court that Colorado's Amendment 2 violated the Equal Protection Clause of the Fourteenth Amendment, it did so for reasons different from those of the lower court. The Colorado Supreme Court subjected Amendment 2 to strict scrutiny and found that it infringed the fundamental right of *sex/gender outsiders* to participate equally in the political process. The U.S. Supreme Court, on the other hand, subjected Amendment 2 to rational-basis scrutiny and found that it bore no rational relation to a legitimate state purpose. By utilizing the lowest level of scrutiny in *Romer*, and by failing to reconsider its 1986 opinion in *Hardwick*, the Supreme Court implicitly rejected the state supreme court's holding that Amendment 2 infringes a fundamental right, and it failed to reconcile the seeming contradiction between *Hardwick* and *Romer*.

88. Sixteen states criminalize consensual, non-commercial same-sex solicitation: Alabama, Arizona, Arkansas, Delaware, Georgia, Kansas, Maryland, Massachusetts, Michigan, Nevada, New York, North Dakota, Ohio, Oklahoma, Rhode Island, and Wisconsin [Hunter, Michaelson, and Stoddard (1992)]. Richard Mohr points out, however, that three of these statutes have been held invalid by state courts. New York's solicitation law was declared unconstitutional "as companion legislation to its unconstitutional consensual sodomy law" in *People v. Uplinger* (1983) [Mohr (1988) at 55 fn.19]. California's and Massachusetts' solicitation laws were voided on due process grounds [*Pryor* (1979) at 645; *Sefranka* (1980); Mohr at 55 fn.20].

89. In 1994, twenty-six states had sodomy statutes on their books: Alabama, Arizona, Arkansas, Florida, Georgia, Idaho, Kansas, Kentucky, Louisiana, Maryland, Massachusetts, Michigan, Minnesota, Mississippi, Missouri, Montana, New York, North Carolina, Oklahoma, Pennsylvania, Rhode Island, South Carolina, Tennessee, Texas, Utah, and Virginia. Of these, four statutes (Kentucky 1992, New York 1980, Pennsylvania 1980, and Texas 1994 with the dismissal of *Morales* (1990)) have been held to violate the respective state's constitution but have not yet been repealed; the constitutionality of two other statutes (Louisiana and Michigan) is unclear. The decision of the Orleans Parish Court in Louisiana, that criminalization of the "crime against nature" is unconstitutional is pending appeal. The two relevant judicial decisions in Michigan conflict with one another. In *Michigan Organization of Human Rights* (1990) the Wayne County Circuit Court held that the "crime against nature" statute, as applied to private, consensual, adult behavior is unconstitutional in Wayne County. No appeal was taken in this case. In *People v. Brashier* (1992) the Michigan Court of Appeals held that the "crime against nature" statute is constitutional outside of Wayne County. Consequently, a decision is needed from the Michigan Supreme Court to determine whether this statute is constitutional. Of the twenty-two sodomy statutes which have been neither repealed nor judicially invalidated, twelve categorize this crime as a felony, while eleven categorize it as a misdemeanor [Summersgill (Internet)].

90. Despite the fact that in *Baehr* (1993) the Hawaii Supreme Court held that the Hawaii marriage law limiting marriage to different-sex couples could only be upheld if the government could demonstrate a legitimate compelling purpose for the classification, in 1997 the Hawaii legislature passed a state version of the national "The Defense of Marriage Act" (DOMA) enacted by the 104th Congress in 1996. As a result, regardless of how the state judiciary rules with regard to Hawaii's marriage law, unless it finds the DOMA statute to be in violation of the Hawaiian constitution—or unless the U.S. Supreme Court finds the national legislation to be in violation of the U.S. Constitution—the ban on same-sex marriage may very well remain intact.

91. Violence against *sex/gender outsiders* takes a multitude of forms, from vituperation to beatings involving torture or mutilation of the victim. Kendall Thomas reports that a physician who treats victims targeted due to their real or perceived gender identity or affectional orientation/preference finds that the attacks are frequently vicious and that the intent seems clearly to kill or maim [Thomas (1992) at 1463]. In the doctor's experience, "[w]eapons include knives, guns, brass knuckles, tire irons, baseball bats, broken bottles, metal chains, and metal pipes. Injuries include severe lacerations requiring extensive plastic surgery; head injuries, at times requiring surgery; puncture wounds to the chest, requiring insertion of chest tubes; removal of the spleen for traumatic rupture; severe eye injuries, in two cases resulting in permanent loss of vision; as well as severe psychological trauma the level of which would be difficult to measure" [*Id.* at 1466].

92. Cory (1951). D'Emilio reports that "after 1965 the pseudonymous Cory ceased to exist and was replaced by Edward Sagarin, a sociologist of deviance" [D'Emilio (1983) at 168].

93. Cory, *id.* at 14, as quoted in D'Emilio, *id.* at 57.

94. *Id.*

95. California, Connecticut, Hawaii, Massachusetts, Minnesota, New Jersey, Vermont, Wisconsin, and the District of Columbia.

96. Badgett (1996) at 32. See: Editors of the *Harvard Law Review* (1989, 1990) at 44–74.

97. See: *Ben-Shalom* (1989) at 1380; *Equality Foundation of Greater Cincinnati* (1994) at 410; *High Tech Gays* (1987) at 1368, (1990) at 377; *Jantz* (1991) at 1551; *Watkins* (1988) at 1349.

98. See: *Baehr* (1991) at 5; *Baker* (1982) at 1144 n.58, (1985) at 292; *Ben-Shalom* (1989); *Childers* (1981) at 147 n.22; *Equality Foundation of Greater Cincinnati* (1994) at 430–434; *High Tech Gays* (1990) at 573–574, (1990) at 376; *National Gay Task Force* (1984) at 1273; *Steffan v. Cheney*, 780 F.Supp. 1, 6–7 (DDC 1991), *rev'd sub. nom. Steffan* (1993); *Woodward* (1989) at 1076.

99. Title VII states: "(a) It shall be unlawful employment practice for an employer—(1) to fail to hire or to discharge any individual, or otherwise to discriminate against an individual with respect to his compensation, terms, conditions, or privileges of employment, because of such individual's race, color, religion, sex, or national origins; or (2) to limit, segregate, or classify his employees or applicants for employment in any way which would deprive or tend to deprive any individual of employment opportunities or otherwise adversely affect his status as an employee, because of such individual's race, color, religion, sex, or national origin." See: 42 U.S.C. §§2000e-2000e-17, §2000e-2(a)(1)(2) (1988). The Equal Employment Opportunity Commission (EEOC) was created to enforce this statute, but the effectiveness of this statute in eliminating race and/or sex discrimination is directly connected to the "teeth" provided by (threatened or actual) lawsuits [Stetson (1991) at 68].

100. See: *Williams* (1976); *Firefighters Institute for Racial Equality* (1977); *Cariddi* (1977); *Miller* (1979); *Henson* (1982); *Craig* (1983); *Weiss* (1984); *Horn* (1985); *Risinger* (1989).

101. The first sexual harassment case to be heard by the Supreme Court was *Meritor Savings Bank* (1986).

102. Catherine MacKinnon (1979) identifies two specific forms of sexual harassment. The first, *"quid pro quo"* harassment, is defined by MacKinnon as "the more or less explicit exchange: the woman must comply sexually or forfeit an employment benefit. The exchange can be anything but subtle, although its expression can be euphemistic" [MacKinnon (1979) at 32]. The second form of sexual harassment, which the courts commonly call "hostile environment" harassment, is labeled "condition of work" harassment by MacKinnon. She defines this type of harassment as a "situation in which sexual harassment simply makes the work en-

vironment unbearable. Unwanted sexual advances [occur], made simply because [an employee] has a woman's body. . . . She may be constantly felt or pinched, visually undressed and stared at, surreptitiously kissed, commented upon, manipulated into being found alone, and generally taken advantage of at work—but never promised or denied anything explicitly connected with her job" [*Ibid* at 40].

103. EEOC decision 76–67, EEOC Decision (CCH) par. 6493 (2 March 1976); EEOC decision 76–75, EEOC Decision (CCH) par. 6495 (2 March 1976); EEOC Decision 76–75, 19 Fair Employment Practice Cases (BNA) 1823, 1824 (1976).

104. *Holloway* (1977); *Smith* (1978); *Voyles* (1975); *Blum* (1979); *DeSantis* (1979); *Valdes* (1980); *Ulane* (1984); *Williamson* (1989). See, however, *Price Waterhouse* (1989) at 1791, wherein the Court held that employment discrimination based on gender non-conformity/sex stereotyping violates Title VII.

105. EEOC Decision 75–76, 19 Fair Employment Practice Cases (BNA) 1823, 1824 (1975).

106. In 1982, the Supreme Court held that, while an EEOC charge is required—except in extraordinary cases—before a Title VII suit is filed, the EEOC filing is not a "jurisdictional prerequisite," since it is subject to "waiver, estoppel, and equitable tolling" [*Zippes* (1982) at 394].

107. EEOC decision 76–75, EEOC Decision (CCH) par. 6495 (2 March 1976) at 4266.

108. *Id.*

109. *Holloway* at 661.

110. The Ninth Circuit Court, at the request of counsel for appellants, consolidated three separate federal district court actions brought by lesbians and gay men that claimed that "their employers or former employers discriminated against them in employment decisions because of their homosexuality" [*DeSantis* at 328]. In *Strailey v. Happy Times Nursery School, Inc.*, the appellant alleged that "he was fired because he wore a small gold ear-loop to school prior to the commencement of the school year." In *DeSantis v. Pacific Telephone & Telegraph Co.*, three males (DeSantis, Boyle, and Simard) claimed that "Pacific Telephone & Telegraph Co. impermissibly discriminated against them because of their homosexuality. DeSantis alleged that "he was not hired when [a company] supervisor concluded that he was homosexual"; Boyle "was continually harassed by his co-workers and had to quit to preserve his health . . . because his supervisors did nothing to alleviate this condition"; Simard was "forced to quit under similar conditions." All three also alleged that company officials "had publicly stated that they would not hire homosexuals." In *Lundin v. Pacific Telephone & Telegraph*, the appellants, both females, alleged that the company "discriminated against them because of their known lesbian relationship and eventually fired them" [*Id.* at 328–329].

111. *DeSantis* at 329.

112. *Id.* at 330.

113. *Id.* at 331.

114. *Id.* at 329–330.

115. *Id.* at 329, citing *Holloway* at 662.

116. In *Griggs*, the U.S. Supreme Court held that "[w]hat is required by Congress [under Title VII] is the removal of artificial, arbitrary, and unnecessary barriers to employment when the barriers operate invidiously to discriminate on the basis of racial or other impermissible classifications" [*Griggs* (1971) at 431].

117. *DeSantis* at 331.

118. *Id.* at 330.

119. Judge Sneed dissented from the holding that the gay men in *DeSantis* had not stated a Title VII claim under the disproportionate impact theories of *Griggs* (1971). According to Judge Sneed, the male appellants were not using *Griggs* "as an artifice to 'bootstrap' Title VII protection for homosexuals under the guise of protecting men generally" [*DeSantis* at 333 (Sneed, J., dissenting)]. Judge Sneed warned, however, that it would be very difficult to establish such a claim, since "the male appellants must prove that as a result of the appellee's practices there exists discrimination against males *qua* males" [*Id.*]. If the appellants were successful in establishing their claim, then males would be protected generally.

120. *Phillips* (1971) at 544. *Phillips* was the first Title VII case heard by the Supreme Court. The Fifth Circuit Court addressed the question of what constituted a *per se* violation of sex discrimination under Title VII. It replied that "a *per se* violation of the Act can only be discrimination based solely on one of the categories, i.e., in the case of sex; women vis-a-vis men. When another criterion of employment is added to one of the classifications listed in the Act, there is no longer apparent discrimination based solely on race, color, religion, sex, or national origin. . . . The evidence presented in the trial court is quite convincing that no discrimination against women as a whole or the appellant individually was practiced by Martin Marietta. The discrimination was based on a two-pronged qualification, i.e., a woman with pre-school age children" [*Phillips v. Martin Marietta Corp.*, 411 F.2d 1, 3–4 (5th Cir. 1969)]. The Supreme Court rejected the line of reasoning put forth by the majority of the Appeals Court and sided with the dissent of Chief Justice Brown. In both the Supreme Court's and Chief Justice Brown's opinion, "a woman with pre-school children may not be employed, a man with pre-school children may. The distinguishing factor seems to be motherhood versus fatherhood. Is this sex-related? . . . The answer is . . . simple: nobody . . . has yet seen a male mother. A mother . . . must then be a woman. It is the fact of being a mother—i.e., *qua* mother—not the age of the children, which denies employment opportunity to a woman which is open to a man" [*Id.* at 1257, 1259–1262 (Brown, Chief Judge, dissenting)].

121. *DeSantis* at 331.

122. *Strailey*, consolidated into *DeSantis* (1979).

123. *Holloway* (1977).

124. *Smith* (1978).

125. *Smith* (1978) at 328.

126. See: *Scott* (1968); *Morton* (1969); *McConnell* (1971); *Holloway* (1977); *Smith* (1975); *Voyles* (1975); *DeSantis* (1979); *Valdes* (1980); *Ulane* (1984).

127. At the present time lesbians, gay men, bisexuals, and transgenderists have no protection from employment discrimination based on affectional orientation/preference under the Civil Rights Act of 1964, the Civil Rights Act of 1972, the Pregnancy Discrimination Act of 1978, the Age Discrimination Act of 1978, or the Americans with Disabilities Act of 1990. Attempts to amend Title VII of the Civil Rights Act of 1964, to add affectional orientation/preference as a prohibited category of discrimination, have been consistently rejected by the national legislature since 1978.

128. *Ulane* at 1084.

129. *Id.* at 1084.

130. *Id.* at 1085.

131. See: *Sommers* (1982); *Holloway* (1977).

132. *Ulane* at 1087.

133. *Id.*

134. *Id.*

135. *Price Waterhouse* at 251.

136. *Id.* at 252.

137. *Id.* at 251.

138. *Dillon* at 28–29.

139. *Id.* at 27 n.5.

140. EEOC Compliance Manual (CCH) §615.2(b)(3) (1987).

141. *Id.*

142. It should be noted that if an employee's supervisor is bisexual and that supervisor harasses members of both sexes, a federal court stated the actions of that "particularly unspeakable cad" would not violate Title VII [*Ryczek* (1995)]. This reasoning was in line with that of the D.C. Circuit Court's opinion which recognized that "[i]n the case of a bisexual supervisor, the insistence upon sexual favors would not constitute [sex] discrimination because it would apply to male and female employees alike" [*Barnes* (1977) at 990 n.55]. For a more detailed examination of bisexual harassment, see MacKinnon (1979) at 200–206.

143. *Pritchett* (1995).

144. *Nogueras* (1995).

145. *McWilliams* (1996). The court noted, however, that its decision in *McWilliams* does not "purport to reach any form of same-sex discrimination claim where either victim or oppressor, or both, are homosexual or bisexual" [*Id.* at 1195 n.4]. See also: *Hopkins* (1996). The refusal of the Fourth Circuit to find a same-sex sexual harassment claim actionable under Title VII, when both parties are presumed to be heterosexual, accurately reflects the position of the Fifth Circuit Court of Appeals in *Garcia* (1994) and *Oncale* (1996).

146. *Wrightson* (1996) at 141. The Eighth Circuit Court of Appeal ruled in *Quick v. Donaldson Co.* that even though both parties comprised heterosexual

males, "a fact-finder could reasonably conclude that the treatment of men at Donaldson were worse than the treatment of women. Thus, Quick raised a genuine issue of material fact as to whether the alleged harassment was gender based" [*Quick* (1996) at 1379].

147. *Barnes* (1977) at 990 n.55.

148. *Saulpaugh* (1993) at 148 (Van Graafeiland, J., concurring).

149. *Baskerville* (1995) at 430.

150. See: *McConnell* (1971); *Singer* (1976); *Sharar* (1992); Chew (1980); Douglas (1988); Heatherly (1986); Wise (1980).

151. See: Choper (1982); Tribe (1978).

152. Tribe (1978) at 826. See: *Davis* (1890) at 341–343 (wherein the Court held that "the term 'religion' has reference to one's views of his relations to his Creator, and to the obligations they impose for reverence for his being and character, and of obedience to his will"); *MacIntosh* (1931) at 633–634 (wherein the Court held that "the essence of religion is belief in a relation to God involving duties superior to those arising from any human relation. . . . One cannot speak of religious liberty, with proper appreciation of its essential and historic significance, without assuming the existence of a belief in supreme allegiance to the will of God").

153. *Kauten* at 708.

154. *Id.*

155. *Seeger* at 166.

156. *Welsh* at 340.

157. *Id.*

158. *Reynolds* at 164.

159. *Davis* at 335–336 n.1, quoting Idaho Rev. Stat. §501 (1844) (territorial statute) (current version at Idaho Constitution art.6 §3).

160. *Id.* at 342, 343.

161. *Late Corporation of the Church of Jesus Christ of Latter-Day Saints* at 49.

162. *Church of the Holy Trinity* at 472.

163. The concept "Judeo-Christian," while accepted almost universally in this country as a stock phrase, is problematic because, first, it implies the subsumption of Judaism by Christianity, thereby erasing the crucial historical, doctrinal, and cultural differences that exist between these traditions; second, this concept implies that Christianity is the natural progression of Judaism. The third problem centers not on the concept itself but on the presumption that this country is a Christian nation that follows that "Judeo-Christian" tradition and, as a consequence, that the law can be used to enforce the belief system. The religion clauses of the First Amendment of the Constitution clearly establish that citizens are not legally mandated to embrace any religious or spiritual values—even those labeled "Judeo-Christian"—or to live their lives in accordance with any religious or spiritual system. Despite these problems, however, the phrase "Judeo-Christian" will

be used in this book to refer to the religious tradition generally associated with this concept.

164. See: Buchanan (1985) at 546–549; Zawadsky (1979) at 701; *Hardwick* (1986).

165. Kozma (1994) at 891–892.

166. See: D'Emilio (1983).

167. *Id.* at 13.

168. *Id.* D'Emilio further observes that although the bible is no longer as central in the lives of many U.S. people in the twentieth century as it once was, "and although modern believers might be less inclined to expect ruin to pour down from heaven," views of sexuality and sexual behavior are still shaped by religious teachings [*Id.*].

169. Feinberg (1996) at 68–73.

170. *Id.* at 68.

171. *Id.* at 71.

172. *Id.*

173. Mark Kohler argues that while the early Christian church expressed little, if any, hostility toward homosexuality, its attitude dramatically changed during the time of St. Thomas Aquinas. At that time, he asserts, "antihomosexual prejudice became firmly entrenched in church doctrine, largely out of an overarching rigidity concerning sexual behavior" [Kohler at 139–140]. For an in-depth analysis of the relationship of Christianity to *sex/gender outsiders*, see: Harvey (1967); Barrett (1979); Ide (1985); Boswell (1980); Comstock (1991) at 120–140; Feinberg (1996).

174. According to Reverend Barrett, the Church turned sinners convicted of "heresy or sodomy over to the secular authorities for execution" when death was the decreed penalty. However, while the king had the authority to execute anyone within his domain, no laws governing homosexual offenders existed in England prior to [Henry VII's] reign, when "the detestable and abominable vice of buggery was deemed a capital felony." This legal pronouncement condemned convicted persons to execution and forfeiture of their estates to the king [Barrett at 1022, 1023, 1024].

Justice Blackmun, in his dissenting opinion in *Bowers v. Hardwick*, observes that "the theological nature of the origin of Anglo-American antisodomy statutes is patent. It was not until 1533 that sodomy was made a secular offense in England. . . . Until that time, the offense was, in Sir James Steven's words, 'merely ecclesiastical.' . . . The transfer of jurisdiction over prosecutions for sodomy to the secular courts seems primarily due to the alteration of ecclesiastical jurisdiction attendant on England's break with the Roman Catholic Church, rather than to any new understanding of the sovereign's interest in preventing or punishing the behavior involved" [*Hardwick* at 211–212 fn.5 (1986) (Blackmun, J., dissenting) (footnotes omitted)].

175. As noted by James E. Andrews, Stated Clerk of the General Assembly of the Presbyterian Church (U.S.A.), "[r]eligious bodies now manifest a spectrum of responses to homosexuality ranging from total acceptance to virulent denunciation" ["*Brief Amicus Curiae* of James E. Andrews . . ." at 12].

For examples of positions assumed by at least some religious bodies, see: (1) "The Petitioners' Religious *Amici Curiae Brief . . .*," which represented the views of: the Christian Life Commission of the Southern Baptist Convention, Lutheran Church-Missouri Synod, and the National Association of Evangelicals; (2) "The Respondents' Religious *Amici Curiae Brief . . .*," which represented the views of: the American Friends Service Committee; the American Jewish Committee; the Federation of Reconstructionist Congregations and Havurot; the Most Reverend Edmond L. Browning, Presiding Bishop of the Episcopal Church; the Reconstructionist Rabbinical Association; the Unitarian Universalist Association; the United Church of Christ Office for Church in Society; and the United Synagogue of Conservative Judaism; (3) "The Brief of *Amicus Curiae* of the Concerned Women for America. . . ."

176. *Hardwick* at 210–211 (Blackmun, J., dissenting). See also: *Hardwick* at 192–194, 196–197 (White, J.); *Hardwick* at 197 (Burger, C.J., concurring); *Hardwick* at 216 (Stevens, J., dissenting); Rubenfeld (1989); Wolfson (1991).

177. In May 1992, a petition was submitted by the requisite numbers of qualified voters to place Amendment 2 on the ballot; on 3 November 1993, Amendment 2 was approved by the Colorado voters by 53.4 percent of the vote. Litigation was commenced by Richard Evans and others on 12 November 1992 to obtain a preliminary injunction to prevent the governor of Colorado and the Colorado attorney general from enacting or enforcing Amendment 2 pending a trial on the merits. The trial court determined that Amendment 2 violated the fundamental right not to have the state endorse and give effect to private bias; the injunction was granted on 15 January 1993. The Colorado Supreme Court held, in response to the state's appeal, that Amendment 2 was subject to strict scrutiny under the Fourteenth Amendment, because it infringed the fundamental right of lesbians, bisexuals, and gay men to participate in the political process; the interim injunction was sustained, and the case was remanded for further proceedings on 19 July 1993. On remand, the state advanced various arguments in an effort to show that Amendment 2 was narrowly tailored to serve compelling interests, but the trial court found none sufficient and enjoined enforcement of Amendment 2 on 14 December 1993. The Colorado Supreme Court, in a second opinion, affirmed the trial court's ruling on 11 October 1994. The state appealed to the U.S. Supreme Court. On 20 May 1994, the U.S. Supreme Court affirmed the judgment of the Colorado Supreme Court on the grounds that Amendment 2 did not bear a rational relationship to a legitimate government purpose and thus violated the Equal Protection Clause. See: *Evans* (1993).

178. "Brief for Petitioners . . ." at 44–45. It should be noted that although transgenderists were not specifically covered by the language of Colorado's Amend-

ment 2, Vera Whisman reports, they were included in a propaganda short entitled *The Gay Agenda,* filmed by The Report—a right-wing Christian organization. The purpose of the video was to manipulate and shock the conservative religious audience for whom it was intended. In an attempt to communicate its message that perverse and public sexuality was central to the anti-ballot initiatives, the centerpiece of the video was scenes from the New York and San Francisco gay pride parades that included what The Report considered negative portrayals of lesbians, gay men, and trans persons: public partial nudity of women, open-mouthed kisses between men, and drag queens who were members of San Francisco's Sisters of Perpetual Indulgence [Whisman (1996) at 1].

179. This argument is most fully developed by Richards (1994).

180. *County of Allegheny* (1989) at 593 (emphasis in original) (quoting *Wallace* at 70 [O'Connor, J., concurring]).

181. For a discussion of the ways in which discrimination against *sex/gender outsiders* violates the Free Exercise Clause and the Establishment Clause of the First Amendment, see: Richards (1989) at 260, 280; Richards, *Toleration* (1986) at 140–146. For a discussion of the ways in which "anti-gay ballot initiatives" violate the religion clauses of the federal constitution, see: Niblock (1993); "Constitutional Limits . . . " (1993); Reing (1990); "Religion and Morality . . . " (1984); Richards (1994).

182. See: *Hatheway* (1981) (the military's sodomy law does not violate Establishment Clause); *National Gay Task Force* (1984) (prohibiting public school teachers from advocating or encouraging homosexual conduct does not violate Establishment Clause); *Baldwin* (1974) (California's sodomy law does not violate Establishment Clause); *Steward v. United States* (1976) (District's sodomy law does not violate the Establishment Clause).

183. Cruz (1994) at 1191–1192.

184. See: Colker (1996); D'Emilio and Freedman (1988); Rich (1980).

185. See: Carrington (1989); Schneider (1988).

186. "There is a religious war going on in this country. It is a cultural war, as critical to the kind of nation we shall be as the Cold War itself, for this war is for the soul of America" [Buchanan 1992].

187. Hunter (1991) at 187.

188. *Id.* at 48.

189. See: American Family Association (Internet); U.S. Senate, 104th Congress (1996); Gallagher (1986); Gramick and Furey (1988); Moore (1986).

190. Hunter (1991) at 50.

191. *Id.* at 51.

192. *Id.* at 320.

193. *Id.* at 321.

194. *Id.* at 322.

195. *Id.* at 322.

196. Bull and Gallagher (1996) at 265–281.

197. *Id.* at 269.
198. Wolfson (1991) at 22 [emphasis added].
199. *Id.* at 23 fn.9.
200. *Id.*
201. Posner (1992) at 346.
202. Salmons at 1258. Although Salmons focuses his arguments exclusively on a comparison between religion and sexual orientation/preference, I believe that the expansion of his comparison to encompass the larger realm of gender identity and affectional orientation/preference [GI/AOP] neither distorts nor undermines his essential arguments.
203. *Id.*
204. *Id.*
205. *Id.* at 1243.
206. *Id.* at 1254. The court recognized in *Ben-Shalom* (1980) that sexual identity is a component of personality and that " 'autonomous control over the development and expression of one's intellect, interest, tastes, and personality' are among the most precious of rights protected by the First Amendment" [*Ben Shalom* at 975 (quoting *Doe* [1973] at 211 [Douglas, J., concurring])].
207. Richards (1994) at 552.
208. Salmons at 1261.
209. *Id.*
210. *Id.*
211. *Id.* at 1263.
212. *Id.* at 1262.
213. *Id.* at 1266.
214. Katz (1976, 1992) at 11.
215. Salmons at 1262–1263.
216. See: Boswell (1980); Card (1995); Childester (1988); Colker (1996); Duberman (1993); Faderman (1991); Feinberg (1996); Gager (1983); Goldstein (1988) at 1081–1087; Katz (1976, 1992); Langmuir (1990a); Langmuir (1990b); Norgren and Nanda (1996); Poliakov (1965–1975); Poliakov (1985); Richards (1993); and Richards (1986).
217. See: Katz (1983) at 355–357, 552, 558–559; Feinberg (1996) at 70–71.
218. At least some courts have rejected the argument that race and sex are immutable characteristics maintaining instead that they are socially constructed. See: *Ortiz* (1982) at 565; *Shaare* (1987); *Saint Francis College* (1987); Halley (1985).
219. See: Arriola (1988) at 154–155 ["making discrete and insular status depend on . . . immutability . . . fails on deeper analysis"]; *Steffan* (1991) at 6, 6 n.12 ("[h]omosexual orientation is neither conclusively mutable nor immutable"; "[w]ithout a definite answer at hand, yet confident that *some* people exercise *some* choice in their own sexual orientation, the Court does not regard homosexuality as being an immutable characteristic"); *Baehr* (1991) ("the issue of whether homosexuality constitutes an immutable trait has generated much dispute in the relevant

scientific community"). For a in-depth critique of the immutability argument as it relates to *sex/gender outsiders* see: Halley (1994).

220. See: *Hardwick* at 203 n.2 (Blackmun, J., dissenting), wherein Justice Blackmun maintained that "[h]omosexual orientation may well form part of the very fiber of the individual's personality"; *Watkins* (1988) at 1446, wherein the court concluded "that allowing the government to penalize the failure [of individuals] to change such a central aspect of individual and group identity [as their sexual orientation] would be abhorrent to the values animating the Constitutional ideal of equal protection." Moreover, the court observed that "[i]t may be that some heterosexuals and homosexuals can change their sexual orientation through extensive therapy, neurosurgery, or shock treatment. . . . But the possibility of such a difficult and traumatic change does not make sexual orientation 'mutable' for equal protection purposes"; *Jantz* (1991) at 1548, wherein the lower federal court asserted that "available scientific evidence . . . strongly supports the view that sexual orientation is not easily mutable." It is important to note that the Ninth District Court's bipolarization of sexual orientations ("heterosexuals and homosexuals") in *Watkins* renders invisible, if not eradicates, the existence of other forms of sexual feelings—i.e., bisexuality.

221. For an discussion of the failure of "insight" therapy, behavior therapy, and religious therapy to reorient gay males, see: Green (1992), at 77–84.

222. Richards (1994) at 508.

223. *Id.*

224. See: *Id.* at 528–530; Cohn-Sherbok (1992); Langmuir (1990a); Langmuir (1990b); Moore (1987). It should be noted that Cohn-Sherbok's study of anti-Semitism, while primarily focusing on the Christian West, indicates that anti-Semitism was not confined to Europe; it existed [and still exists] in this country [*Id.* at 188–192].

225. See: Debo (1970); Deloria (1970, 1988); Jaimes (1992); Matthessen (1980, 1983); Messerschmidt (1983).

226. See: Channing (1882, 1970).

227. See: Bradley (1993); Ellsworth (1992); Hansen (1981); Renteln (1994); Wells (1978).

228. Richards (1994) at 508.

229. Richards (1994) at 509.

230. See the *Amici Curiae* briefs filed in *Bowers v. Hardwick*, 478 U.S. (1986) No. 85–140: The Presbyterian Church (U.S.A.), the Philadelphia Yearly Meeting of Friends Service Committee, the Unitarian Universalist Association, the Office for Church and Society of the United Church of Christ, the Right Reverend Paul Moore, Jr., and the American Jewish Congress.

231. See: Richards (1986).

232. The Court stated that "[t]he law . . . is constantly based on notions of morality, and if all laws representing essentially moral choices are to be invalidated

under the Due Process Clause, the courts will be very busy indeed" [*Hardwick* at 196].

233. See: *Plessy v. Ferguson*, 163 U.S. 537 (1896).

234. For example: the congressional apology to Japanese-Americans for their internment during World War II; *Brown v. Board of Education*, 347 U.S. 483 (1954).

235. Richards (1993) at 61.

236. See: *Id.* at 63–73; Richards (1986) at 67–117.

CHAPTER 4

Speech, Hate, and (Non-) Discrimination

In accordance with the equality principle of Title VII and the Equal Protection Clause of the Fourteenth Amendment, civil rights adherents would insist that equality ought to take precedence over free speech in the hierarchy of values,[1] for "equality . . . [is] . . . a precondition to free speech."[2] Yet as demonstrated in the previous chapter, *sex/gender outsiders* are not automatically guaranteed refuge in the equality and anti-discrimination principles of either the Equal Protection Clause or Title VII. While these legal principles, in the abstract, may be instrumental in alleviating discrimination or oppression based on race and sex, they have little direct impact on discrimination or oppression based on gender identity or affectional orientation/preference. Despite the fact that "a kind of war is waged on [*sex/gender outsiders*] daily,"[3] there is currently little room for lesbians, gay men, bisexuals, or transgenderists in the equality or anti-discrimination principle as interpreted by the judiciary with regard to gender identity or affectional orientation/preference.

For lesbians, gay men, bisexuals, and transgenderists, legal protection from discrimination is not, and has never been, readily available. As self-identified or presumed *sex/gender outsiders*, they are relegated to the most remote periphery of the legal system, if that, and thus are deprived of their legal, political, and human rights, consistently and unapologetically, by the government and society.[4] The complex and vehement nature of social, political, and legal discrimination and violence based on gender identity or affectional orientation/preference is firmly entrenched in this society. Myths, stereotypes, and half-truths—created and disseminated about *sex/gender outsiders* by the dominant culture through official institutions—remain the primary socio-political construct which supports the designation of lesbians, gay men, bisexuals, and transgenderists as less than full citizens.

It is the government, according to Kendall Thomas, that sanctions discrimination and violence against lesbians, gay men, bisexuals, and transgenderists.[5] By legislatively and judicially depicting *sex/gender outsiders* as "outlaws" or "perverts" in debates, statutory laws, and judicial decisions, the government implies that lesbians, gay men, bisexuals, and transgenderists are unworthy of full legal, political, or social protection.[6] Terry Kogan would articulate the government's responsibility much more forcefully.[7] In his opinion, the government is a vital accomplice in the perpetuation of the violence and discrimination that *sex/gender outsiders* experience. Because all legislatures possess the power and the opportunity to depict the "truth" about *sex/gender outsiders* to the general public, it is their portrayals of lesbians, gay men, bisexuals, and transgenderists that transmutes *sex/gender outsiders* into "outlaws" or "perverts" deserving violent treatment, both officially and unofficially.[8] The government's bi-genderist and heterosexist denigration of lesbians, gay men, bisexuals, and transgenderists facilitates the uncritical acceptance of bi-genderist and heterosexist beliefs by average citizens. This in turn allows citizens to assuage their own responsibility for the perpetuation of discrimination and violence against *sex/gender outsiders*.[9]

One way the government implicitly endorses the physical and emotional violence wreaked upon *sex/gender outsiders* is through the continued existence of solicitation[10] and sodomy[11] laws. Essentially, these laws place *sex/gender outsiders* at the mercy of those in the legal establishment who possess the capricious power to enforce or refrain from enforcing these sex statutes. *Sex/gender outsiders* are thus in the ambiguous position of being arbitrarily targeted and metamorphosized into the involuntary prey of government agents empowered to surreptitiously or blatantly watch the activities of lesbians, gay men, bisexuals, and trangenderists. As a result, many *sex/gender outsiders* live under the threat of harassment, arrest, indictment, conviction, or incarceration under existing solicitation or sodomy laws. Moreover, all lesbians, gay men, bisexuals, and transgenderists live under the shadow of institutionalized censorship, as illustrated by the National Endowment of the Arts (NEA) controversy.

The primary common denominator linking these sex statutes and the NEA controversy is that each attempts to criminalize sexual expression between consenting adults. The bias against *sex/gender outsiders* encoded in the sex statutes and the NEA controversy serve as the foundation for discrimination against lesbians, gay men, bisexuals, and transgenderists in other areas of law. The more restricted the expressive component of *sex/gender outsiders'* speech, the less they are able to portray realistically their communities and the more likely it is that the prevailing myths, stereotypes, and lies about lesbians, gay men, bisexuals, and transgenderists will be believed by the majority of citizens. A consequence of these misconceptions is violence directed against *sex/gender outsiders*. While the federal Hate Crimes Statistics Act is intended to document this violence, which it does, it also communicates society's ambivalence with regard to eliminating totally discrimination against lesbians, gay males, bisexuals, and transgenderists.

SOLICITATION LAWS

Laws that criminalize the solicitation of an adult to engage in consensual, non-commercial, sexual activity exist in sixteen states. As the editors of the *Harvard Law Review* point out, "[i]n practice, loitering and solicitation statutes . . . provide the primary means of regulating [same-sex] activity."[12] They further note that frequently the validity of a solicitation statute rests on the constitutionality of the state's sodomy law, since it is illegal to solicit an individual to commit a crime.[13] This, however, is not always the case. Some courts have upheld the validity of solicitation statutes even when the state has decriminalized sodomy, on the grounds that such laws are intended to protect the public from offensive conduct or protect public sensibilities.[14]

The proffered rationale of the state for the existence of solicitation laws seems deceitful. According to Jon Gallo, "[s]ocietal interests are infringed only when a solicitation to engage in a homosexual act creates a reasonable risk of offending public decency. The incidence of such solicitations is statistically insignificant. The majority of homosexual solicitations are made only if the other individual appears responsive and are ordinarily accompanied by quiet conversation and the use of gestures and signals having significance only to other homosexuals."[15] For a solicitation to occur, literal speech and symbolic speech are essential on the part of both individuals. Unless the individual solicited understands the ritual involved, the solicitation will not occur; the person solicited must first signal his or her interest and availability to the solicitor. As Richard Mohr explains, "sexual solicitations for 'public' sex acts, as in washrooms and parks, are conspiratorial rituals in which the one person's predisposition to commit a crime becomes a specific intent to do so here-and-now *only if* the other person also has the same intention."[16]

Individuals who honestly participate in the ritual would probably not have their sensibilities offended; individuals who do not participate would probably not be exposed to conduct they might find offensive. A more forthright rationale for solicitation laws by the state might be that they restrict the speech expression of those persons interested in finding a sexual partner of the same sex. Under this rationale, the state makes the price of that speech high for, as Mohr points out, the "solicitation laws frequently have devastating personal, social, and economic effects on those arrested, even though criminal penalties typically are slight and even if charges are ultimately dropped or a not-guilty verdict reached."[17] Individuals who unwittingly solicit police decoys, after the decoys have willing participated in the ritual, may be shocked by the accusation that they offended the officer by the ritual—as exemplified by *Ohio v. Phipps.*

According to the facts in *Phipps,* as provided in the syllabus of the Ohio Supreme Court's decision[18] and supplemented by the trial transcript,[19] Kenneth Phipps stopped his car at a downtown corner in Cincinnati on 27 October 1976 and motioned to the only individual standing on the nearby sidewalk. When the adult male approached the car, Phipps said, "Hop in, let's go have sex." The stranger looked into the back seat and Phipps retorted: "You look paranoid, come on in, I want to suck your dick." After the person got into the car, Phipps made a similar proposal, along with some other conversation, which included Phipps telling the officer that he was "handsome," "beautiful," and that Phipps "really liked him." At that point the individual identified himself as a police officer and arrested Phipps. At the trial, the officer testified that he was offended by the conversation and consequently Phipps was convicted by the Hamilton County Municipal Court under the solicitation statute. This statute provided that "[n]o person shall solicit a person of the same sex to engage in sexual activity with the offender, when the offender knows such solicitation is offensive to the other person, or is reckless in that regard."[20]

The Hamilton County Court of Appeals overturned Phipps's conviction on the grounds that the challenged statute was unconstitutionally overbroad in violation of the First Amendment, inasmuch as it proscribed protected speech without establishing a compelling state interest and failed to proscribe unprotected speech. It also held that the statute was unconstitutionally vague and thus violated Phipps's due process rights under the Fourteenth Amendment. The Ohio Supreme Court disagreed. Judge Locher, writing for the majority, dismissed the due process challenge on the grounds that a person of ordinary intelligence is provided adequate notice of the conduct prohibited by the statute. After systematically defining the key words of the statute—"sexual activity," "knows," "offensive," and "reckless"—he concluded that it would be "difficult to conceive of a more clearly and precisely written statute" than §2907.07(B) of the Ohio Revised Code.

Yet whether the statute is as "clearly and precisely written" as Judge Locher contends depends upon the factual circumstances of the case. The key words as defined by Judge Locher, contrary to his assertion, provide neither clear nor precise notice of what is specifically proscribed by the statute. According to the definitions he uses, the word "know" is defined: "A person 'knows' or has knowledge of . . . a fact when he has actual knowledge of it. 'Discover' or 'learn' or a word or phrase of similar import refers to knowledge rather than to reason to know."[21] The definitions he uses of "offensive" and "reckless" are as follows: "offensive" refers to "that which is disagreeable or nauseating or painful because of outrage to taste and sensibilities or affronting insultingness";[22] "reckless" refers to "lacking in caution[,] . . . irresponsible, wild[;] . . . careless, heedless, inattentive; indifferent to consequences."[23] Nothing in these definitions indicates how the person making the solicitation is to determine in advance if the individual addressed will find the request "disagreeable or nauseating or painful," or if naming what is desired is being "irresponsible." This information is ascertained through the response of the person addressed. If the adult male Phipps' addressed were interested in same-sex activity, there is no reason to assume that he would find the solicitation offensive. But, even if he were not interested in Phipps' suggestion, there still is no reason for Phipps to assume that the man would find the solicitation offensive.

The facts of the case do not substantiate the assumption that the vice officer's initial reaction to the solicitation was one of offense or anger. If anything, his reaction might be characterized as anxious, as illustrated by Phipps' remark, "you look paranoid, come on in."[24] Phipps' "knowledge" that the person was anxious, however, does not meet the standard articulated by the court—it does not establish that Phipps had "actual knowledge that the solicitation [would] be outrageous to the taste and sensibility of the person solicited, which [might] cause that person to resist, or [that Phipps] act[ed] heedlessly and indifferently to the consequences."[25] The fact that the solicited person voluntarily got into Phipps' car might have indicated to Phipps that the individual was interested in participating in the activity Phipps had proposed to him. One who found the solicitation outrageous to his taste and sensibility would hardly be expected willingly to enter the solicitor's motor vehicle, in light of the proposed activity.

Judge Locher conceded, as he had to, that the statute on its face is overbroad. In order to save the challenged statute, the court announced that the construction of the statute be limited or the statute had to be partially invalidated, to ensure that constitutionally protected speech is not jeopardized. Judge Locher noted that speech covered under the First Amendment can be regulated if the state articulates a compelling reason for the regulation. One purpose for the solicitation statute that he considered is the state's interest in protecting its citizens' privacy, protecting them from language that is personally offensive and violates their right to be let alone. In his opinion, this is a legitimate state interest. Indeed, he asserted that "[t]hose who would have this court believe that the average citizen would not find homosexual solicitations of the nature described by R.C. 2907.07(B) to be offensive are guilty of murky thinking. The type of expression proscribed in the statute may have been acceptable in a more barbarous age when human dignity had not reached the level expected by citizens in our modern society."[26] However worthy he found this purpose, however, Judge Locher did not find it compelling enough to outweigh Phipps' First Amendment rights.

He then turned to a second consideration—whether the statute can be narrowly construed to proscribe only unprotected speech. This Judge Locher determined can be done by narrowing the construction of the statute in order for it "to proscribe only the 'fighting words' category of unprotected speech."[27] He then recast the statute to read: "a person may be punished under R.C. 2907.07(B) if the solicitation, by its very utterance, inflicts or is likely to provoke the average person to an immediate retaliatory breach of the peace."[28] In the eyes of Judge Locher, same-sex solicitations are *per se* offensive and "likely to provoke the average person to retaliation and thereby cause a breach of the peace."[29]

From his perspective, it is not surprising that he found Phipps' solicitation to be equivalent to "fighting words." But Judge Locher's construction of the statute is at odds with the facts presented in *Phipps*. As S. Adele Shank correctly points out, "[o]ne sincerely interested in having a sexual encounter would not try to achieve that goal by addressing the prospective partner with personally abusive insults or epithets."[30] Given the compliments paid to the vice officer by Phipps, it is difficult to see how these statements would be considered insulting or offensive within the meaning of the Ohio Revised Code §2907.07(B). A justification for such a finding seemingly resides in the Ohio Supreme Court's heterocentric and heterosexist attitudes.[31] It is not Phipps' words that are problematic, it is the fact that he said them to another male that automatically renders them offensive for the Ohio Supreme Court.

Judge Locher also fails to explain how the words spoken by Phipps satisfies the incitement-to-violence aspect of the "fighting words" doctrine. Why is it taken as a given that if one man says to another "you are handsome and beautiful" it will "incite an immediate breach of the peace"?[32] The Technical Committee's assertion that "[t]he rationale for prohibiting indiscreet solicitation of deviate conduct is that the solicitation in itself can be highly repugnant to the person solicited, and there is *a risk* that it *may* provoke a violent response,"[33] does not provide an complete answer. There is no evidence in *Phipps* that an unavoidable relationship exists between the words spoken by Phipps and a violent response. Shank contends that since Phipps' remarks were addressed to a member of the vice squad who was officially on duty, and since the officer acknowledged at the trial that he had heard the type of solicitation that Phipps made on other occasions from other men, "it is ridiculous to apply the fighting words rationale" in *Phipps*.[34] By expanding Shank's position, it can be argued that Phipps offended no one who was not already predisposed to being offended[35] by a same-sex solicitation.

If one dismisses the logic or validity of Shank's conclusion regarding the actual likelihood that the police officer was offended by Phipps' words, as the Ohio Supreme Court seemingly does, the unavoidable relationship between Phipps' solicitation and a violent response is still not established by the government in *Phipps*. The Ohio Supreme Court merely assumed the existence of such a relationship.[36] As a result, the "men of common intelligence" standard[37] applied by Judge Locher contains an inherent bias. As the editors of the *Harvard Law Review* observe, "the 'average person' [is framed] in a traditional, heterosexual, male-dominated role . . . [that] legitimates anti-gay violence by placing the burden of proof on gay persons to avoid a violent heterosexual response to their sexual orientation."[38] Through such a construction, the Ohio Supreme Court legitimates heterocentric, heterosexist, and homophobic attitudes and behavior within society.

Beneath Judge Locher's understanding of the "average person" is the unspoken rule that an individual is proscribed from using any language to establish same-sex contacts that is not "palatable to the most homophobic members of society."[39] This requirement places an extreme burden on the free speech rights of *sex/gender outsiders* by functioning like the "heckler's veto,"[40] whereby the injury sustained by the person solicited need exist only in his or her own mind. By accepting such a broad restriction on the speech of *sex/gender outsiders*, Judge Locher permits "the freedom of those whose ideas[,] . . . lifestyle, or . . . physical appearance is resented by the majority of their fellow citizens"[41] to be curtailed.

Judge Locher's construction of the "fighting words" doctrine, which encompasses both prongs of the *Chaplinsky* rule,[42] was four years out of date with respect to the U.S. Supreme Court's ruling in *Gooding v. Wilson*. In *Gooding*, Justice Brennan maintained that "fighting words" are limited to words that "have a direct tendency to cause acts of violence by the person to whom, individually, the remark is addressed."[43] The first prong of *Chapinsky*—the infliction of injury through words—is eliminated in *Gooding*, yet Judge Locher not only retains that part of the test in *Phipps*, he relies on it more heavily than the incitement-to-direct-violence aspect of the test.[44] Although Judge Locher believes that the injury caused by words can be equivalent to that caused by physical violence,[45] he never takes the next step required by *Gooding*—determining the real potential that the person solicited would respond violently.[46] As Judge Sweeney accurately states in his dissenting opinion, "this court seems willing to equate offensive speech with fighting words. To this writer, the majority's stance appears as a dangerous narrowing of First Amendment freedoms."[47]

By restricting the scope of the First Amendment through its "contorted" interpretation of the solicitation statute,[48] the Ohio Supreme Court represses the speech of *sex/genders outsiders* which it labels "injuriously offensive,"[49] "scurrilous,"[50] and "emotionally disturbing."[51] In addition, it indirectly legitimates the expression of sexual attraction between individuals of different sexes while censuring an expression of sexual attraction between individuals of the same sex. By interpreting §2907.07(B) in this "contorted" manner, Judge Locher reinforces sex discrimination, inasmuch as the entire scope of the crime revolves around the sex of the person who solicits and the person being solicited. A man soliciting another man for sexual activity is, for Judge Locher, an affront to human dignity[52] that finds no protection under the First Amendment. A greater offense against human dignity—one which he fails to recognize—is suffered by *sex/gender outsiders* through the enforcement of solicitation laws: by penalizing consensual, non-commercial, adult, same-sex solicitations, the government systematically and officially insults and injures *sex/gender outsiders* by denying them equal respect and casting aspersions upon their status.

SODOMY LAWS

An identical affront to the dignity of *sex/gender outsiders* is perpetrated through sodomy laws. By legally restricting the dissenting expression that lesbians, gay men, bisexuals, and transgenderists communicate through their gender identity or affectional orientation/preference, sodomy laws attempt to silence speech that questions the norm. As a form of government-sanctioned discrimination, these laws function to legitimate private, public, governmental, and military bigotry against *sex/gender outsiders* within society regardless whether particular individuals actually engage in the activity proscribed by a specific statute.[53] This is because sodomy is an activity that possesses neither a universal nor fixed definition when state laws are compared with one another; each state establishes its own criminal laws and legal language to name the crime prohibited—for instance, "buggery," "crime against nature," "sexual misconduct," or "unnatural sexual intercourse."[54]

Sodomy laws serve as an official declaration of what is moral or right within society. Through such laws, society attempts to control the lives of *sex/gender outsiders* in a way that would not be tolerated if the choices of persons who conform to traditional conceptions of gender identity or affectional orientation/preference were limited in a similar manner.[55] Yet these laws need not be enforced to accomplish their main purpose: insulting or injuring lesbians, gay men, bisexuals, and trangenderists.[56] The states, for their part, maintain that one of the primary reasons for their uneven enforcement of same- and cross-sex sodomy statutes is that they have a moral interest in deterring, or a moral abhorrence toward, *sex/gender outsiders*—which, while seldom acknowledged, is explicitly intertwined with the myths, stereotypes, and prejudices that exist regarding lesbians, gay men, bisexuals, and transgenderists. Another justification offered by the states for the uneven enforcement of these laws is that same-sex sodomy violates traditional Judeo-Christian values—presumably in a manner that cross-sex sodomy is no longer deemed to do.

The Georgia Attorney General's justification for the non-enforcement of its sodomy law, as Justice Steven notes in *Bowers v. Hardwick*, is that the law serves a symbolic purpose[57]—as a value judgment regarding the worth or morality of those persons believed most likely to engage in the specific type of behavior prohibited. Richard Mohr agrees. As he points out, "when no attempt is made to enforce sodomy laws, the dubious 'educational function' of stigmatizing gays as a class seems to be their main purpose."[58] Indeed, Mohr argues, sodomy laws "stigmatize individuals *quite independently* of legal sanctions."[59] They project the ideas that *sex/gender outsiders* are "unapprehended felons" whom society is "entitled" to make scapegoats by "casting all gay acts as felonies."[60] Through sodomy laws the citizenry of a state is symbolically "afforded an opportunity . . . to express its 'raw hatred' of [*sex/gender outsiders*] without having publicly to discuss and so justify that hatred."[61]

Sodomy statutes thus elevate the gender identity of those who conform to societal expectations and the affectional orientation/preference of heterosexuals. Simultaneously they subordinate the gender identity and affectional orientation/preference of *sex/gender outsiders*. In many instances the mere existence of sodomy laws, even if they do not exist in one's own state and regardless of the official enforcement policy if they do, manipulate the conditions under which individuals make personal intimate choices. They function as a propaganda or terrorist tool, according to Mohr, insomuch as they methodically convey the societal message that *sex/gender outsiders* "are scum" who possess "bad" moral character.[62] By legitimating this assessment regarding the morality of *sex/gender outsiders* through the validation of sodomy statutes, the courts symbolically condone other material and rhetorical forms of discrimination and violence.[63] Such judicial decisions "serve notice" to lesbians, gay men, bisexuals, and transgenderists that police protection against violence and discrimination has not been and may continue not to be readily available to them.[64]

Sodomy laws do not merely reinforce and perpetuate the gender polarities upon which sex discrimination hinges, by mirroring socially prescribed sex and gender roles.[65] They also operate to increase aggression toward, dehumanization of, and discrimination against *sex/gender outsiders*, while simultaneously justifying the denial of lesbians', gay men's, bisexuals', and transgenderists' civil rights and liberties. Although it is recognized that "civil rights and liberties do not create human rights nor award special benefits,"[66] Evan Wolfson maintains, they can "attempt to preclude the most frequent bases of discrimination [i.e., race, sex, gender identity, and affectional orientation/preference] that accompany . . . dehumanization."[67] But laws that may appear to be facially neutral are frequently employed by all levels of the government to draw unjust and illegal distinctions between persons in similar circumstances. Consequently, as Wolfson notes, "equality on its face is not equality in fact"[68]—which is conclusively demonstrated by the U.S. Supreme Court's decision in *Hardwick* concerning the constitutionality of Georgia's facially neutral sodomy statute.

§16–6–2 of the Georgia Annotated Code states, in pertinent part, that anyone who "performs or submits to any sexual act involving the sex organs of one person and the mouth or anus of another" commits the offense of sodomy. As codified, this law is neutral with regard to the sex or the affectional orientation/preference of the individuals who engage in the defined activity. Whether the persons are same-sex or cross-sex, single or married, female or male, the statute declares that any "person convicted of the offense of sodomy shall be punished by imprisonment for not less than one nor more than 20 years." The neutrality of this statute disappears, however, in the state's application of it. Justice Blackmun points out that the state of Georgia, "both in its brief and at oral argument" before the U.S. Supreme Court, attempts "to defend §16–6–2 solely on the grounds that it prohibits homosexual activity,"[69] despite the broad language contained in the actual statute. By narrowing the statute in this manner, Georgia, in effect, validated the dismissal of John and Mary Doe's challenge to the constitutionality of its sodomy statute for lack of standing. As the District Court stated and the Court of Appeals affirmed, "the couple neither sustained, nor were in immediate danger of sustaining, any direct injury from the enforcement of the statute" against them as a married couple, notwithstanding their allegation "that they wished to engage in the sexual activity prohibited in §16–6–2 in the privacy of their home, but . . . had been 'chilled and deterred' from engaging in the activity by the existence of the statute and by Hardwick's arrest."[70]

This constriction of the statute to same-sex sodomy allowed Justice White, representing the Court majority,[71] to frame the issue in *Hardwick* as "whether the Federal Constitution confers a fundamental right upon homosexuals to engage in sodomy and hence invalidate the laws of the many States that still make such conduct illegal and have done so for a very long time."[72] The narrowness of Justice White's question starkly contrasts with the broad conceptualization of the issue by Justice Blackmun[73] in his dissenting opinion. In Justice Blackmun's view, the issue raised in *Hardwick* involveed " 'the most comprehensive of rights and the right most valued by civilized men,' namely 'the right to be let alone;' "[74] and "the fundamental interest all individuals have in controlling the nature of their intimate associations with others."[75]

In addressing the issue as he posed it, Justice White asserted that both the court of appeals and Hardwick misconstrued the Supreme Court's earlier decisions that established a constitutional right to privacy. He maintained that the Court's prior cases establish the right to privacy only in the areas of family relationships, (heterosexual) marriage, procreation, contraception, child rearing and education, and abortion[76]—areas wherein "no connection . . . to homosexual activity . . . has been demonstrated."[77] By constructing the Court's precedent in this manner, Justice White's miserly interpretation of privacy rights contrasts sharply with the expansive reading of Justice Blackmun. According to Justice Blackmun's reading of the cases cited by Justice White, the Court's privacy cases establish "a privacy interest with reference to certain *decisions* that are properly for the individual to make . . . [and] a privacy interest with reference to certain *places* without regard for the particular activities in which the individuals who occupy them are engaged."[78]

While Justice Blackmun envisioned *sex/gender outsiders* as autonomous moral agents,[79] Justice White conceived of them as inherently immoral beings.[80] Thus, *Hardwick* becomes a judicial vehicle through which the long dehumanizing history of *sex/gender outsiders* is voiced and legitimated by the Supreme Court. Justice White's almost exclusive reliance on history and religion furnished a necessary textual foundation for affirming societal "permissions to hate" and for tacitly validating the continued deprivation of fundamental human and legal rights for *sex/gender outsiders*. In essence, the Supreme Court figuratively places its seal of approval on individual and institutionalized denigration of *sex/gender outsiders* as "sub-human, *untermenschen*, animal, and alien."[81] By positing a constitutionally deformed image of *sex/gender outsiders* as "second class citizens"—undeserving of the rights and liberties accorded the popular majority—the Court deprives them of their "human rights [by robbing them] of [their] birthright to equal civil rights and liberties."[82]

This judicial thievery is sustained and perpetuated, at least in part, by three factors. First, Justice White equates consensual sodomy with "homosexuality" *per se*, criminal activity,[83] and all "homosexual conduct."[84] The Court's "obsessive focus on homosexual activity"[85] is not accidental. Janet Halley argues that the Court's focus throughout the *Hardwick* decision on same-sex "acts . . . depends on a less obvious focus on persons"—the person of the *sex/gender outsider* takes precedence over "homosexual conduct or acts," which frequently means same-sex sodomy. While the Court "only fleetingly acknowledge[s] heterosexual identity," and asserts its neutrality with regard to "*all* [affectional]-orientation identities," it is firmly situated (at a sub-textual level) in heterosexuality.[86] Justice White's equation of sexual identity (status) with sexual behavior (conduct) in *Hardwick* reflects other legal opinions at both the Supreme Court and lower federal court level.[87] Through the conflation of status and conduct, the judiciary affirms that status is defined by (presumed) conduct, despite the fact that "acts do not translate one-for-one into identities,"[88] as illustrated by the loopholes contained in the most recent military policy.[89]

This conflation of status and conduct is one of the most subtle, yet notorious, strategies utilized to maintain *status quo* discrimination and violence against those individuals who are, or who are assumed to be, *sex/gender outsiders*. The government, by criminalizing same-sex sodomy, communicates at least two important messages regarding the ordering of affectional identities—that the identities of *sex/gender outsider* are subordinate, while those of heterosexuals are superordinate;[90] and that the identity politics of lesbians, gay men, bisexuals, and transgenderists are interlocked with the act of sodomy.[91] Thus, *sex/gender outsiders*—especially those who self-identify with a sense of pride, dignity, and self-respect—are generally perceived (and treated) as "sodomites" by institutions and individual members of society.[92] Identification of one's affectional orientation/preference is assumed to be sufficient evidence for a "reasonable inference" to be made that one engages in or has a penchant to engage in same-sex sodomy.[93]

Blurring the distinction between status (affectional orientation/preference) and conduct (sexual behavior) is a principal means by which the judiciary rationalizes the degree, type, and form of punishment legally meted out to *sex/gender outsiders*. It is also an ancillary means of absolving the courts of their culpability in utilizing and upholding disingenuous arguments, policies, practices, and laws that insult and injure *sex/gender outsiders*.[94] By rhetorically sanctioning heterocentric/heterosexist/homophobic attitudes and images that imply that *sex/gender outsiders* have few human rights, civil rights, or civil liberties that the government is obligated to acknowledge or protect, the courts brand lesbians, gay men, bisexuals, and trangenderists as "acceptable" targets for abuse, insults, and malevolence.

Another factor that permits judicial thievery of the equal rights and liberties of *sex/gender outsiders* is the Supreme Court's own condemnation of same-sex affectional orientation/preference. It expresses this in *Hardwick* through its obsession with same-sex sodomy,[95] and its unwillingness to differentiate "between laws that protect public sensibilities and those that enforce private morality."[96] In Justice White's opinion, Georgia's criminalization of same-sex sodomy, while reflecting millennia of moral teaching, is rationally related to the majoritarian belief that "homosexual sodomy is immoral and unacceptable."[97] Rather than articulate a secular justification underlying Georgia's decision to codify religious teachings, Justice White takes refuge in archaic prejudices. He reiterates that "[p]roscriptions against [the right of same-sex couples to engage in acts of consensual sodomy] have ancient roots"[98] and that "the law . . . is constantly based on notions of morality."[99] Thus Justice White upholds the criminalization of same-sex consensual adult sodomy merely because it does not conform to the majority's moral standards. In his estimation, those standards provide ample justification for the state of Georgia to penalize a specific form of sexual expression—same-sex consensual adult sodomy.

Through "willful blindness,"[100] Justice White denies the individual autonomy of *sex/gender outsiders* as moral agents. He accepts the right of Georgia to judge arbitrarily individuals who engage in same-sex consensual sodomy as felons, without requiring it to substantiate its invective of *sex/gender outsiders*. He also accedes to Georgia's refusal to allow individuals who engage in same-sex consensual sodomy to make their own moral decisions about this conduct. Justice White's acceptance of Georgia's elevation of religious moral standards to the level of law, without compelling the state to provide a compelling secular justification for infringing the conscience of the affected minority, is tantamount to assaulting the dignity and self-respect of at least a segment of the lesbian, gay male, bisexual, and transgender communities.[101] In so doing, he violates the expressive association rights of *sex/gender outsiders* guaranteed in the Constitution.

Justice White's conclusion arises from his predisposition to ignore the precise language of the Georgia law, to rely on "misleading and in some cases inaccurate" historical accounts,[102] and to constrict and contort the Court's former privacy decisions. His decision exhibits a resistance to challenging or undermining patriarchal power, which is intrinsically entangled with, and inseparable from, the ideological institutions of sex/gender identity and heterocentrism or heterosexism. By aligning himself with the state of Georgia, Justice White shields the Court from (symbolically) dismantling the sexual identity of male heterosexuals and from legitimating one means of sexually expressing same-sex affectional orientation/preference.

Justice White reflects and adheres to the dominant culture's bias against *sex/gender outsiders* by alleging that deference to the Georgia legislature is necessitated by the Court's status as a non-political branch of the government. He thus retreats behind the facade that the judiciary lacks the authority necessary to confer rights on *sex/gender outsiders* that are not explicitly stated in the Constitution.[103] To reach beyond the Constitution in order to accommodate *sex/gender outsiders*, Justice White asserts, would require the Court to engage in extra-legal measures—that is, the Justices would have to impose their "own choice of values on the States and the Federal Government."[104] He decides to violate the neutrality principle articulated in *Palimore v. Sidoti*[105] and impose his values on *sex/gender outsiders* instead.

As a consequence, Justice White places the Court in a situation analogous to bashers and bigots in general. He accepts the construction of rigid boundaries that segregate acceptable and unacceptable persons and activities, and then designates *sex/gender outsiders* to be the "proper" receptacles of the doubt, insecurities, internalized self-hatred, and panic experienced individually and collectively regarding the instability of one's identity or place within society. By overlooking or ignoring the fact that "normal" and "deviant" (or "heterosexual" and "homosexual") are relational terms—the meaning of these terms being derived from the subjective reference and existence of each to the other—Justice White utilizes the Court's institutionalized authority and position to lend credence to the vilification, harassment, or punishment of individuals whose "deviant" gender identity and affectional orientation/preference are envisioned as potentially destructive to the very structure and fabric of U.S. culture.

The Court's equating of private consensual adult same-sex sodomy with other "victimless crimes" (possession or use of illegal drugs, firearms, or stolen goods) or with "adultery, incest, or other sexual crimes"[106] provides the third factor permitting the judicial thievery of the equal rights and liberties of *sex/gender outsiders*. Why these activities are grouped together by Justice White, however, remains unexplained. If one attempts a serious comparison of these activities—that is, "victimless crimes" and sexual conduct less sodomy, versus private consensual adult same-sex sodomy—with one another, it becomes apparent that the Court's equation is wrong. A more accurate (and honest) comparison would dictate that the Court compare private consensual adult same-sex sodomy with crimes truly lacking a victim or with private consensual adult cross-sex "activity by unmarried persons or . . . with oral or anal sex within marriage"[107]

The Court's failure to explain the rationale by which it chose the selected categories prompted Justice Blackmun to criticize its negligence. As he accurately noted, one of the problems inherent in the Court's comparison of "victimless or other sexual crimes" and consensual sexual activities is that the "victimless crimes" identified by the Court involve activities that are intrinsically or physically dangerous to the participants or to third parties, or they wrongfully deny others of their own property.[108] Consensual adult same-sex sodomy, on the other hand, fails to violate the harm principle with regard to either consenting participants or "innocent" third parties.[109]

The flaw in the Court's likening of consensual adult same-sex sodomy to "other sex crimes," first of all, is that "adultery, incest, or other sexual crimes" lack the requisite elements of consent, non-injury, and voluntariness to the participants or to potentially unsuspecting third parties. Since adultery intimates the breaking of a legal contractual agreement between marital parties regarding sexual fidelity, it suggests that an unaware individual, whose ignorance renders consent impossible, is victimized or betrayed regardless of whether a partner's extra-marital affair is ever revealed or discovered. Individuals who engage in same-sex consensual adult sodomy, in contrast, leave behind neither victims, betrayals, nor broken contracts, unless one of the participants is "having an affair." In the case of "an affair," however, the issue is similar to adultery on the part of a married participant and fornication on the part of a non-married participant, not to same-sex adult consensual sodomy.

The second flaw is that incest between a parent and a minor child *never* fulfills the consent, voluntariness, or non-injury requirements. If the incestuous relationship involves individuals who have reached the age of legal adulthood, then "consent" must be evaluated in relation to at least four questions: (1) Did the incestuous relationship begin prior to the age of majority for at least one participant? (2) Has there been, or does there continue to be, a parent/child relationship between the two individuals such that "consent" is problematic, if not impossible, to ascertain? (3) Does the familial relationship entail an unequal distribution of power or resources between the two parties such that coercion rather than "true" consent occurs? (4) Has the incestuous activity between the participants resulted in or will it result in injury or harm to either of the participants or to a third party? These question do not arise when non-incestuous adult consensual sodomy is under consideration. Such activity by definition connotes the idea that the participating adults (regardless of their affectional orientation/preference) are autonomous, mature, rational beings who are legally capable of giving consent.

Finally, the Court's reference to "other sexual crimes" fails to identify the specific types of crime to which this phrase applies. Since the Court does not bother to define the scope of this phrase, the question arises as to which sexual practices are included: fornication; cunnilingus; fellatio; tribadism; indecent exposure, public lewdness, open and gross lewdness, or lascivious behavior; solicitation (involving only same-sex sexual activity without monetary exchange); same-sex kissing, caressing, or hand-holding; any bodily contact for the purpose of satisfying one's sexual desire; mutual masturbation; bestiality. Obviously, judicial interpretations of a state's criminal statutes and the legal code of the state within which one engages in any or all of the named sexual practices determine the actual or potential criminality of each activity. Insofar as each state's criminal code is independent of every other state's, neither universal condemnation nor acceptance of any or all of these activities exists, even if the participants are *sex/gender outsiders*. Thus, regardless of whether the Court's phrase "other sexual crimes" includes the sexual activities noted above or others, the Court's employment of this phrase ostensibly infuses "truth" into the stereotypical portrayal of *sex/gender outsiders* as "immoral, perverse, deviant, or criminal sexual predators" whose sexual activities are different from or inferior to those of individuals who engage in cross-sex affectional activities.

The legacy of *Hardwick* might be summed up by Halley's assessment that "[s]odomy . . . is such an intrinsic characteristic of [*sex/gender outsiders*], and so exclusive to us, that it constitutes a rhetorical proxy for us. It is our metonym."[110] The Court's reasoning in *Hardwick* has been extended to anchor even further denials of the civil and human rights of lesbians, gay men, bisexuals, and transgenderists, most notably in the arena of "state imposed penalties on identity."[111] As Jane Schacter states, "[b]ecause sexual behavior is seen as the defining aspect of gay and lesbian life, homosexuality is all 'doing' and no 'being.' Because civil rights laws protect people only for who they 'are' and not for what they 'do,' homosexuality is not entitled to civil rights protection."[112]

INSTITUTIONALIZED CENSORSHIP

The denial of rights and liberties to *sex/gender outsiders* on the basis of "self-identifying expression"[113] has a long history in this country. The most recent attempts to restrict identify speech include the Briggs Initiative (1978),[114] the Helms AIDS Education Amendment (1987),[115] the National Endowment for the Arts (NEA) controversy (1989),[116] and legislative initiatives designed to eliminate civil rights laws protecting *sex/gender outsiders* (1990s).[117] Each of these legislative actions seek to suppress core political speech about gender identity or affectional orientation/preference in violation of the First Amendment. Although the specific provocation for these four legislative proposals differ, the underlying stimulus is similar—to penalize individuals who seek to self-represent their gender identity or affectional orientation/preference through "a message that one has not merely come out, but that one intends to *be* out—to act on and live out that identity" as *sex/gender outsiders*.[118]

The precarious position occupied by *sex/gender outsiders* who discuss or portray their gender identity or affectional orientation/preference in an explicit manner is seen most clearly in the NEA controversy.[119] At the center of the firestorm over the use of taxpayers' money for art funding was a $30,000 grant the NEA gave to the Institute of Contemporary Art—part of the University of Pennsylvania—under the NEA's museum program. This grant was used to help support a retrospective exhibition, "Robert Mapplethorpe: The Perfect Moment," which covered the photographer's entire twenty-one-year career from the late 1960s to 1988. The exhibit's "X,Y,Z Series"[120] consisted of about one hundred and seventy photographs, of mostly floral arrangements and portraits, approximately thirteen of which portrayed "homosexual and heterosexual erotic acts and explicit sadomasochistic practices in which black and white, naked or leather-clad men and women assume erotic poses."[121] An attack was launched immediately in both houses of Congress on the individuals and institutions who had supported this "inappropriate" use of NEA funds, with extensive attacks specifically targeting *sex/gender outsiders*.[122]

The outcome was the Helms Amendment, part of the Interior Department Appropriations Act, which attempted to legislate "proper social morality." This Amendment stated: "None of the funds authorized to be appropriated for the National Endowment for the Arts . . . may be used to promote, disseminate, or produce material which in the judgment of the National Endowment for the Arts . . . may be considered obscene, including, but not limited to, depictions of sadomasochism, homoeroticism, the sexual exploitation of children, or individuals engaged in sex acts and which, when taken as a whole, do not have serious literary, artistic, political, or scientific value."123 While the Amendment contained a portion of the *Miller* criteria for determining obscenity, it neither mirrored nor paralleled that standard. Indeed, there was only one part of the Helms Amendment which is identical to the language found in the third prong of the *Miller* test. In *Miller v. California*, the Supreme Court ruled that "the basic guidelines for the trier of fact [are]: (a) whether 'the average person, applying contemporary community standards' would find that the work, taken as a whole, appeals to the prurient interests; (b) whether the work depicts or describes, in a patently offensive way, sexual conduct specifically defined by the applicable state law; and (c) whether the work, taken as a whole, lacks serious literary, artistic, political, or scientific value."124

There are several significant differences between the Helms Amendment and the *Miller* standard. The Helms Amendment eliminates the "average person" as the measure of whether material is to be prohibited. It substitutes the judgement of the NEA chair for that of the "average person" and "contemporary community standards," which raises the possibility of decisions based on arbitrary discretion. Further, the Amendment does not use "applicable state law" as the determinate of whether the sexual conduct portrayed is illegal. Since the Amendment is federal legislation, presumably the federal standard for determining obscenity is to be utilized. But since the wording of the Amendment differs from the federal standard articulated in *Miller*, what exactly the Amendment relies upon to determine obscenity is unclear. Nor does the Amendment require that "the work, taken as a whole, appeal to prurient interests," unless one assumes that the examples of obscenity provided in the Amendment inevitably appeal to such interests.

Essentially, the Amendment elides the distinction between obscenity and sex that may be considered merely shocking or offensive. By making the portrayal of the latter seemingly synonymous with the former, the Helms Amendment enlarged the *Miller* criteria by conceivably prohibiting both constitutional and unconstitutional speech. Moreover, the key terms—"sadomasochism," "homoeroticism," "individuals engaged in sex acts," and "the sexual exploitation of children"—remain undefined in the Amendment. Thus, it is unclear whether the Amendment considers each element *per se* to be obscene or whether the mere inclusion of these activities in otherwise non-obscene works disqualifies the work from receiving NEA funds. If these elements are deemed *per se* to be obscene, the Helms Amendment seems to stand in tension with established judicial decisions,[125] for under this Amendment, artists "cannot reasonably steer between lawful and unlawful conduct, with confidence that they know what its terms prohibit."[126]

If one takes a larger view of the Helms Amendment, two radically different arguments can be made. One is that by selecting only some forms of obscenity—sadomasochism, homoeroticism, the sexual exploitation of children, or individuals engaged in sex acts—as opposed to all forms of obscenity, the Helms Amendment endorses content and viewpoint discrimination, in violation of the First Amendment.[127] The second argument is that since the awarding of an NEA grant is an acknowledgement of artistic value, no projects funded by the NEA can violate the conditions of the Helms Amendment. Since the existence of artistic value removes the work from the realm of the obscene, either no NEA works will contain the depictions of those elements listed as examples of obscenity, or the inclusion of these elements will be deemed to be of artistic value.

The uncertainty generated by the Helms Amendment—whether it would prevent the NEA from funding another Mapplethorpe-like exhibit—fueled the battle between artists, interest groups, and Congress. Hence, when the reauthorization hearings for the NEA began the following year, Representative Pat Williams, as chair of the House Education and Labor Committee's Subcommittee on Select Education and Post-Secondary Education, focused on a central question: could a balance be found between the First Amendment rights of artists and the responsibility of Congress to oversee all expenditures of federal funds? The answers received by the committee, in addition to the vehement debate raging both inside and outside of the legislature, did little to assuage the apprehensions of either supporters or opponents of the NEA.

Once more *sex/gender outsiders* were targeted in the NEA debates. For example, Representative Rohrabacher, in his criticism of the NEA's funding policy, entered into the *Congressional Record* an article which had appeared in the *New York City Tribune* that criticized "weird funding by the NEA," included the "$60,000 [given] to three lesbian writers to help fund their homoerotic writings about their lesbian lifestyles. One of the poems reads in part, 'for my methods, indecent and unnatural, of gratifying a depraved and perverted sexual instinct.'"[128] These same three authors were singled out again in a letter sent by Senator Helms to Charles A. Bosher, the Comptroller General of the General Accounting Office, less than one month later. Helms's letter of 6 March 1990 contained a table of contents which, as quoted by Minnie Bruce Pratt, "lists, under 'Questionable NEA Activities,' eleven items including: 'D: Three NEA $20,000 Creative Writing Fellowships to Audre Lorde, Minnie Bruce Pratt, and Chrystos.' "[129] These authors were named for no discernable reason except the fact that in their writings each of them challenges the heterocentric and heterosexist attitudes of the dominant culture, dares to name herself lesbian, and exposes the political, social, legal, physical, emotional, and psychic costs associated with living one's life openly and honestly in this society.

Others artists who drew attention and wrath during this time included David Wojnarowicz and the "NEA Four" (Karen Finley, John Fleck, Holly Hughes, and Tim Miller). In 1990, Wojnarowicz wrote an angry essay that was included in the exhibition catalogue to accompany "Witnesses: Against Our Vanishing," an art show pertaining to AIDS. In his essay, Wojnarowicz "expressed his 'feeling of rage' about having AIDS and watching his friends die of the disease"[130] and attacked the AIDS policies of Senator Helms, Senator D'Amato, Representative Dannemeyer, and Cardinal O'Connor. The reaction of NEA chair John E. Frohnmayer to the essay was to refuse to allow the executive director of the gallery Artist Space, Susan Wyatt, to use any of her $10,000 from the NEA to pay for the catalogue. He did, however, eventually permit the gallery to use its grant money to exhibit the work of the twenty-three artists in "Witnesses."

Another incident involving Wojnarowicz revolved around a multimedia retrospective exhibit of his work that was funded by the NEA at the University of Illinois. In his work, "Tongues of Flame," Wojnarowicz embedded some homoerotic scenes in his painting, photography, and printed material. After selectively cropping "Tongues of Flame" to focus on same-sex lovemaking, Reverend Donald Wildmon of the American Family Association reproduced the modified artwork, under a heading denouncing the use of tax dollars to fund such "works of art," and mailed it to members of Congress, the clergy, and the media.[131]

In an attempt to avoid having either the spirit or the letter of the Helms Amendment violated by future grant recipients or having Congress decide to defund the NEA rather than reauthorize it, Frohnmayer instituted a policy which required all grant applicants to certify that their proposed works of art would not be obscene.[132] The controversy sparked by his "anti-obscenity oaths" was exacerbated by his rejection of the grant recommendations of the NEA theater panel to four performance artists—Karen Finley, John Fleck, Holly Hughes, and Tim Miller—without explaining why. Frohnmayer wanted artists who received NEA grants to avoid confrontational work. If an artist's work caused shock or offered societal insights, then it was considered to be obscene or out of conformance with general standards of decency. In either case, the NEA would not fund that work.

As Hughes points out, the work of the four named artists "*is* controversial. . . . [A]t different times there are different targets, and at the time that these grants were turned down the buzzwords were 'pornography' and 'obscenity' and this whole equation; and, you know, just being gay makes you 'obscene.' By the very definition . . . Jesse Helms is denying my very existence."[133] In her opinion, the NEA was trying to stop artists who were openly and identifiably *sex/gender outsiders* or who challenged traditional sex or gender roles from doing their art.

In October 1990, Representatives Williams and Coleman offered a proposal intended to guarantee the continuation of the NEA in some form, as part of the 1991 Interior Appropriation Act. This legislation, which replaced the Helms Amendment, acknowledged that the government must be "sensitive to the nature of public sponsorship" and that public funds must ultimately serve congressionally defined public purposes. In order to realize this goal, the legislation altered the structure of the application procedure; strengthened the role of the NEA Chair; shifted determination of obscenity to the court; changed the advisory board's role, responsibilities, and composition; and mandated the submission of GAO reports to Congress. In addition, the Williams-Coleman proposal stated that "the Chairman of the [NEA] is required to ensure that artist excellence and artistic merit are the criteria by which applications are judged, taking into consideration general standards of decency and respect for the diverse beliefs and values of the American public."[134]

While both sides of the debate simultaneously applauded and criticized the new law, seldom was it publicly acknowledged that the difference between the two laws was, overall, more a matter of degree than substance. Many of the problems associated with the Helms Amendment were neither adequately addressed nor resolved by the Williams-Coleman proposal. In essence, the new legislation left intact the spirit, if not the content, of the Helms Amendment. By conditioning the receipt and use of federal funds in the manner prescribed in the proposal, Congress still risked violating the First Amendment rights of grant recipients and imposing an illegal system of government censorship. Questions regarding prior restraint, vague and uncertain standards of approval, content restrictions, and threats of freedom of expression remained, albeit in a subtler form. Thus, the Williams-Coleman proposal was no less susceptible to constitutional challenge on these grounds than the Helms Amendment. Moreover, while the Williams-Coleman proposal may have been either politically necessary or politically expedient, a sword of Damocles still hangs over the cultural life of the entire nation, and not only over the heads of grant applicants whose forms of artistic expression fail the litmus test of "cultural values." The symbolic effect of this proposal is to make the government the sponsor of art while also giving it the role of censor.

The generalizing language in the Williams-Coleman proposal, rather than eliminating the threat to expression by *sex/gender outsiders,* merely made the threat less overt. Instead of frontal attacks, it launched a more subtle assault via the phrases "general standards of decency" and "respect for diverse beliefs and values of the American public"—the new code words for continued social and legal attacks on positive images and messages of *sex/gender outsiders.*[135] The theme of this attack was articulated by Republican Senator Trent Lott of Mississippi, who declared: "All lifestyles are not equal. We must decide that the institution of traditional marriage is preferable and superior, and our policies should reflect that conclusion and its moral imperative."[136] His position was reiterated by Patrick Buchanan, Pat Robertson, and others at the 1992 Republican National Convention in Houston.

Attempts to suppress the expression of individuals whose gender identity or affectional orientation/preference does not correspond to what the dominant culture deems acceptable, or who resist or critique traditional sex and gender roles or cross-sex affectional orientation/preference, violate the anti-discrimination principles contained in the Equal Protection Clause and Title VII and the free speech principle embodied in the First Amendment. While politicians are free to disagree with *sex/gender outsiders,* they ought not be permitted to legislate their heterocentric or heterosexist biases by limiting the civil and human rights of lesbians, gay men, bisexuals, and transgenderists. Legislation which restricts or denies the rights and liberties of *sex/gender outsiders* conveys the message that the value of the lives of lesbians, gay men, bisexuals, and trangenderists is not equal to that of the lives of individuals who mirror the gender identity or affectional orientation/preference endorsed by the majority. A consequence of such communication is the perpetuation of hate crimes against those who are, or are assumed to be, *sex/gender outsiders.*

HATE SPEECH AND HATE CRIMES

Sex/gender outsiders do not conform to societal norms that define and enforce permissible attitudes and behaviors governing gender identity or affectional orientation/preference within this society. Because of this difference, lesbians, gay men, bisexuals, and trangenderists are systematically devalued and stigmatized. By denigrating *sex/gender outsiders* for transgressing the binary parameters recognized by society, the dominant community gives tacit consent for the victimization of lesbians, gay men, bisexuals, and trangenderists by means of violence, hostility, discrimination, harassment, and intimidation.[137] While the specific manner of attack on *sex/gender outsiders* may vary, the consequences for the victims are similar. The individual's gender identity or affectional orientation/preference, according to Linda Garnets, Gregory Herek, and Barrie Levy, frequently becomes "directly linked to the heightened sense of vulnerability that normally follows victimization."[138] It is not uncommon, following an attack, for *sex/gender outsiders* to experience internalized homo-, bi-, or trans-phobia; a diminished sense of self-esteem, or an intensified sense of self-blame. Indeed, the more "invisible" a person has been regarding her/his gender identity or affectional orientation/preference prior to being victimized, the more publicly exposed an individual may feel by the attack and the less community support networks s/he may have access to while recovering from the physical and psychological repercussions of the attack.[139]

While the bodily injuries resulting from a physical assault may be obvious, the psychic or emotional harms of being verbally assaulted may not be readily apparent. As Garnets, Herek, and Levy have observed:

verbal abuse constitutes a symbolic form of violence and a routine reminder of the ever-present threat of physical assault. Its "cost" to the perpetrator in time, energy, and risk is minimal, yet it reinforces the target's sense of being an outsider in American society, a member of a disliked and devalued minority, and a socially acceptable target for violence.[140]

This message is communicated by the perpetrator not only to the person directly assaulted but also to everyone who shares the victim's gender identity or affectional orientation/preference.

The federal Hate Crimes Statistics Act[141] requires the Justice Department to collect data on crimes perpetrated against individuals on the basis of the race, religion, affectional orientation/preference, and ethnicity of the victims. It is one of the first pieces of federal legislation to use the term "sexual orientation" in a federal statute or to protect the status of at least some *sex/gender outsiders* with regard to the collection of data. As a consequence of the training provided to representatives of local police departments throughout the U.S. by the Federal Bureau of Investigations, this law indirectly increased the sensitivity and awareness of the police regarding the seriousness of hate crimes based on an individual's known or presumed identity in a designated group, and intimated that affectional orientation/preference is irrelevant in the reporting of hate crimes.

The ability of even such well-meaning legislation to help *sex/gender outsiders* counter the heterocentric and heterosexist or homophobic[142] outlook of the legislature, judiciary, and society, however, is weakened in several major ways. The first flaw in the federal Hate Crimes Statistics Act is that it fails to include discrimination based on gender identity or sex. As a result, no data is required to be collected for crimes against women or transgenderists, regardless of their affectional orientation/preference, who are victims of a bias-motivated attack due these characteristics. A second weakness is contained in the Act's definition of "sexual orientation." Because the statute states that " 'sexual orientation' means consensual homosexuality and heterosexuality,"[143] the scope of this term is confined to the two sexual orientations/preferences listed, thus implying that no other sexual orientations/preferences exist—for example, bisexuality.

From this definition several difficulties arise. The initial issue concerns the ambiguity which results from the placement of the qualifying adjective "consensual"; a question arises whether the adjective modifies both identified orientations/preferences or only that of same-sex individuals. If it modifies only the latter, then the statute implies that a majority of the sexual encounters involving same-sex couples are non-consensual while those involving cross-sex couples are consensual. Yet, non-consensual crimes, such as rape, incest, sexual abuse, and molestation (to name but a few), are predominately committed by heterosexuals. If it modifies both orientations/preferences, then a related problem becomes apparent due to the definition's equating of homosexuality and heterosexuality. By suggesting that these two orientations/preferences are equivalent, the Act obfuscates the legal and social reality that homosexuality and heterosexuality are not treated as equally desirable or acceptable in this country. It also distorts reality given that the power and privileges held by heterosexuals versus that held by *sex/gender outsiders* are not equal. Indeed, the statistics regarding who generally perpetrates violence against whom, and the dominant status of heterosexuals in this society—as illustrated by the second-class citizenship experienced by *sex/gender outsiders*, as well as the innumerable discriminations firmly held in place by most levels and branches of the government—bear witness to the disparate power relationship existing between members of these groups.

The third flaw is in the Act's statement that "[n]othing in this section creates a cause of action or a right to bring an action, including an action based on discrimination due to sexual orientation."[144] This segment of the statute explicitly prevents hate crime victims attacked due to their known or perceived sexual orientation/preference from obtaining a judicial remedy to the violence perpetrated upon them, while it implicitly condones government discrimination based on sexual orientation/preference through the paucity of laws prohibiting such discrimination. Moreover, *sex/gender outsiders* who are victims of hate crimes may be prevented from seeking or pursuing other legal remedies to the violent assaults, since there exist almost no legal protections that can negate the fear of exposure or the consequences resulting from such exposure.

Official approval of violence against *sex/gender outsiders* is also inherent in the congressional finding regarding "American family life," which constitutes the fourth flaw in this statute. Despite the fact that Helms Amendment 1251 was never adopted,[145] the final statutory version of the federal Hate Crimes Statistics Act of 1990 stresses the centrality of the "American family": "Congress finds that—(1) the American family life is the foundation of American Society; (2) Federal policy should encourage the well-being, financial security, and health of American family life; (3) schools should not de-emphasize the critical value of American family life."[146] The implicit message this congressional finding conveys is that *sex/gender outsiders* are not included in this official declaration of a fundamental social and legal institution, given that same-sex marriages, with very few exceptions,[147] are not legally recognized,[148] and that the phrase "American family life" as currently used excludes same-sex partnerships.

Coupled with this imperfection is a fifth flaw—a disclaimer which proclaims that "[n]othing in this Act shall be construed, nor shall any funds appropriated to carry out the purpose of the Act be used, to promote or encourage homosexuality."[149] In effect, this Act is equivocal with regard to eradicating discrimination based on sexual orientation/preference and to obliterating violence against those who are known or presumed to be lesbians or gay men. It clearly communicates the unspoken message that although crimes against *sex/gender outsiders* will be recorded, such crimes are less important or serious than crimes committed against other victims encompassed by this statute. A second message symbolically transmitted through this disclaimer is that *sex/gender outsiders* are, to some degree, responsible for the violent attacks against them.[150]

A final flaw contained in the Hate Crimes Statistics Act is its failure to recognize a claim based on the intrasectionality of identity. Individuals who fall between the recognized categories protected under this statute are forced to pick a single identifier to represent their reality. This requirement violates their integrity as complete persons. For example, if a Japanese-American, Buddhist lesbian is raped, and if during the attack the rapist denigrates her ethnicity, religion, affectional orientation/preference, and sex, how is the crime to be counted? Obviously, the aspersions cast on the basis of sex would be excluded automatically, since sex is not a recognized category under this statute. But the remaining characteristics cannot be so readily dismissed, as they are specifically named in the law. To reflect accurately the crime in one sense—to list it under all three potential categories—misrepresents the crime in another sense—the crime on one individual, marked under three categories, is triple counted. Yet, who determines which of the three possible motives is to be counted, and how is that determination reached? To pick any one identity to the exclusion of the remaining two, as required by law, requires that her identity be fragmented and compartmentalized into neat, isolated categories. But law and reality are not congruent under these circumstances. Two aspects of her identity cannot be discounted merely because legislators could conceptualize only unidimensional individuals.

Due to these flaws, *sex/gender outsiders* find little in the federal Hate Crimes Statistics Act to suggest that this statute will stem the tide of discrimination, harassment, or violence against lesbians, gay men, bisexuals, and transgenderists. As Ruthann Robson properly observes, the Act operates on a symbolic level, since "[a]s a rule of law, the act is neither rule nor law. It provides no rights, no remedies, no penalties. . . . Many believe that symbolism is insufficient to deter the violence against us."[151] The law does not criminalize or increase penalties for bias-motivated crimes; it merely requires the collection of data by the U.S. Attorney General, who has delegated responsibility to the Uniform Crime Reporting Section of the Federal Bureau of Investigation. But statistics can only be collected *after* a person or group has been victimized.

Since the purpose of this statute is to collect data, its effectiveness is necessarily limited by the quality of the data available. The issue then is what statistics will be collected. When a person is attacked because of her/his perceived or known affectional orientation/preference, whether or not the attack will count as a hate-motivated crime depends on: (a) the willingness of the victim to report the crime;[152] (b) the willingness of the police to classify the action as a hate-motivated crime;[153] or (c) the willingness of the Community Relations Service operators who handle hate crime calls to record the information provided by individuals reporting crimes against them, as opposed to hanging up.[154] Initial evidence suggests that the collection process has the potential of becoming bogged down by the prejudices of those involved in the classification and collection phases of the program.[155] But if accurate statistics cannot be collected due to interference by the very social institutions designated to assist lesbians and gay men, how likely is it that a speech code enacted to protect *sex/gender outsiders* from "fighting words" or words that inflict intentional emotional distress will be successful? Indeed, the experience of *sex/gender outsiders* suggests that when speech is suppressed, they are frequently the victims.[156]

It is conceded that *some* statistics will be collected by individuals who are not prejudiced, who are conscious of their prejudices and consciously work to overcome them, or who do not allow their prejudices to compromise their job duties. It follows, then, that ultimately at least some hate crimes directed at *sex/gender outsiders* will be recorded. It is further conceded that hate crime laws may help to ameliorate a deeply embedded, widespread problem for *sex/gender outsiders*, since there is a very real difference between a law that fails to solve a problem and one which helps to alleviate a problem—which could be said about many laws—without totally solving it. But to the extent that such laws embody flaws similar to those in the federal Hate Crimes Statistics Act, the latter possesses a very real potential to do more harm than good for the lesbian, gay male, bisexual, and transgender communities in the long run (and perhaps in the short run as well).

NOTES

1. Matsuda (1989); Delgado (1982); Lawrence (1990).
2. Lawrence, *Id.* at 467.
3. Pratt (1991), at 240.
4. See: Chapter One *infra*.
5. Thomas (1992) at 1481–1482.
6. *Id.*
7. Kogan (1994).
8. *Id.* at 209.
9. Thomas (1992) at 1482.
10. See Chapter Three, note 88.

11. See Chapter Three, note 89 for a list of states with sodomy statutes on their books. It should be noted that of the twenty-four sodomy statutes, twelve states categorize this crime as a felony, while eleven consider it a misdemeanor. [Summersgill (Internet)].

As Kate Bornstein notes, "[a] dominant culture tends to combine its subcultures into manageable units. As a result, those who practice non-traditional sex are seen by members of the dominant culture (as well as by members of sex and gender subcultures) as a whole with those who don non-traditional roles and identities" [Bornstein (1994) at 38]. According to Bill Stuart, "[m]ost transvestites are heterosexual. . . . Many psychologists say that transvestites are no more gay or straight than the non-transvestite segment of the male population. . . . The male-[to-]female transsexual population is roughly 50 percent oriented towards males. The female-[to-]male transsexual population is more oriented towards females, but some [female-to-males] have relationships with gay men" [Stuart at 6 (Internet)]. Despite this information, the general perception is that transvestites and transsexuals are lesbians or gay men, regardless of their actual orientation/preference. The same is true for transgenderists.

    12. Editors of the *Harvard Law Review* (1989, 1990) at 27.

    13. But see *Brandenburg* (1969) at 447, wherein the Supreme Court stated that "the constitutional guarantees of free speech . . . do not permit a state to forbid or proscribe advocacy of . . . law violation except where such advocacy is directed to inciting or producing imminent lawless action and is likely to incite or produce such action."

    14. Editors of the *Harvard Law Review* at 28 fn.136.

    15. Gallo (1966) at 795–796.

    16. Mohr (1986/1987) at 48 n.21 (emphasis in original).

    17. *Id.* at 49.

    18. *Phipps* at 1130.

    19. As provided in: Shank (1980) at 553–554.

    20. §2907.07(B) of the Ohio Revised Code, as cited in *Phipps* at 1131.

    21. *Phipps* at 1131.

    22. *Id.*

    23. *Id.*

    24. *Id.* at 1130.

    25. *Id.* at 1131.

    26. *Id.* at 1133.

    27. *Id.*

    28. *Id.* at 1134.

    29. *Id.* at 277. In *Logan* (1985), decided six years after the *Phipps* case, the Alabama Supreme Court held that an employee's statement that plaintiff was "as queer as a three dollar bill" did not violate the torts of outrage and invasion of privacy. The Court held that "to create such a cause of action, the conduct must be such that would cause mental suffering, shame, or humiliation to a person of ordinary sensibilities, not conduct which would be considered unacceptable merely by homosexuals" [*Logan* at 124]. The Court relied upon Professor Prosser's summary of the tort of outrage: "The plaintiff cannot recover merely because he has had his feelings hurt. Even the dire affront of inviting an unwilling woman to illicit intercourse has been held by most courts to be no such outrage as to lead to liability—'the view being, apparently,' in Judge Margruder's well-known words, that 'there is no harm in asking'" [*Logan* at 124]. It is interesting to note what *Phipps* and *Logan* have to say about solicitation, despite the fact that they focus on two different laws (First Amendment and tort of outrage) in two different jurisdictions (Ohio and Alabama). When considered side-by-side, the implication is that legally only *sex/gender outsiders* can cause harm by asking. In both cases the courts reaffirm a heterocentric social outlook: for the Ohio court, same-sex solicitation denotes "fighting words" despite the circumstances—by definition it is deemed

highly repugnant to the person solicited; for the Alabama court, heterosexual solicitation does not rise to the level of outrage (and thus, one might assume, would
not satisfy the criterion of "fighting words") regardless of circumstances—it constitutes "one of those relatively trivial insults for which the law grants no relief"
[*Logan* at 124].

   30. Shank at 572.

   31. See: *The State ex rel. Grant v. Brown* (1974). *Grant* asked the question: is
the Secretary of State required to file the articles of incorporation for the Greater
Cincinnati Gay Society? In a *per curiam* decision, the Ohio Supreme Court answered no. The Court's reason for denying the requested writ of mandamus was
that "[a]lthough homosexual acts between consenting adults are no longer statutory offenses since the new Criminal Code came into effect, . . . [w]e agree with
the Secretary of State that the promotion of homosexuality as a valid life style is
contrary to the public policy of the state" [at 113–114]. Judge Stern, in his dissenting opinion, notes that "as of January 1, 1974, when Amended Substitute House
Bill 511 became effective, [the Secretary of State's] objection to [the Greater Cincinnati Gay Society's] articles of incorporation are moot. Sodomy and solicitation
of acts of sex perversion, are no longer crimes in this state" [at 115]. He also points
out that "[a] fair reading of the [Society's] enunciated purpose indicates that they
hope to foster community acceptance of *themselves*, as individuals, and not that
they seek to convert the community to homosexuality, as suggested by the majority" [at 114 n.1 (emphasis in original)]. It is interesting to note that Judge Stern's
assertion that solicitation is no longer a crime in Ohio occurred two years prior to
Kenneth Phipps being arrested and convicted for soliciting an undercover police
officer in violation of §2907.07(B) of the Revised Ohio Code.

   32. *Chapinsky* at 569.

   33. *Phipps* at 1134 (emphasis added).

   34. Shank at 573.

   35. See: Gerety (1977).

   36. *Phipps* at 1134.

   37. *Id.* at 1130.

   38. Editors of the *Harvard Law Review* at 29–30.

   39. Shank at 570.

   40. The Court defined this term in *Terminiello*: the "heckler's veto" permits
the arrest or conviction of a speaker if the listeners are stirred to anger, invited to
dispute publicly, or brought to a condition of unrest by the speaker [1949]. See:
Feiner (1951); *Nationalist Movement* (1992).

   41. *Coates* (1971) at 612.

   42. The "fighting words" doctrine, as stated in *Chaplinsky*, encompasses
"words which by their very utterance inflict injury or tend to incite an immediate
breach of the peace" [at 572].

   43. *Gooding* at 522.

   44. *Phipps* at 1135.

45. Judge Locher states that "solicitation of the type proscribed by the statute are often 'grossly offensive and emotionally disturbing.' They are very likely to cause injury in a very real, if only emotional, sense. Many times the shock to one's sensibilities and the sense of affront, resulting in injury to one's mind and spirit, are as great from such speech as from a physical assault" [*Id.* at 1134].

46. *Gooding* at 528.

47. *Phipps* at 1135 (Sweeney, J., dissenting).

48. *Id.*

49. *Id.* at 1134.

50. *Id.*

51. *Id.*

52. *Id.* at 1133.

53. See: Bernstein (1995); Dyer (1990); Koppleman (1988); Nava and Dawidoff (1994); Mohr (1986/1987); Rist (1990); Rubenstein (1993); Thomas (1993).

54. States which still have sodomy laws as part of their legal code use the following classifications: BUGGERY: South Carolina; CONSENSUAL SODOMY: New York; CRIME AGAINST NATURE: Arizona, Idaho, Louisiana, Massachusetts, Michigan, North Carolina, Oklahoma, Rhode Island, Virginia; DEVIANT SEXUAL CONDUCT: Montana; HOMOSEXUAL ACTS: Tennessee, Texas; LEWD AND LASCIVIOUS ACTS: Arizona; LEWDNESS: Utah; SEXUAL MISCONDUCT: Alabama, Missouri; SODOMY: Arkansas, Georgia, Kansas, Kentucky, Maryland, Minnesota, Utah; UNNATURAL INTERCOURSE: Mississippi; UNNATURAL AND LASCIVIOUS ACTS: Florida, Massachusetts; VOLUNTARY DEVIANT SEXUAL INTERCOURSE: Pennsylvania. Note that states may be listed more than one time due to the fact that they have different names for similar behavior or for various aspects generally conceptualized as "homosexual sex."

55. See: *Hardwick* at 2458 n.10 (1986) (Stevens, J., dissenting), wherein Justice Stevens states that "the Georgia Attorney General concedes that Georgia's statute would be unconstitutional if applied to a married couple . . . because of the 'right of marital privacy as identified by the Court in *Griswold.*' "

56. Mohr (1988) at 59.

57. *Hardwick* at 2859 n.12 (Stevens, J., dissenting).

58. Mohr (1988) at 108.

59. *Id.* (emphasis in original).

60. *Id.* at 107–108. Despite the perception that sodomy is always a felonious act, of the twenty-four sodomy statutes which have not been legislatively repealed or judicially invalidated by the state's highest court, only thirteen are classified as felonies (Georgia, Idaho, Louisiana, Maryland, Massachusetts, Michigan, Mississippi, Montana, North Carolina, Oklahoma, Rhode Island, South Carolina, and Virginia), while eleven are classified as misdemeanors (Alabama, Arizona, Arkansas, Florida, Kansas, Minnesota, Missouri, Tennessee, Texas, and Utah).

61. Mohr (1986/1987) at 60.

62. *Id.* at 53.

63. See: Kogan (1994); Thomas (1992).

64. See: Comstock, "The Police as Perpetrators . . ." (1991); Feinberg (1996); Herek and Berrill (1992).

65. See: Koppelman (1988); Koppelman (1994); Pharr (1988).

66. Wolfson (1991) at 34.

67. *Id.*

68. *Id.*

69. *Hardwick* at 201 (Blackmun, J., dissenting). Justice Stevens makes a similar point, noting that the state attorney general affirmed during oral argument that "Georgia's statute would be unconstitutional if applied to a married couple . . . because of the 'right of marital privacy as identified by the Court in Griswold'" ["Trial of Oral Argument" at 8, as quoted in *Id.* at 217 n.10 (Stevens, J., dissenting)].

70. *Id.* at 188 n.2.

71. Chief Justice Burger and Justices O'Connor, Powell, and Rehnquist joined Justice White's majority opinion. Both Chief Justice Burger and Justice Powell filed separate concurring opinions.

72. *Id.* at 190.

73. Justices Brennan, Marshall, and Stevens joined in Justice Blackmun's dissenting opinion. Justice Stevens also filed a separate dissenting opinion, which was joined by Justices Brennan and Marshall.

74. *Hardwick* at 201 (Blackmun, J., dissenting) (citing *Olmstead* at 478 (Brandeis, J., dissenting)).

75. *Id.* at 206 (Blackmun, J., dissenting).

76. *Id.* at 189.

77. *Id.* at 190–191.

78. *Id.* at 203 (Blackmun, J., dissenting) [emphasis in original].

79. *Id.* at 204–205 (Blackmun. J., dissenting).

80. *Id.* at 186, 190, 192, 194; *Id.* at 196–197 (Burger, C.J., concurring); *Id.* at 205, 214 (Blackmun, J., dissenting); *Id.* at 219 (Stevens, J., dissenting).

81. Wolfson (1991) at 21.

82. *Id.* at 34.

83. The equating of same-sex adult consensual sodomy with criminal activity persists, despite the fact that sodomy statutes have been repealed or ruled unconstitutional in twenty-eight states and the District of Columbia notwithstanding one's sexual orientation/preference. Indeed, if the total population in the United States for 1990 (approximately 249 million regardless of sexual orientation; approximately 5 million of whom are presumed to be *sex/gender outsiders*—using a very conservative estimate of 2 percent of the population) is compared with the population in (a) the sixteen states with gender-neutral sodomy statutes (approximately 77 million regardless of sexuality, 2 percent or 1.5 million of whom are

presumed to be *sex/gender outsiders*); (b) the six states with only same-sex sodomy statutes (approximately 20 million regardless of sexuality, 2 percent or 400 thousand of whom are presumed to be *sex/gender outsiders*); and (c) the twenty-eight states without sodomy statutes (approximately 152 million regardless of sexuality; 2 percent or 3 million of whom are presumed to be *sex/gender outsiders*), two conclusions can be drawn. First, approximately 61 percent of all U.S. citizens live in jurisdictions with no legal prohibition against *any* consenting adults engaging in sodomy; and second, either (a) sodomy is not the sole sexual conduct engaged in by approximately 39 percent of United States citizens who live in the sixteen jurisdictions that criminalize sodomy regardless of the sexual orientation/preference of the participant(s) and in the six jurisdictions that criminalize only same-sex sodomy; or (b) sodomy statutes are seldom (if at all) enforced in these twenty-two states; or (c) sodomy is not the sole sexual conduct engaged in, and sodomy statutes are seldom (if at all) enforced. See: *Webster's II New Riverside Desk Reference* (1992) at 17, citing information collected from Department of Commerce (1991).

84. See: "Brief of Respondent Hardwick #85–140: Complaint: Joint Appendix" at 3; "Brief of Respondent Hardwick #85–140: Opposition to Petition for a Writ of Certiorari" at 1; *Hardwick* at 188.

85. *Hardwick* at 200 (1986) (Blackmun, J., dissenting).

86. Halley (1993) at 1766–1767.

87. Cammermeyer (1993); *Inman* (1951); *Meinhold* (1993); *Petition of Nemetz* (1980); *Pruitt* (1987); *Saal* (1980); *Steffan* (1990).

88. Halley (1993) at 1738 fn.51.

89. See: "National Defense Authorization Act For Fiscal Year 1994" (1993).

90. Halley (1993) at 1731.

91. A common stereotype is that all lesbians, gay men, and bisexuals (when involved in a same-sex relationship) engage in some form of oral or anal sexual activity. Moreover, even transgenderists, who perceive themselves as having a cross-sex orientation/preference, may be believed to have a same-sex orientation/preference by members of society—especially if genital surgery has not occurred (regardless of the reason). If surgery has occurred, an individual who legally married prior to surgery and did not obtain a divorce may also be believed to be a lesbian or gay male by members of society, regardless of how the individual self-defines her or his affectional orientation/preference.

92. *Baker* (1982); *Ben-Shalom* (1989) at 464 (7th Cir. 1989); *High Tech Gays* (1987); *Woodward* (1989) at 1076 n.10. The assumption in each of these cases is that all or most lesbians and gay men engage in sexual activities that are inevitably linked to sodomy—regardless of whether they ever have engaged in this act, whether they intend to continue participating in this act, or whether the "sexual majority" (i.e., heterosexuals) is permitted to do so with impunity. Frequently, under military and civilian law, the term "sodomy" is used interchangeably with the broader term "homosexual conduct" [See: Wells-Petry (1993) at 26–27, 45, 47,

136]. What is frequently not acknowledged, however, is that while the sexual practices of *sex/gender outsiders* may include sodomy, "homosexual conduct" is not limited to sodomy nor is sodomy confined to *sex/gender outsiders*. Sodomy occurs between individuals regardless of their affectional orientation/preference (For example: *Fagg* (1992); *Moseley* (1989); *Schochet* (1990)).

But even if, for the sake of argument, the sexual conduct of *sex/gender outsiders* does primarily include consensual same-sex adult sodomy, it would not change the fact that sexual behavior is but one aspect of their total identity. While it may be an important, perhaps even essential, component, it is not the sole dimension or expression of their identity. Affectional orientation/preference, regardless of how an individual might conceptualize it, influences multiple aspects of one's life—friends, living space, religion, family relations with regard to coupling or building families, social activities, self-image, self-worth or acceptance, the perception of others, and the potential for sustaining physical, social, legal, political, economic, or psychological harm.

93. See: *Rich* (1981); *Ben-Shalom* (1989).

94. See: Crittenden (1957); Sarbin and Karols (1990); McDaniel (1990).

95. *Hardwick* at 200 (Blackmun, J., dissenting).

96. *Id.* at 211 (Blackmun, J., dissenting).

97. *Id.* at 196.

98. *Id.* at 192 (White, J., majority opinion); *Id.* at 196 (Berger, C.J., concurring), *Id.* at 203 (Stevens, J., dissenting).

99. *Id.* at 196 (White, J., majority opinion); *Id.* at 201 (Blackmun, J., dissenting).

100. *Id.* at 205 (Blackmun, J., dissenting).

101. See: Mohr (1986/1987) at 52.

102. See: Goldstein (1988) at 1074.

103. *Hardwick* at 194–195.

104. *Id.* at 191.

105. A unanimous Supreme Court stated: "The question . . . is whether the reality of private biases and the possible injury they might inflict are permissible considerations. . . . We have little difficulty concluding that they are not. The Constitution cannot control such prejudices but neither can it tolerate them. Private biases may be outside the reach of the law, but the law cannot, directly or indirectly, give them effect" [*Palimore* at 433].

106. *Hardwick* at 195–196.

107. *Id.* at 209, 209 fn.4 (Blackmun, J., dissenting).

108. *Id.*

109. *Id.*

110. Halley (1993) at 1737.

111. Hunter (1995) at 1718.

112. Schacter (1994) at 294.

113. Hunter (1995) at 1718.

114. Permitted schools to dismiss employees for "advocating, soliciting, imposing, encouraging, or promoting of private or public homosexual activity directed at, or likely to come to the attention of, schoolchildren and/or other employees."

115. Forbids the Center for Disease Control to use any funds "to provide AIDS education, information, or prevention materials and activities that promote or encourage, directly or indirectly, homosexual sexual activity."

116. A law arising out of this controversy was the Helms Amendment, discussed below.

117. For example, Colorado Constitution, Article II, §30b (1992): "No Protected Status Based on Homosexual, Lesbian, or Bisexual Orientation. Neither the State of Colorado, through any of its branches or departments, nor any of its agencies, political subdivisions, municipalities or school districts, shall enact, adopt or enforce any statute, regulation, ordinance or policy whereby homosexual, lesbian, or bisexual orientation, conduct, practices or relationships shall constitute or otherwise be the basis of or entitle any person or class of persons to have or claim any minority status, quota preferences, protected status or claim of discrimination. This Section of the Constitution shall be in all respects self-executing."

118. Hunter (1995) at 1696.

119. For a complete history of the battle over NEA reauthorization and the attacks on *sex/gender outsiders* in both chambers of Congress, see the *Congressional Record* (1989–1991). See also: the hearings held by the Subcommittee on Postsecondary Education (1990).

120. The complete photographs of the "X" segment of Mapplethorpe's work are reproduced in Storr (1991) at 14–28.

121. Glueck (1989) at 1 col.3.

122. See the following segments of the *Congressional Record* for additional examples: S6858 (19 June 1989), H3181 (27 June 1989), H3511 (29 June 1989), H5635 (13 September 1989), H5819 (21 July 1989), S12111 and S12131 (28 September 1989), S12968–12969 and S12985 (7 October 1989), E358 (22 February 1990).

123. "Helms Amendment."

124. *Miller* at 24.

125. See, for example: *Farger* (1982), wherein the Court held that photographs of nude children are constitutionally protected; *Osburne* (1990), wherein the Court ruled that "depictions of nudity, without more, constitute protected expression."

126. *American Booksellers Association, Inc.* (1984) at 1339.

127. See, for example: *Cohen* at 24, wherein the Court held that government bodies may not prescribe form or content of individual expression; *Mosley* at 95, wherein the Court maintained that under the First Amendment the government has no power to restrict expression on the basis of ideas, subject matter, or content; *Widmar* (1981) at 276, wherein the Court asserted that the most exacting scrutiny is required when the state undertakes to regulate speech on the basis of content; *Reagan* (1984) at 648–649, wherein the Court stated that a federal statute regulat-

ing photographic reproductions of currency is unconstitutional, in part because it discriminated on the basis of content. More recently, in light of Justice Scalia's reasoning in *R.A.V.* (1992), discussed in Chapter Five *infra*, the Helms Amendment would appear to violate the Constitution.

128. Dannemeyer (1990) at 99–100. The poem from which Representative Dannemeyer quotes (out of context, and thus misrepresents) is "Crime Against Nature," by Minnie Bruce Pratt (1990).

129. Pratt (1991) at 243 fn.5 (letter, on file with Minnie Bruce Pratt).

130. deGrazia (1992) at 644.

131. Selcraig (1990) at 24–26.

132. See: *Bella Lewitzky Dance Foundation* (1991). Lewitzky maintained that because the determination of obscenity was to be decided by the NEA, the obscenity pledge was unconstitutionally vague. On 9 January 1991, Judge John G. Davies held that the obscenity pledges contained unconstitutionally vague provisions, violated the First Amendment protection against the chilling of artistic expression, and contained none of the procedural safeguards required by prior Supreme Court precedents, such as *Speiser* (1958). While Judge Davies acknowledged that the government could put restrictions both on whom and how it subsidizes, he stated that "once the government moves to subsidize, it cannot do so in a manner that carries with it a level of vagueness that violates the First and Fifth Amendments" [*Bella Lewitzky Dance Foundation* at 784–785].

133. deGrazia at 662 (emphasis in original).

134. "Summary for Williams-Coleman Proposal Reauthorizing the National Endowment for the Arts."

135. For example: Senate debate on Helm's Amendment (#1653) to the Higher Education Amendment Bill, in February 1992; Senate debate on the Public Broadcasting Reauthorization Bill, in June 1992; speeches delivered at the Republican National Convention in Houston, 1992; congressional debate on the Hate Crimes Statistics Act of 1989; and congressional debate on the amendments written by Senator Helms and Representative Dannemeyer on AIDS funding in 1988.

136. Keen (1992) at 1, 17.

137. Berrill (1990); Herek (1989); Herek (1991).

138. Garnets, Herek, and Levy (1993) at 583. See also: Feinberg (1996); Pharr (1988); Pratt (1995).

139. Garnets, Herek, and Levy at 583–584.

140. *Id.* at 586.

141. The Hate Crime Statistics Act, in pertinent part, reads:

An Act to provide for the acquisition and publication of data about crimes that manifest prejudice based on certain group characteristics.

. . .

(b) (1) Under the authority of section 534 of title 28, United States Code, the Attorney General shall acquire data, for the calendar year 1990 and each of the succeeding 4 calendar years, about crimes that manifest evidence of prejudice based on race, religion, sexual orientation, or ethnicity, including where appropriate the crimes of murder, non-negligent manslaughter; forcible rape; aggravated assault, simple assault, intimidation; arson; and destruction, damage, or vandalism of property.

. . .

(3) Nothing in this section creates a cause of action or a right to bring an action, including an action based on discrimination due to sexual orientation. As used in this section, the term "sexual orientation" means consensual homosexuality or heterosexuality. This section does not limit any existing cause of action or right to bring an action, including any action under the Administrative Procedure Act or the All Writs Act.

(4) Data acquired under this section shall be used only for research or statistical purposes and may not contain any information that may reveal the identity of an individual of a crime.

. . .

Sec.2. (a) Congress finds that—

(1) The American family life is the foundation of American Society,

(2) Federal policy should encourage the well-being, financial security, and health of the American family,

(3) Schools should not de-emphasize the critical value of American family life.

(b) Nothing in this Act shall be construed, nor shall any funds appropriated to carry out the purpose of the Act be used, to promote or encourage homosexuality.

142. Sylvia Law aptly defines the difference between these two concepts. The term homophobia "suggests a fear of homosexuals and an individual pathological hatred of them;. . . heterosexism is a much broader phenomenon, structured into basic familial, economic, political relationships. Heterosexism shapes the lives, choices, beliefs and attitudes of millions of people who experience neither fear nor hatred of gay and lesbian people" [Law (1988)]. Janet Halley pushes Law's definitions further by arguing that "[a] key rational for antihomosexual discrimination . . . is anxiety about the ambiguity of heterosexual interactions, about a potential for mutability that undermines heterosexual identity" [Halley (1985) at 956]. In essence, the term homophobia effectively absolves the bearer of responsibility, insofar as it is generally believed that one cannot be held accountable for "irrational fears"; heterosexism places responsibility for the hatred, discrimination, and violence experienced by *sex/gender outsiders* squarely on the ideology woven into the very fabric of society and manifested in its official institutions. See also: Blumenfeld and Raymond (1988); Lorde (1984); Neisen (1990); Wittig (1992).

143. §534 (b)(3).

144. *Id.*

145. Helms Amendment 1251 states that: "(1) the homosexual movement threatens the strength and the survival of the American family as the basic unit of society; (2) State sodomy laws should be enforced because they are in the best interest of public health; (3) the Federal government should not provide discrimination protections on the basis of sexual orientation; and (4) school curriculums

should not condone homosexuality as an acceptable lifestyle in American society." (This amendment was defeated in the Senate by a vote of 77–19.)

146. This act was approved by a vote of 92–4 and signed by President George Bush on 23 April 1990 at a public ceremony attended by lesbian and gay male activists.

147. See: Eskridge (1996). Eskridge concedes that if Native American tribes are excluded from consideration, then technically no state in the U.S. has ever adopted a marriage law approving same-sex unions [at 95]. He further notes that in every state in the Union, a biological male cross-dressed as a female is legally permitted to marry a biological female dressed either as a male or female, but a biological female cross-dressed as a male is not legally permitted to marry a biological female—due solely to their sexual organs, hormones, or chromosomes [at 94]. Yet, despite these observations, Williams contends that "there is no way to draw the sex-and-gender line consistently enough to deny that states have repeatedly recognized same-sex marriages. If a male-to-female transsexual's marriage to a man is same-sex, then New Jersey has recognized a form of same-sex marriage, as have the various states that have given marriage licenses to people whose chromosomal pattern did not match their genitals at birth. If it is cross-sex, then other states have recognized same-sex marriages between male-to-female transsexuals to women." He explains in a footnote that if a male-to-female transsexual presents an official birth certificate that indicates her birth gender to be male, then regardless of whether the individual's self-identification matches the documented information—that is, the transsexual's outward appearance and self-presentation is female—a marriage license can be officially issued [at 94].

148. The Defense of Marriage Act refuses, in essence, to recognize same-sex marriages at the federal level and grants states the right to determine for themselves whether to recognize a same-sex marriage performed within their own borders or in another state.

149. "Hate Crimes Statistics Act of 1990" at §534, §2(b).

150. See: Bagnall, Gallagher, and Goldstein (1984); Comstock (1991); Comstock (1989); Herek (1991); Herek and Berrill (1992); National Gay & Lesbian Task Force (1988); National Gay & Lesbian Task Force Policy Institute (1990).

151. Robson (1992) at 149.

152. Whether victims are willing to report a crime is based on (a) personal experiences or perceptions that the police will be heterosexist, (b) fear that the police will be abusive, or (c) fear of public disclosure of their sexual orientation/preference. See: Committee of the Judiciary (1986); Committee of the Judiciary (1983); Comstock (1991); Comstock (1989); Harry (1982); Herek and Berrill (1992).

153. Id.

154. Coward (1992) at 1.

155. Id.

156. In the United States, censorship of lesbian and gay male speech has occurred on numerous occasions. In the words of Ruthann Robson, "when the speech

that is supposedly free is lesbian [and gay male] speech, the government routinely suppresses it" [Robson (1992) at 154]. Examples of government suppression of same-sex speech can be found in the 1920s [see *Before Stonewall: The Making of a Gay and Lesbian Community*, a documentary]. A more recent series of events surrounded the reauthorization and funding of the National Endowment for the Arts between 1989 and 1990 [see: the National Gay and Lesbian Task Force (1992) at 2]. See also: Cossman, Bell, Gotell, and Ross (1997); LeMarche and Rubenstein (1990) at 524.

CHAPTER 5

Judicial Response to Hate Regulations

While freedom of speech is not an absolute right under the Constitution, the government is not permitted arbitrarily to restrict it; if the government seeks to regulate the fundamental rights protected by the First Amendment, it must demonstrate a compelling state interest. One such interest that the Supreme Court has recognized is the government's concern for maintaining peace. By focusing on the social value of expression, Judge Murphy, writing for a majority, established the "fighting words" doctrine in *Chaplinsky v. New Hampshire*. He stated that certain classes of speech could be prevented or punished by the government without violating the Constitution. "These include the lewd and the obscene, the profane, the libelous, and the insulting or fighting words—those which by their very utterance inflict injury or tend to incite an immediate breach of the peace."[1] Expressions such as these are not, in his opinion, an essential part of discourse and possess such negligible social value that the government's interest in law and order outweighs the right of citizens to express themselves through such expressions. With this dictum, Justice Murphy's categorical approach divided expression into speech that possesses social value and is protected under the First Amendment, and speech that does not, and is not.

Fifty-five years after its inception, albeit in a narrowed form that encompasses only the words "which by their very utterance . . . tend to incite an immediate breach of the peace," the "fighting words" doctrine is at the center of legal discourse regarding hate speech regulations. These regulations have grown in popularity across the country, especially on university campuses, since the late 1980s. The purpose served by speech codes, however, is ardently disputed. On the one hand, supporters maintain that they reinforce society's commitment to the values of tolerance and equality. Opponents, on the other hand, argue that these codes censor and repress ideas. The courts find themselves in the midst of this conflict as they judge the constitutionality of various hate speech regulations.

DOE V. UNIVERSITY OF MICHIGAN

The first case to challenge a university's hate speech policy on First Amendment grounds was *Doe v. University of Michigan.* At issue in this case was the University of Michigan's "Policy on Discrimination and Discriminatory Harassment of Students in the University Environment." Under this policy, penalties or sanctions could be levied against individuals who, while in educational and academic centers, engaged in either verbal or physical behavior that "stigmatizes or victimizes an individual on the basis of race, ethnicity, religion, sex, sexual orientation, creed, national origin, ancestry, age, marital status, handicap, or Vietnam-era veteran status."[2] This policy encompassed behavior in the form of express or implied threats to an individual's "academic efforts, employment, participation in University sponsored extra-curricular activities or personal safety," and behavior that "creates an intimidating, hostile, or demeaning environment."[3]

Doe, a biopsychology graduate student,[4] fearing he might be found in violation of the University's policy if he taught the controversial theories in his field of study, sued in district court for a preliminary injunction against the policy. He argued that the policy was unconstitutionally vague and overbroad and that it chilled speech and conduct protected by the First Amendment.

Judge Cohn, writing for the court, began his opinion by distinguishing between the First Amendment's protection of "pure speech" and of conduct.[5] Blatant forms of discriminatory conduct—assault and battery, depriving another of her/his constitutionally guaranteed rights, and sexually abusive and harassing conduct—are not protected under the First Amendment.[6] These forms of conduct are, moreover, punishable under various federal and state statutes. Certain forms of "pure speech" (such as "fighting words," offensive speech, speech sufficient to establish a state claim for the tort of intentional infliction of emotional distress,[7] legally obscene speech, speech capable of inciting lawless action and "racial and ethnic epithets, slurs, and insults" that fit into one of the previously mentioned categories) are also outside of First Amendment protection.[8] While the University of Michigan could regulate some categories of speech (such as those identified by the court), it could not prohibit speech because the University disagreed with the ideas or messages the speech sought to convey, or because the University found the expression extremely offensive.[9] Prohibitions of speech based on either orthodoxy or offense, in Judge Cohn's view, were contrary to judicial precedents with regard to content neutrality, protection of offensive speech, and "the special significance [these principles acquire] in the university setting, where the free and unfettered interplay of competing views is essential to the institution's educational mission."[10] But according to the University's own memorandums, it deliberately sought to restrict speech that was constitutionally protected due to the reluctance of the courts and the common law to recognize the personal damage to individuals within the community caused by discriminatory and offensive speech.[11]

Once the court had defined the scope of permissible regulations, it moved to a consideration of whether the University's policy was overbroad, either facially or as applied. Judge Cohn noted that a statute regulating speech is overbroad if, in addition to unprotected speech, it embraces a substantial amount of protected speech.[12] While acknowledging empathy with the University's obligation to provide an equal educational opportunity to all students and with its attempts to eliminate discrimination on its campus, Judge Cohn found fault with the implementation of its anti-discrimination policy. He recited numerous incidents wherein the University's Interim Policy Administrator had censored unpopular but constitutionally protected views. For example, a School of Social Work student had been investigated for stating the belief that "homosexuality was a disease and that he intended to develop a counseling plan for changing gay clients to straight."[13] Another student had been reproved for reading a homophobic limerick in a business administration class.[14] A third incident involved a student who had been censured for repeating what he had heard about the treatment of minority students by a particular minority faculty member in the Dental School.[15] Based on these and other episodes involving students charged with violating the University's policy, the court concluded that the University did not exempt comments made in the context of classroom discussion, even though they caused no threat of imminent violence.[16] It thus held that the policy was consistently applied to sanction protected speech.

Judge Cohn next considered Doe's vagueness argument. By definition, a statute is unconstitutionally vague if it fails to give adequate notice of the proscribed conduct or to establish explicit standards for the enforcement of the statute. The court observed that the vagueness doctrine has particular force when it produces a chilling effect on constitutionally protected speech.[17] Nowhere in the policy did the University articulate a principled method of distinguishing protected from unprotected speech. As a result, students "of common intelligence"[18] were forced to guess at what verbal conduct was sanctionable under the policy. Analyzing both the cause and effect clauses within the policy, the court noted the ambiguity of critical concepts. In the cause section,[19] the terms "stigmatize" and "victimize" eluded precise definitions; in the effect clauses,[20] conduct that constitutes a "threat" or which "interferes" with an individual was not clearly identified. That neither the University attorneys nor the interpretive guide (which was later withdrawn by the university as inaccurate) could articulate the definite scope of the policy suggested to Judge Cohn that the University had no idea what the limits of its own policy were and that rules for enforcing the policy were spontaneous. Thus, Justice Cohn concluded that "[t]he terms of the Policy were so vague that its enforcement would violate the due process clause."[21] Quoting Thomas Cooley,[22] Judge Cohn asserted that an expansive reading of the First Amendment was necessary because regardless of whether speech "exceeds all the proper bounds of moderation, the consolation must be that the evil likely to spring from the violent discussion will probably be less, and its correction by public sentiment more speedy, than if the terrors of the law were brought to bear to prevent the discussion."[23]

In an addendum to the his decision Judge Cohn noted that the court had been unaware of a paper presented by Mari J. Matsuda[24] at the University of Michigan's Law School until after the *Doe* decision had already been signed and filed. He indicated that earlier awareness of her paper "would have sharpened the court's view of the issues" in *Doe*.[25] In his opinion, her attempt to find a valid First Amendment solution to the problem of hate speech through the "criminalization of a narrow, explicitly defined class of racist speech, to provide public redress for the most serious harm, while leaving many forms of racist speech to private redress"[26]—was important for "a broader perspective of the issues put by the [University of Michigan] Policy and the court's holding of unconstitutionality under the First Amendment."[27] It seems, however, that even if the court had had time to reflect on Matsuda's arguments, its decision regarding the overbreadth and vagueness of the university's policy would have been unchanged, for several reasons.

First, the Michigan Supreme Court and Matsuda begin from different premises with regard to the scope of the First Amendment vis-a-vis public universities. Judge Cohn holds that an expansive interpretation of the First Amendment is necessary to prevent the harm that would arise from judicial miscalculation and misdeeds[28] and to prevent the universities from getting into the business of censorship.[29] He also advocates a liberal reading of the

First Amendment, because the evil springing from discussion of the hate speech would be less, and the correction of public sentiment faster, than if speech were suppressed.[30] Matsuda, on the other hand, begins from the premise that universities have a duty to their students to provide an environment wherein individuals can grow and develop socially, intellectually, and personally. Hence, toleration of hate speech by the universities causes greater harm than that caused by similar toleration in society at large, as such toleration violates the principles and goals articulated by universities.[31]

Judge Cohn and Matsuda also differ on their views regarding the consequences of hate speech. For Judge Cohen, "the free and unfettered interplay of competing views is essential to the institution's educational mission."[32] It is the uniqueness of the university setting that provides students exposure to a multitude of ideas and beliefs. This setting allows students to explore, analyze, and discuss issues with one another and to confront opposing viewpoints. Matsuda would counter that many of the new students who live and study at the major universities are psychologically vulnerable. When a university tolerates hate speech, it effectively sides with the abuser, thereby abandoning the targeted students and compounding the injury caused by that speech.[33] In addition, because of their vulnerability, new students may not be capable of "processing" the hate speech in a manner that would allow them to engage the attacker verbally.

Finally, Judge Cohn and Mastuda disagree on the scope of impermissible speech. Judge Cohn requires that unprotected speech be confined primarily to "fighting words" and speech that creates a hostile or abusive working environment, in violation of Title VII. Matsuda enlarges the scope of unprotected speech. She asserts that "racist speech should be treated as a *sui generis* category, presenting an idea so historically untenable, so dangerous, and so tied to perpetuation of violence and degradation of the very classes of human beings who are least equipped to respond that it is properly treated as outside the realm of protected discourse."[34] Under her analysis, the worst forms of racist speech would be messages of racial inferiority, directed against a historically oppressed group; these messages are persecutorial, hateful, and degrading.[35] She states unequivocally that prosecuting someone for racist speech requires the existence of all three elements in her/his message.[36]

Matsuda's theory would not have solved the problems that the University of Michigan's anti-discrimination policy was designed to solve. The discrimination and hate speech the University sought to eliminate was much broader than that which could be addressed under Matsuda's theory. The only speech conduct that is definitely sanctionable using Matsuda's *suis generis* category is (a) where hateful speech is directed against a subordinated, as opposed to a dominant, group member; (b) anti-semitic hate propaganda;[37] and (c) wordless speech in the form of swastikas, Klan robes, burning crosses, and other symbols or signs whose historically known to convey the message of persecution based on race.[38]

It is unclear, however, whether hate speech directed against individuals on the basis of sex, affectional orientation/preference, creed, national origin, ancestry, age, marital status, handicap, or Vietnam-era veteran status, all of which the University seeks to regulate, would violate Matsuda's standard. Based on her definitions and examples, it would seem that hate speech directed at individuals on the basis of the last four characteristics should be left to private remedies, such as counter-speech, social disapprobation, boycott, and persuasion. Hate speech attacks based on creed, national origin, and ancestry would be actionable only if they could satisfy the requirements of the *sui generis* category. In the majority of instances, a case-by-case determination would probably be required to determine the history and context, and also the community standard of the recipient's group with regard to the attack. Verbal behavior on the basis of sex or affectional orientation/preference is deliberately not addressed by Matsuda on the grounds that these issues require a separate analysis.[39] It can be inferred, however, that since discrimination on the basis of sex or affectional orientation/preference is neither "universally condemned"[40] nor has "achieved world consensus either for or against,"[41] hate speech on the basis of these two characteristics would be considered the equivalent of core political speech.[42]

If the four scenarios presented in *Doe* are reexamined in light of Matsuda's theory, the majority of students who were censured by the University should not have been. In the case of the biopsychology student, Matsuda would contend that the University could deny him a forum for his controversial theories regarding the biologically based difference between the sexes and races *if* his theories can neither be sustantiated nor meet the requisite professional standards.[43] *If*, however, his biologically based theories are supported by credible evidence and presented in a manner that is "free of any message of hatred and persecution," then the student should be permitted to teach his theories free from the threat of punishment.

The University of Michigan would not have disciplined the graduate student in the School of Social Work class who voiced the belief about lesbians and gay men, or the student in the School of Business Administration class who read the "homophobic limerick." As previously argued, the first incident would be deemed core political speech, and thus protected speech. In the second incident, regardless of how the limerick is conceptualized—as "satire or stereotyping that avoids persecutorial language,"[44] the equivalent of ethnic humor, or core as political speech—Matsuda would protect its expression. The only sanction the speaker might be subjected to would be that of private redress.

Finally, in the case of the student who repeated information about a specific minority faculty member's treatment of minority students in the Dental School, the student might not have been disciplined by the University. Since the court's reporting of the incident did not indicate that the student's statement would satisfy the requirements of *sui generis* category defined by Matsuda, it would seem that the student's speech would not be sanctionable by the University. If, however, his comment did in fact meet the criteria it seems the race of the student would be a determining factor in whether his speech would be punishable. If a minority student raised the issue, then—because a minority professor would be involved—history, context, and the judgment of other minority faculty members would determine the outcome of this case.[45] If, on the other hand, a non-minority student raised the issue, then the student could be sanctioned for the remark, since the professor's "well-being and status . . . is related to the status of the individual's group."[46]

UWM POST, INC. V. UNIVERSITY OF WISCONSIN

Two years after *Doe*, a second major case came before the courts involving the constitutionality of a university hate speech policy. The policy under consideration in *UWM Post, Inc.* v. University of Wisconsin was narrower than the one challenged in *Doe*. Under the University of Wisconsin's anti-discrimination policy, a student could be disciplined for speech in a non-academic setting, for racist or discriminatory comments, epithets, or other expressive behavior or physical conduct directed at an individual, or on separate occasions at different individuals, that intentionally "demeans the race, sex, religion, color, creed, disability, sexual orientation, national origin, ancestry or age of the individual or individuals; and creates an intimidating, hostile or demeaning environment for education, university-related work, or other university-authorized activity."[47] In the brochure which accompanied this rule, the University advised students that proscribed speech would include racial slurs or jokes, written material placed in a person's living quarters or work area, or damage to or destruction of property of a member of the university community or of a guest on the basis of the characteristics listed in the policy.[48] However, the guidelines noted that within an academic setting, students would not be held in violation of the University's non-discrimination policy for stating their beliefs or opinions, provided the remarks were not addressed at specific individuals with intent to demean them and create an intimidating environment.[49]

In *UWM Post,* Judge Warren, the senior district judge who wrote the court's opinion, gave serious consideration to the Board of Regent's arguments that its anti-discrimination policy, contrary to the challenge raised by the plaintiffs, did not violate the First Amendment. The first issue addressed by the court was whether the policy was facially overbroad, as maintained by the challenging students. In its defense, the Board asserted that its rule fell within the "fighting words" doctrine developed by the U.S. Supreme Court. In their opinion, "it is understandable to expect a violent response to discriminatory harassment because such harassment demeans an immutable characteristic which is central to the person's identity."[50] The court, however, pointed out that only two types of fighting words were identified under *Chaplinsky*—"those which by their very utterance inflict injury *or* [those which] tend to incite an immediate breach of the peace."[51] The first part of the test is associated with preventing psychological injury, "primarily in the form of emotional upset and injury to the 'sensibilities' of addressees;"[52] the second part deals with preventing physical retaliation which is "likely to cause an immediate breach of the peace."[53] Although these two types of speech are correctly designated as "fighting words" in *Chaplinsky*, Judge Warren noted the Supreme Court had significantly narrowed the "fighting words" doctrine through its subsequent rulings in *Cohen v. California,*[54] *Gooding v. Wilson,*[55] *Lewis v. City of New Orleans,*[56] and *Texas v. Johnson.*[57] He argued that

[s]ince *Chaplinsky*, the Supreme Court has narrowed and clarified the scope of the fighting words doctrine in at least three ways. First, the Court has limited the fighting words definition so that it now only includes its second half [—words which tend to incite an immediate breach of the peace]. Second, the Court has stated that in order for words to meet the second half of the definition they must "naturally tend to provoke violent resentment." Finally, the Court has held that fighting words must be "directed at the person of the hearer."[58]

In reviewing the University of Wisconsin's policy, Judge Warren found that its rule reached speech in excess of the scope permitted under the modified fighting words doctrine. The University's first requirement, that the speech be racist or discriminatory, failed to meet the fighting words test, because although it described the content of the speech to be regulated, it did not demand that the speech be inclined to cause a breach of the peace. While its second requirement, that the speech must be directed at an individual, met the specification that the speech be directed at the hearer and suggested the criterion that the speech must trigger a violent reaction to be proscribed, it failed to require that the speech always incite a violent reaction. As a result, it encompassed speech that would not breach the peace contrary to the fighting words doctrine. The third requirement set out in the policy, that the speech demean an individual on the basis of certain named characteristics, was inherently invalid. It regulated speech contained in the now-defunct first part of the *Chaplinsky* fighting words doctrine, without addressing the concerns of the still valid second part. Finally, the fourth requirement, that the speech create an intimidating, hostile, or demeaning environment, reached not only speech that tends to incite a violent reaction but also speech that does not. Overall, although all four of the University's policy requirements governed speech which may cause a violent reaction, they also covered speech which may not cause such a reaction and thus "fail[ed] to meet the requirements of the fighting words doctrine."[59]

The second argument offered by the Board was that since its rule "only regulates speech with minimum social value and which has harmful effects,"[60] it was not in conflict with the First Amendment. In fact, in their opinion, the policy conformed to the balancing test utilized by the Supreme Court in *Chaplinsky*. Although Judge Warren agreed that the Court employed a balancing approach to determine that certain categories of speech do not deserve protection under the First Amendment, he observed that the district court "may employ a balancing approach to determine the constitutionality of the UW Rule only if it is content neutral."[61] Because the University's policy was a content-based restriction—it disciplined only those comments, epithets, and other expressive behaviors which demeans the addressee on the basis of the characteristics specified in its policy, as opposed to speech that demeans on the basis of any characteristic—the court could not use the balancing approach in its evaluation.

The court noted, however, that even if one did utilize the balancing test, the arguments put forth by the University for its policy would not be saved by either the benefits or the costs side of this test. With regard to the benefits side, the court believed that the type of speech restricted by the University's policy, contrary to the University's claim, "[was in fact] intended to convince the listener of the speaker's discriminatory position."[62] But were the court to accept that this intention did not exist, the speech proscribed by the University would still be protected under the First Amendment since it expresses the emotions of the speaker. In addition, while the University had asserted that the speech it prohibited was unanswerable, the court responded that "the Constitution does not make the dominance of truth a necessary condition of freedom of speech. To say that it does would be to confuse an outcome of speech with a necessary condition for the application of the amendment."[63] Moreover, regardless of whether the restricted speech constitutes a form of verbal assault as the Board alleged, the Supreme Court had stated that such speech is still worthy of First Amendment protection. That the speech proscribed by the policy might perhaps incite a violent response was not enough—the Supreme Court limits unprotected speech to that "which by it very utterance tends to incite an immediate breach of the peace."[64]

On the costs side of the balance, the court observed that the policy failed to assist the Board in achieving its compelling interest of increasing minority representation. The anti-discrimination policy obstructed the very diversity of ideas so essential to the achievement of this purpose. Furthermore, since the Board's policy was directed at the actions of students, and students are not state actors, its anti-discrimination policy did not satisfy the University's compelling interest in providing an equal protection remedy to unequal educational opportunities. Nor did the Board's policy qualify as a proper time-place-and-manner restriction on speech that might disrupt the University's compelling interest in providing educational activities. By restricting the content of speech which inflicted psychological injury but might not provoke a violent reaction, the policy was contrary to the fighting words doctrine. As a consequence, the court held that the University's policy failed both the balancing test proposed by the Board of Regents and the fighting words doctrine, and that the University of Wisconsin's anti-discrimination policy was overbroad, in violation of the First Amendment.

The Board's final argument, in its attempt to disprove that its policy was overbroad, was that its rule prohibiting "discriminatory speech which creates a hostile environment [had] parallels in the employment setting" under Title VII law.[65] While the court found this argument persuasive, it also detected three key flaws in it. In the first place, Title VII applies to employment, not educational, settings; this statute only pertained to the University in its capacity as an employer, not as a provider of community services. Second, even if Title VII did apply to educational settings, the University by the Supreme Court's decision of *Meritor Savings Bank v. Vinson*, still could not be held liable for the discriminatory actions of its students, because students are not agents of the school and do not represent it. Finally, even if the University's policy could be deemed parallel to Title VII, the fact remained that "[s]ince Title VII is only a statute, it cannot supersede the requirements of the First Amendment."[66] What the court did not address was the fact that the University's policy was *not* parallel to Title VII: the latter regulates discriminatory conduct rather than speech content, whereas the former does the opposite, regulating the content of the students' speech rather than their conduct.

While the court did concede that neither the phrase "discriminatory comments, epithets, and abusive language" nor the term "demean," as used in the University's policy, suffered from vagueness difficulties, that did not rescue the policy from constitutional problems. As Judge Warren pointed out, the vagueness of the anti-discrimination rule stemmed from the ambiguity regarding "whether the regulated speech must actually demean the listener and create an intimidating, hostile or demeaning environment for education or whether the speaker must merely intend to demean the listener and create such an environment."[67] Although the court could have limited the University's policy to alleviate the ambiguity, such a solution would not have remedied the rule's difficulties with regard to overbreadth. Accordingly, Judge Warren found that the University of Wisconsin's policy violated the overbreadth doctrine and was unduly vague, in violation of the First Amendment.

What both the University of Michigan and the University of Wisconsin's anti-discrimination policies had in common was that they were content-based regulations that selectively proscribed speech on the basis of specific characteristics. Both policies suffered similar difficulties inasmuch as neither was sufficiently narrow or precise to encompass only that speech that threatens an imminent breach of the peace. In both instances, every single example provided by the two universities in defense of their anti-discrimination policies involved acts of expression or association protected by the First Amendment to some degree—either absolutely or almost so. Since neither university chose to appeal the decision rendered by the respective district courts, the Supreme Court did not consider the question of hate speech regulations until 1992.

R.A.V. V. CITY OF ST. PAUL

The U.S. Supreme Court's entry into the political fray of hate speech codes came in its decision to hear *R.A.V. v. City of St. Paul*. The facts of this case[68] are that Robert Viktora (referred to as R.A.V. by the courts) and several other teenagers assembled a two-foot cross, by taping together broken furniture legs, and wrapped it in terrycloth doused with paint thinner. They then planted the cross inside the fenced yard of Russell and Laura Jones—an African-American couple who, with their five small children, lived across the street from where Viktora was staying—and set it on fire at approximately 2:30 on the morning of 21 June 1990. Although this conduct could have been punished under any of a number of laws (those against, for instance, terroristic threats, arson, or criminal damage to property), one of the two provisions under which the city of St. Paul chose to charge the teenagers was the St. Paul Bias-Motivated Crime Ordinance. This statute provided that "[w]hoever places on public or private property a symbol, object, appellation, characterization or graffiti, including, but not limited to, a burning cross or Nazi swastika, which one knows or has reasonable ground to know arouses anger, alarm, or resentment in others on the basis of race, color, creed, religion, or [sex] commits disorderly conduct and shall be guilty of a misdemeanor."

Arthur M. Miller, one of the teenagers charged along with Viktora, was sentenced to thirty days in jail after pleading guilty, but Viktora moved to have his own charges dismissed. He argued that the St. Paul ordinance was substantially overbroad and impermissibly content-based, and thus facially invalid under the First Amendment.[69] The trial court granted his motion, but the Minnesota Supreme Court reversed that ruling. Viktora then appealed to the U.S. Supreme Court which, agreeing with the trial court, unanimously ruled that the St. Paul Biased-Motivated Crime Ordinance was unconstitutional. The justices vigorously disagreed, however, as to why the ordinance violated the First Amendment. While Justice Scalia, writing for a five-judge majority,[70] accepted the Minnesota Supreme Court's narrowing of the ordinance to "reach only those expression that constitute 'fighting words' within the meaning of *Chaplinsky,*"[71] he argued that the statute was facially unconstitutional because "it prohibits otherwise permitted speech solely on the basis of the subjects the speech addresses."[72] Not only did the ordinance restrict speech on the basis of its content, but it also limited speech in a viewpoint-discriminatory manner—it regulated the use of fighting words on the basis of the government's approval or disapproval of the underlying message expressed by the speaker.[73] Justices White, Blackmun, O'Connor, and Stevens, joining for the minority concurrences, countered that the St. Paul statute was fatally overbroad because it criminalized both unprotected and protected expression.[74]

According to Justice Scalia, while a limited category of speech "may be regulated *because of their constitutionally proscribable content* (obscenity, defamation, etc.),"[75] these categories of speech are not "entirely invisible to the Constitution, so that they may be made the vehicles for content discrimination unrelated to their distinctively proscribable content."[76] Under the categorical approach, upon which both courts relied in *Doe* and in *UWM Post*, restrictions on speech must be content-neutral even in those areas believed to be "of such slight social value as a step to truth that any benefit that may be derived from them is clearly outweighed by the social interest in order and morality."[77] Based on this conception of the categorical approach, Justice Scalia stated that the reason fighting words are excluded from First Amendment protection, notwithstanding their expressive content, is that "the unprotected features of the words are, despite their verbal character, essentially a 'nonspeech' element of communication."[78] By characterizing fighting words in this manner, Justice Scalia was at odds with the concurring justices, who defined fighting words as words intended to provoke violence and inflict injury.[79]

In answer to the accusations of the concurring justices[80] that he was setting forth a new First Amendment principle on underinclusiveness[81] and endorsing an "all or nothing" approach to content discrimination,[82] Justice Scalia asserted that while a state may not prohibit constitutionally proscribable speech based on content under the First Amendment, this limitation is not absolute.[83] In fact, he identifies three exceptions to the prohibition. The first is "[w]hen the basis for the content discrimination consists entirely of the very reason the entire class of speech at issue is proscribable."[84] The second exception occurs when "the subclass [of proscribable speech] happens to be associated with particular 'secondary effects' of the speech, so that the regulation is *justified* without reference to the content of the . . . speech,' "[85] or "when a particular content-based subcategory of a proscribable class of speech can be swept up incidentally within the reach of a statute directed at conduct rather than speech."[86] The third exception arises when "the nature of the content discrimination is such that there is no realistic possibility that official suppression of ideas is afoot."[87]

Justice Scalia, without adequately explaining how or why,[88] concludes that because the St. Paul ordinance failed to fit into these exceptions it was unconstitutional. He maintains that while the Bias Motivated Crime Ordinance proscribes all fighting words based on race, color, creed, religion, or sex, regardless of whether they are threatening or merely obnoxious, it permitted abusive invectives that threaten individuals based on unprotected characteristics.[89] This selectivity created the possibility that the government was seeking to silence speech on the basis of its content.[90] Under such circumstances, the St. Paul ordinance "goes even beyond mere content discrimination, to actual viewpoint discrimination."[91]

Justice Scalia further argued that the government's desire, to communicate to individuals or groups who are particularly vulnerable to victimization that the majority does not condone the "group hatred" aspect of a speaker's fighting words, is unjustifiable.[92] In his opinion, the effect hate speech has on listeners is not a "secondary effect" of the type the Court had referred to in *Renton v. Playtime Theatres, Inc.*[93] Moreover, even though the state interests promoted by the ordinance were compelling, according to Justice Scalia, the danger of censorship requires that the government meet a more stringent test—"that [the content discrimination] . . . be employed [only] where it is 'necessary to serve the asserted [compelling] interest.' "94 Since content-neutral alternatives exist by which the government can achieve it objectives, Justice Scalia refused to uphold the Minnesota Supreme Court's ruling based on either overbreadth or strict scrutiny.

The concurring justices vehemently disagreed with Justice Scalia's reasoning. In their opinion, his reasoning "disregards two established principles of First Amendment law [the categorical approach and strict scrutiny] without providing a coherent replacement theory."95 By so doing, Justice Scalia had inexplicably turned "First Amendment law on its head,"96 even as he tried to salvage his argument regarding the First Amendment's prohibition on content-based discrimination. Yet, in the concurring justices' view, there were several major flaws in Justice Scalia's argument.

One problem with his argument was that he necessitated an "all or nothing" approach to fighting words,97 which, as Justice White pointed out, meant that "[s]hould the government want to criminalize certain fighting words, the Court now requires it to criminalize all fighting words."98 In Justice White's opinion, it was inconsistent to maintain that the government can proscribe an entire category of speech but cannot proscribe a subset of that category without violating the First Amendment: if the content of the entire category is worthless, then the "content of the subset is by definition worthless and undeserving of constitutional protection."99 For Justice Scalia seriously to hold such a position, in Justice White's view, conflicted with common sense100 and violated precedent by a renunciation of strict scrutiny in favor of doctrinal revisionism.

Justice White noted that even though the majority conceded that the state interest promoted by the ordinance is compelling, Justice Scalia "treats strict scrutiny analysis as irrelevant to the constitutionality of the legislation,"101 contrary to the Court's plurality decision in *Burson v. Freeman,*102 reached one month prior to the Court's *R.A.V.* decision. In *Burson,* wherein the issue was the constitutionality of a content-based statute (which only prohibited political speech, by banning the solicitation of votes and the display or distribution of campaign materials within one hundredfeet of the entrance to a polling place)103 Justice White declared that "seven of the eight participating members of the Court agreed that the strict scrutiny standard applied."104 The dissenting justices in *Burson* had complained not that the plurality applied strict scrutiny but that they felt the plurality was not rigorous enough in its review.105 On the basis of *Burson,* Justice White found puzzling Justice

Scalia's invalidation of the St. Paul ordinance on the grounds that the statute could have been drafted in broader, content-neutral terms. Justice Scalia's alteration of the strict scrutiny test through the addition of the necessity prong, as Justice White made clear, prevented "a narrowly drawn, content-based ordinance [from ever passing] constitutional muster if the object of that legislation could be accomplished by banning a wider category of speech."[106]

Justice Scalia might have countered Justice White's criticism by observing that he did not totally reject the utilization of strict scrutiny analysis when evaluating content-based discrimination. Rather, he merely heightened the requirements of strict scrutiny when legislators attempt to silence the expression of specific messages.[107] Thus, he might have argued, his decision in *R.A.V.* was consistent with his concurrence in *Burson*, wherein he held that the challenged statute "though content-based, is constitutional [as] a reasonable, viewpoint-neutral regulation of a nonpublic forum."[108] While he willingly admitted that presumptive invalidity is not synonymous with invariable invalidity, as an explanation of his *Burson* concurrence,[109] he dismissed the validity of the "revolutionary proposition that the suppression of particular ideas can be justified when only those ideas have been a source of trouble in the past."[110]

To accept that Justice Scalia was merely employing a heightened form of strict scrutiny in *R.A.V.* because viewpoint-based discrimination was at issue, which had been unnecessary in *Burson* because the statute was viewpoint neutral, becomes problematic in light of his position in *Rust v. Sullivan*. In this 5–4 decision, in which he joined with Chief Justice Rehnquist (who wrote the opinion) and Justices Kennedy, Souter, and White, Justice Scalia voted to uphold a "gag rule" that prohibited clinics receiving federal funds from counseling pregnant women about abortions or even broaching the subject. As Justice Brennan noted in his dissenting opinion, the "gag rule" amounted to a content- and viewpoint-based restriction on the free speech rights of both the doctor and the patient, by impermissibly "manipulating the content of the doctor/patient dialogue."[111]

But even if one overlooks Justice Scalia's stance in *Rust*, Justice White might submit that all Justice Scalia has proven by his decision in *R.A.V.*, versus *Burson*, is that he places fighting words on the same constitutional level as political discourse, thereby devaluing the latter category.[112] Justice Stevens would argue that Justice Scalia's elevation of fighting words, through his "arid, doctrinaire interpretation,"[113] entitles them to more protection than either commercial speech or possibly even core political speech.[114] As a result Justice Scalia merely "obscures the line between speech that could be regulated freely on the basis of content (i.e., the narrow categories of expression falling outside the First Amendment) and that which could be regulated on the basis of content only upon a showing of a compelling state interest (i.e., all remaining expression)."[115]

By revising the categorical approach, Justice Scalia managed to avoid the consequences of his own analysis, according to Justice White. Justice Blackmun, on the other hand, believes that Justice Scalia's abandonment of the categorical approach enabled him to manipulate doctrine in order to strike down an ordinance he specifically opposed. In Justice Blackmun's view, Justice Scalia's invalidation of the St. Paul ordinance offers an example of the Court being "distracted from its proper mission by the temptation to decide the issue over 'politically correct speech' and 'cultural diversity.' "[116] The end result of his dismissal of the traditional categorical approach, as Justice Stevens pointed out, is that the Court "wreaks havoc in an area of settled law."[117]

In an attempt to stave off the criticisms levied by the concurring justices regarding his revision of the categorical approach, Justice Scalia offered three exceptions for permissible content discrimination within proscribable categories.[118] His *ad hoc* limitations, however, cannot withstand the concurring Justices' scrutiny nor adequately justify his conclusion that the St. Paul ordinance was unconstitutional because it fell outside all of his exceptions. For instance, the example Justice Scalia relied upon to validate his first exception was the right of the federal government to "criminalize only those threats of violence that are directed against the President . . . since the reasons why threats of violence are outside the First Amendment . . . have special force when applied against the President."[119] What he fails to explain, however, is how the "special force" component for prohibiting violent threats against the president "consists entirely of the very reason the entire class of speech is proscribable," when threats against other (either government or non-government) persons are not included in this exception. Justice Scalia might argue that if the president is threatened, the security of the nation as a whole is jeopardized and thus, at least symbolically, a threat directed at the president is a threat against society as a whole. Since placing threats of violence outside the First Amendment protects individuals from the fear of violence, from the disruption that such fear engenders, and from the possibility that the threatened violence will occur, the magnitude of such fears is greater when the threat is directed against the entire nation than when it is directed against a single individual or even a single group.

However, if Justice Scalia's argument is required to fit the parameters he himself has dictated, then his exception violates his own rule. Under his heightened strict scrutiny test, threats against the president are no more severe than threats against any other person within society. By establishing a regulation which targets only threats against the president, Justice Scalia's test violates the requirement that not only must the regulation be narrowly tailored to serve compelling state interests but that the regulation must also be necessary to the asserted state interest. Although proscribing threats against the president may serve the compelling government interest of protecting society from the fear of violence that threats against the president might engender, such a regulation is unnecessary, since the same compelling government interest could be achieved by enacting a statute proscribing all threats against all persons within society regardless of their relationship to the government. Justice Scalia fails to explain as well why threats of violence against the president entail more severe consequences than threats against individuals or groups who historically have been subjected to discrimination.[120]

As Justice Stevens correctly understands, "[j]ust as Congress may determine that threats against the President may entail more severe consequences than other threats, so St. Paul's City Council may determine that threats based on the target's race, religion, or [sex] cause more severe harm to both the target and to society than other threats."[121] Justice White substantiates this observation. He notes that the reason fighting words are outside the First Amendment's protection is that the fear of violence—which results from the disruption that such fear engenders and from the possibility that the violence will occur—carries a special force of magnitude when the threat is directed against individuals or groups who have been historically subjected to discrimination within society. Indeed, threats of violence against historically subjugated individuals or groups place the stability of the entire nation at risk.[122] Fighting words based on race, color, creed, religion, or sex carry "special force" when flung in the face of a individual(s) who claims membership in one (or more) of these groups. Contrary to the majority's suggestion that fighting words are "simply a mode of communication,"[123] they are in fact a content-based category which bans "a class of speech that conveys an overriding message of personal injury and imminent violence."[124]

Justice Scalia contends as well that under his first exception, while "[a] State might choose to prohibit only that obscenity which is the most patently offensive in its prurience . . . it may not prohibit . . . only that obscenity which includes offensive political messages."[125] The validity of his example, however, is questionable under the obscenity standard established in *Miller v. California*: "to be obscene, expression must be found by the trier of fact 'to appeal to the prurient interest, . . . depict or describe, in a patently offensive way, sexual conduct, and taken as a whole, lack serious literary, artistic, political or scientific value.' "[126] As Justice Stevens accurately states, obscene anti-government messages are an oxymoron—if they are anti-government, by definition they cannot lack serious political value and thus they cannot be obscene.[127]

Justice Scalia's example is potentially saved only by his further example of a hard-core pornographic movie containing a model who sports a political tattoo: it could be found to lack serious value when considered as a whole.[128] But the conditional qualifier "could be" allows for the contrary possibility as well—the tattoo could be found *not* to lack serious value within the context of the movie as a whole. The determination of the tattoo's "value" would presumably depend upon whether, within the parameters of the entire movie, its message was substantial enough to counterweight the pornographic aspects of the movie and thereby exhibit a "serious literary, artistic, political, or scientific value."

Justice Scalia's second exception fares no better than his first, for St. Paul's statute also falls within its boundaries, due to the similarity between the ordinance and Title VII.[129] Although Justice Scalia asserts that Title VII is primarily concerned with conduct, with the "secondary effect" of this statute being speech regulation, he overlooks the fact that St. Paul's ordinance also focused primarily on conduct, with a corresponding "secondary effect" on speech.[130] Indeed, as Justice White observed, Title VII and the St. Paul statute both "focus on what the majority would characterize as [a disfavored topic]" as opposed to prohibiting harassment or discrimination generally.[131] If the St. Paul ordinance failed because it concentrates on "messages of bias-motivated hatred,"[132] then Title VII should also be invalid, since according to Justice Scalia it concentrates on "sexually derogatory 'fighting words.' "[133] Indeed, a comparison of the texts of Title VII and the St. Paul Bias-Motivated Crime Ordinance illustrates that the primary difference is the scope of the protection offered by each—Title VII covers only employment discrimination based on race, color, religion, sex, or national origin; whereas the St. Paul ordinance shields against all displays of hatred based on race, color, creed, religion, or sex. With the exception of Title VII omitting creed and the St. Paul statute omitting national origin, the characteristics specified in these two pieces of legislation are identical. There is, of course, the possibility that because Title VII is restricted to workplace environments, the regulation of speech under this statute is analogous to protecting a captive audience. The St. Paul ordinance, on the other hand, restricts discriminatory speech on specific subjects within the entire city and as such does not protect a captive audience. Most individuals are confined to the work environment for a minimum of eight hours a day and cannot leave; most individuals within the city's limits can find refuge even if they do not leave the city by averting their eyes or by leaving the immediate area where the expression is occurring.[134] While Title VII might operate as a time, place, and manner restriction, the St. Paul ordinance has no such constraints. Finally, a further distinction between Title VII and the St. Paul statute is that the primary emphasis of Title VII is deemed to be conduct, while that of the St. Paul ordinance is expression.

Justice Scalia's final exception also fails to exclude the St. Paul ordinance from its boundaries. Since the fighting words proscribed by the statute are not (fully) protected by the First Amendment, their regulation is guided by the Fourteenth Amendment's Equal Protection Clause.[135] The statute's proscription of an explicit subset of fighting words, according to the minority concurrences,"reflects the City's judgment that harms based on race, color creed, religion, or [sex] are more pressing public concerns than the harms caused by other fighting words. In light of our Nation's long and painful experience with discrimination, this determination is plainly reasonable. Indeed, as the majority concedes, the interest is compelling."[136]

Even if one were to grant the validity of Justice Scalia's example (i.e., that there may be no First Amendment interest that would stand in the way of a state's prohibiting only those obscene motion pictures with blue-eyed actresses),[137] it would *not* necessitate the conclusion that a First Amendment interest may exist that prevents a state from prohibiting only those fighting words that are "so threatening and so directed at an individual as to 'by [their] very [execution] inflict injury.' "[138] Justice Scalia recognizes, as he must, that "a prohibition of fighting words . . . directed at certain persons or groups . . . would be facially valid."[139] Yet he steadfastly resists the idea Justice Stevens posits, that the ordinance regulates "expressive conduct . . . [which] is no less than . . . the first step in an act of assault . . . perhaps the ultimate expression of 'fighting words.' "[140]

If Justice Scalia insists that his exceptions stand without encompassing the St. Paul ordinance,[141] several (unintended) conclusions might conceivably be drawn from the his opinion. First, as Justice White notes, the majority holding would "necessarily signal that expressions of violence, such as the message of intimidation and racial hatred conveyed by burning a cross on someone's lawn, are of sufficient value to outweigh the social interest in order and morality that has traditionally placed such fighting words outside the First Amendment. Indeed, by characterizing fighting words as a form of 'debate' . . . the majority legitimatize hate speech as a form of public discussion."[142] A second possibility, according to Justice Blackmun, is that the majority opinion would be "regarded as an aberration"[143]—since Justice Scalia seemingly goes out of his way to address the issue of "politically correct" speech, rather than merely rest his decision on the traditional argument that "[t]he First Amendment generally prevents government from proscribing speech . . . because of disapproval of the ideas expressed."[144] Because Justice Scalia so disapproves of "political correctness" he may have been more focused on invalidating what appeared to be a "politically correct" statute than on preserving the underlying values of the First Amendment.[145] The final prospect is that the *R.A.V.* ruling would be read as expanding the scope of permissible speech regulations and censorship by the government. Justice Scalia's call for the proscription of all fighting words and of vicious or severe, abusive invectives[146] leaves unanswered how these terms are to be defined and by whom. In addition, his "First Amendment 'absolutism' blurs the line between speech which the government may freely regulate and that which could be regulated on the basis of content only upon a showing of a compelling state interest."[147] It thus raises the specter of sweeping government incursions into areas of speech that heretofore have been protected.

Yet despite these criticisms of Justice Scalia's reasoning for invalidating St. Paul's Bias-Motivated Crime Ordinance, the concurring justices also found the statute to be unconstitutional. They did so not because it utilized a content-or viewpoint-based regulation,[148] since the statute regulated verbal conduct on the basis of that conduct fitting into the unprotected category of "fighting words"[149]—which by definition are (in a sense) "non-speech"—but because the ordinance went beyond the fighting words category by punishing speech 'that by its very utterance' causes 'anger, offense, or resentment.' "[150] By prohibiting such a broad range of expression, the St. Paul ordinance moved "beyond fighting words to speech protected by the First Amendment."[151] As a result, the concurring justices deemed the statute to be constitutionally overbroad.

A major difference between the analyses of the majority and that of the concurring justices seemingly arises from the ideological focal lens informing their judgments—the majority decision reflects a civil libertarian approach, whereas the concurring opinions leans toward an accomodationist position.[152] The majority's standpoint centers on the specific language of the St. Paul Biased-Motivated Crime Statute. Justice Scalia pointed out that even with the Minnesota Supreme Court's narrowed construction of the St. Paul statute, the ordinance still reached only fighting words directed at specific persons or groups that contain bias-motivated messages of hatred based on notions of supremacy. Through this selective limiting of prohibited speech, Justice Scalia maintained, the statute moved beyond content discrimination to actual viewpoint discrimination. Because such censorship is impermissible, he proclaimed that "St. Paul has no such authority to license one side of a debate to fight freestyle, while requiring the other to follow Marquis of Queensbury Rules."[153] Thus, his protest to the contrary,[154] Justice Scalia did embrace an "all or nothing" stance: either all fighting words must be prohibited or none can be proscribed; anything else seemingly endorses content- or viewpoint-based government speech regulations.[155] Consequently, he rejected the constitutionality of the St. Paul ordinance while simultaneously declaring the petitioner's actions to be "reprehensible."[156]

The concurring justices, on the other hand, concentrated on the racial facts of the case. For example, Justice White referred to "the message of intimidation and racial hatred conveyed by burning a cross on someone's lawn,"[157] to "our Nation's long and painful experience with discrimination,"[158] and to "a message that is at its ugliest when directed against groups that have long been the targets of discrimination;"[159] while Justice Blackmun referenced the "racial threats and verbal assaults"[160] and the "race-based fighting words."[161] From Justice Blackmun's vantage point, he saw "no First Amendment values that are compromised by a law that prohibits hoodlums from driving minorities out of their homes by burning crosses on their lawns, but I see great harm in preventing the people of St. Paul from specifically punishing the race-based fighting words that so prejudice their community."[162] In a similar fashion, Justice Stevens concentrated on the fact that it seemed eminently reasonable and realistic on the part of St. Paul to believe that "harms caused by racial, religious, and [sex]-based invective are qualitatively different from that caused by other fighting words."[163] In his opinion, "[t]he cross-burning in this case—directed as it was to a single African-American family trapped in their home—was nothing more than a crude form of physical intimidation."[164]

Throughout their evaluation of the Bias-Motivated Crime Ordinance's legitimacy, the concurring justices stress the importance of the civility (or lack thereof) of the discourse rather than the content of the message. For Justice Blackmun, no First Amendment values are compromised when a state regulates the form a message may take when the state is attempting to stop the use of hate-based fighting words intended to drive minorities from their homes.[165] Justice Stevens agreed with this sentiment. In his view, "conduct that creates special risks or causes special harms may be prohibited by special rules."[166] Indeed, in the opinion of all the concurring justices, St. Paul's statute was comparable to Title VII, since both extended anti-discrimination protection to minorities. Moreover, as Justice Stevens accurately declared, the St. Paul ordinance did not prevent individuals from espousing their beliefs about racial supremacy or from burning crosses or displaying swastikas—provided that these opinions were expressed in a manner that "is not so threatening and so directed at an individual as to 'by its very (execution) inflict injury.' "[167]

Justice Stevens is the only concurring justice who directly addressed Justice Scalia's charge that the statute manifested viewpoint discrimination. Contrary to Justice Scalia's position, Justice Stevens asserted that

[t]he St. Paul ordinance is evenhanded. In a battle between advocates of tolerance and advocates of intolerance, the ordinance does not prevent either side from hurling fighting words at the other on the basis of their conflicting ideas, but it does bar both sides from hurling such words on the basis of the target's "race, creed, religion, or [sex]." To extend the Court's pugilistic metaphor, the St. Paul ordinance simply banned punches "below the belt"—by either party. It did not favor one side of any debate.[168]

Moreover, Justice Stevens's denial that viewpoint discrimination was at the heart of the St. Paul ordinance highlights a major difference between his and Justice Scalia's perspective of the statute. For Justice Stevens, the statute "regulates speech not on the basis of its subject matter or the viewpoint expressed, but rather on the basis of the harm the speech causes."[169] Thus, contrary to the majority's assertion, all the ordinance regulated was a subcategory of expression that causes injury based on specific characteristics; it did not regulate a subcategory of expression that involves discussions concerning those specific characteristics.[170] Justice Scalia, however, accused Justice Stevens of engaging in "word-play." In his view, "nothing makes anger, fear, sense of dishonor, etc., produced by violation of this ordinance distinct from the anger, fear, sense of dishonor, etc., produced by other fighting words [except] . . . that it is caused by a distinctive idea, conveyed by a distinctive message."[171] Agreement between these two justices is not likely as long as one (Justice Stevens) focuses on the fact that the expression regulated by the statute primarily conveys an emotion of hatred without any (or at least very little) "exposition of ideas,"[172] while the other (Justice Scalia) focus on the fact that the expression regulated by the statute primarily conveys "the intellectual message of 'bias motivated' hatred and in particular, as applied in this case, a message 'based on virulent notions of racial supremacy.' "[173]

The majority opinion in *R.A.V.*, rather than the concurring opinions, is the logical extension of the arguments articulated by the district courts in *Doe* and *UWM Post*. All three courts are in agreement that neither the government nor an agent of the government (such as public universities) can differentiate on the basis of expressive content. If fighting words are to be banned, the legal sanctions must apply in every individual case, not just in those cases where the fighting words are based on characteristics mentioned within a specific statute. The unwillingness of the courts to distinguish between speech and conduct in these three cases is not absolute, however, as demonstrated by a Supreme Court decision one year after it delivered its *R.A.V.* decision in *Wisconsin v. Mitchell.*

WISCONSIN V. MITCHELL

Todd Mitchell, an African-American male, was convicted for aggravated battering of a Caucasian male. Ordinarily, the maximum imprisonment for an individual sentenced in Wisconsin for this crime is two years. However, because the jury concluded that Mitchell had intentionally selected his victim on the basis of the victim's race, the maximum possible sentence was seven years. Sentenced to four year in prison, Mitchell sought post-conviction relief. When it was denied to him, he appealed his conviction and sentence. He challenged the constitutionality of Wisconsin Statute §939.645(1)(b), which provided that the penalties for a crime are increased if an individual "[i]ntentionally selects the person against whom the crime . . . is committed or selects the property which is damaged or otherwise affected by the crime . . . because of the race, religion, color, disability, sexual orientation, national origin, or ancestry of that person or the owner or occupant of that property."[174] He maintained that the provisions of §939.645(1)(b) violated his First Amendment rights on the ground that the sentence-enhancement statute punished what the legislature deemed to be offensive thoughts. He further claimed that the statute was overbroad, because it permitted the evidentiary use of a person's prior speech, thereby having a chilling effect through fear of prosecution for offenses on the basis of that speech through the penalty-enhancement statute.

The State Court of Appeals rejected Mitchell's challenge regarding the constitutionality of the statute, but the Wisconsin Supreme Court ruled in his favor. Relying on the U.S. Supreme Court's decision in *R.A.V.*, the Wisconsin Supreme Court concluded that through the penalty-enhancement statute the state punished an individual's subjective mental processes. It thus rejected the state's position that the statute punished only the conduct of the intentional selection of a victim. As the Wisconsin Supreme Court pointed out, "the statute punishes the 'because of' aspect of the defendant's selection, the *reason* the defendant selected the victim, the *motive* behind the selection."[175] In its opinion, the legislature is forbidden under *R.A.V.* to criminalize bigoted thought with which it disagrees. Moreover, the Wisconsin Supreme Court found the statute to be unconstitutionally overbroad, because proof of the motive for selecting a particular victim required the state to introduce the defendant's speech uttered prior to the commission of the crime.

The question the U.S. Supreme Court addressed was whether the First Amendment prohibited the state from punishing conduct motivated by animosity based on a protected status more severely than conduct motivated by animosity based on an unprotected status or by no reason at all.[176] Justice Rehnquist, who wrote the unanimous opinion, necessarily distinguished between speech and conduct to explain why he believed the Wisconsin Supreme Court misinterpreted the *R.A.V.* decision. He began the decision in *Mitchell* by noting that "however obnoxious to most people, [a defendant's abstract beliefs] may be taken into consideration by a sentencing judge."[177] As Justice Rehnquist stated, referring to *Dawson v. Delaware*, there exists no *per se* barrier to the admission of evidence concerning an individual's beliefs or associations, at the sentencing phase of the judicial process, merely because such beliefs or associations are protected by the First Amendment.[178] He also noted that in *Barclay v. Florida* the Court had permitted a sentencing judge to take into consideration the beliefs and associations of the defendant because they were pertinent to the crime of which he had been convicted.[179]

Justice Rehnquist rejected Mitchell's contention that *Dawson* and *Barclay* were not applicable to his situation since neither case had involved a penalty-enhancement statute. He asserted that these cases were relevant, because they established the proposition that the legislature may validly require judges to consider bias-motivated beliefs and associations where the circumstances are such that they are relevant to the commission of a crime.[180] Indeed, he argued motive serves the same function in penalty-enhancement statutes that it does in anti-discrimination laws, which the Court consistently upholds against constitutional challenges—both types of laws are permissible content-neutral regulations of conduct.

Justice Rehnquist further denied the validity of Mitchell's assertion that penalty-enhancement statutes are targeted against bigoted thought as opposed to conduct. While he acknowledged that there are some forms of conduct which can be labeled "speech," since it is through conduct that one may express certain ideas, he stated that not all varieties of conduct constitute "speech." He reiterated the Court's finding in *Roberts v. United States Jaycees* that "violence or other types of potentially expressive activities that produce special harms distinct from their communicative impact . . . are entitled to no constitutional protection."[181] Because he considered the Wisconsin statute to be aimed at conduct, rather than speech, that the legislature believes inflicts greater individual and social harms than other types of conduct, Justice Rehnquist disagreed with the Wisconsin Supreme Court's conclusion that the U.S. Supreme Court's decision in *R.A.V.* necessitated the rejection of Wisconsin's penalty-enhancement statute. As Justice Rehnquist clearly stated, "[n]othing in our decision last Term in *R.A.V.* compels a different result here. . . . Because the ordinance [in *R.A.V.*] only proscribed a class of 'fighting words' deemed particularly offensive by the city . . . we held that it violated the rule against content-based discrimination. . . . But whereas the ordinance struck down in *R.A.V.* was explicitly directed at expression . . . the statute in this case is aimed at conduct unprotected by the First Amendment."[182]

With regard to Mitchell's overbreadth challenge, Justice Rehnquist asserted that the potential chilling effect that the penalty-enhancement statute might have had on speech was so "attenuated and unlikely" that it was simply too speculative to support Mitchell's argument. Consequently, the U.S. Supreme Court held that Wisconsin's penalty-enhancement statute neither violated Mitchell's First Amendment rights nor had a chilling effect on free speech. Under the First Amendment, admissions of previous declarations or statements to establish the elements of a crime or to prove motive or intent was permitted "subject to the evidentiary rules of relevancy, reliability, and the like."[183]

Although Justice Rehnquist distinguished the law that was invalidated in *R.A.V.* from the one upheld in *Mitchell*, the distinction between the two laws seems contrived. It could be argued that a Caucasian male burning a cross on the lawn of an African-American family is as much an act of conduct as an African-American male beating up a Caucasian male is an act of conduct. Indeed, just as the actions of the Caucasian male in *R.A.V.* cannot be understood as an invitation to the African-American family to participate in a dialogue or an exchange of ideas with the cross burner, so the actions of the African-American male in *Mitchell* cannot be understood as an invitation to the Caucasian male to participate in a dialogue or an exchange of ideas with his attacker. Conversely, the burning of a cross on the lawn of an African-American family is as much an expression of racial animus by the Caucasian male in *R.A.V.* as the beating of a Caucasian male is an expression of racial animus by an African-American male in *Mitchell*. Based on the facts of these two cases, it seems clear that neither of the two males who were arrested would have engaged in their respective activities if not for the race of the victim each selected.

It is only if one insists that the St. Paul Bias-Motivated Crime Ordinance emphasized symbolic speech while the Wisconsin Penalty Enhancement Statute underscored criminal activity, and one ignores the conduct aspect of

St. Paul's ordinance and the thought-control aspect of Wisconsin's statute, that the distinction between these two laws is as clear as Justice Rehnquist indicates in *Mitchell.* The laws at issue in *R.A.V.* and *Mitchell* are similar inasmuch as they are both content-based, despite the Court's suggestion to the contrary—they focus on discrimination based on a set of protected characteristics listed by the legislators. A difference between these two laws, however, is that the former proscribes speech outside the parameters of the fighting words doctrine, while the latter does not. The Court's determination of the statute's operative effect—whether the Court defines the statute as primarily governing hate speech or hate crimes—defines the focal lens it utilizes for weighing the degree to which the law infringes the First Amendment rights of the defendant. In instances when the Court focuses on the speech underlying the bias-motivated conduct, it provides an expansive reading of the First Amendment that requires the government to prove that its compelling interest can *only* be achieved by employing content discrimination—as demonstrated in *R.A.V.*[184] But when the Court focuses on the behavior arising from bias-motivated beliefs, it uses a narrow reading of the First Amendment that permits the government to stress the consequences of the conduct at issue—as demonstrated in *Mitchell.*[185] The aim ascribed to the regulation by the Court—whether it views the law as being directed primarily at speech or at conduct—determines the degree of risk to *sex/gender outsiders* posed by its enforcement. But regardless whether laws similar to the St. Paul Bias-Motivated Crime Ordinance (in an expanded version that includes gender identity and affectional orientation/preference within its protected categories) or ones similar to the Wisconsin penalty enhancement statute are used as models, the problems encountered by lesbians, gay men, bisexuals, and transgenderists are not eliminated.

While a broad consensus against racist and sexist speech may arguably exist in this country, the same is not true with regard to heterosexist/homophobic speech. As Toni M. Massaro accurately states, "[heterosexist/]homophobic speech is often unacknowledged as such, even by otherwise 'politically correct' people."[186] Slurs against *sex/gender outsiders* are so habitual in our society[187] that the usage of many vile and derogatory words has "degenerate[d] to a widespread, thoughtless activity," according to Penelope.[188] Verbal bigotry against *sex/gender outsiders* may be unrecognized as such even by those who "have themselves adopted and endorsed opprobrium toward [lesbians, gay men, bisexuals, and transgenderists] and used that opprobrium as a justification for denying any [legal] redress," according to SeLegue.[189] As a result, the harms suffered by *sex/gender outsiders* who are subjected to these heinous and vicious words are frequently ignored, merely because, in Justice Maddox's words, they "have been used for a long time by those outside of the community."[190]

Under such circumstances, *sex/gender outsiders* assume a disproportionate share of the costs associated with securing protection—the liberty of lesbians, gay men, bisexuals, and transgenderists is curtailed, in an attempt to avoid a hate speaker's verbal assault, by "choosing" to alter the patterns of one's life. Each "choice" made to avoid confrontation, however, results in further constrictions on the zones of safety available until, as Toni M. Masarro reports, "the lives of potential targets of bigotry become more stunted and unnatural. . . . Fear of verbal harassment, no less than fear of physical assault, may change one's work patterns, jogging paths, choice of evening entertainment, and social patterns."[191] As a means of self-defense, *sex/gender outsiders*, like any individuals or groups who are targets of verbal abuse or intimidation—even if not directed at them personally—adopt a strategy of avoiding situations or occasions where they might be vulnerable to such attacks. Consequently, their daily activities become restricted in order to facilitate their own safety and circumvent abuse.[192]

The perception that lesbians, gay men, bisexuals, and transgenderists are appropriate targets of abuse is communicated through a variety of instruments. Marshall Kirk and Hunter Madsen identify a subtle conveyance of this tenet in a seemingly innocuous commercial:

The Kellogg Company launched a cereal named Nut and Honey Crunch in 1987, with the help of a TV advertising campaign. The commercials played off the social mischief that might arise when one fellow asks another what's for breakfast, and he seems to reply, "Nuttin' honey." In one vignette, a sheepish soldier is compelled to reply "Nuttin', honey" to a sneering sergeant. In another, a chuckwagon cook finds himself making the same reply to a surrounding gang of cowpokes, who react with displeasure and immediately draw their pistols.[193]

While the ad is intended to be amusing, Kirk and Madsen indicate that the not-so-humorous aspect of this commercial is what it teaches the audience: "the proper way to react to apparent homosexuals—with contempt and, if necessary, violence."[194]

A more overt form of this message is provided in the Doctrinal Congregation's Letter to Bishops.[195] Cardinal Joseph Ratzinger and Archbishop Alberto Bovone, the signatories of a Vatican-approved letter dated 1 October 1986, began by expressing benevolent sentiments: "It is deplorable that homosexual persons have been and are the object of violent malice in speech or in action. Such treatment deserves condemnation from the church's pastors wherever it occurs. It reveals a kind of disregard for others which endangers the most fundamental principles of a healthy society. The intrinsic dignity of each person must always be respected in word, in action, and in law."[196] Their compassion, however, perceptibly evaporated in their next set of remarks. In statements which are commonly interpreted as condoning violence against *sex/gender outsiders*, but which do not fall within the fighting words doctrine, the two representatives of Pope John Paul II made it clear that "the proper reaction to crimes committed against homosexual persons should not be to claim that the homosexual condition is not disordered. When such a claim is made and when homosexual activity is consequently condoned or *when civil legislation is introduced to protect behavior to which no one has any conceivable right, neither the church nor society at large should be surprised when other distorted notions and practices gain ground, and irrational and violent reactions increase.*"[197] This position was repeated verbatim six years later by Jaquin Navarro-Valls, a Vatican spokesman.[198] After reiterating his predecessors' comments, he asserted four paragraphs later, that " '[s]exual orientation' does not constitute a quality comparable to race, ethnic background, etc., in respect to non-discrimination. Unlike these, homosexual orientation is an objective disorder . . . and evokes moral concern. . . . Homosexual persons, as human persons, have the same rights as all persons . . . [but] these rights are not absolute. They can be legitimately limited for objectively disordered external conduct. This is sometimes not only licit but obligatory."[199]

A much more blatant procedure for transmitting societal tolerance for the systematic abuse of *sex/gender outsiders* is achieved through executive policies (e.g., President Clinton's "Don't Ask, Don't Tell" military policy), legislative statutes (e.g., the "Defense of Marriage Act," Colorado's "Amendment 2," the NEA's "Helms Amendment," solicitation and sodomy laws, or the Hate Crimes Statistics Act), and judicial decisions (e.g., *Hardwick, Kirpatrick,* and *Rowland*). Each of these forums provide a channel for disseminating official pronouncements regarding the degree of stigma, dehumanization, and abuse the government authorizes, directly and indirectly, with respect to citizens who are, or are presumed to be, *sex/gender outsiders.* Each informs members of the dominant culture of the relative value the government attaches to the lives of lesbians, gay men, bisexuals, and transgenderists. Each discloses which rights, liberties, and privileges can be denied or abridged with virtual impunity. The success of the government's message is reflected by the results obtained from 2,823 surveyed New York high school students, as documented in the Governor's Task Force on Bias-Related Violence:

One of the most important findings in the youth survey is the openness with which the respondents expressed their aversion and hostility toward [*sex/gender outsiders*]. While racism and ethnocentrism were found to be very much alive among the youth of New York it was rarely openly advocated. The young people are aware that bias based on race and ethnicity can no longer be overtly condoned. There is no such awareness concerning the rights of [*sex/gender outsiders*] and the students were quite emphatic about their dislike for these groups and frequently made violent, threatening statements. [*Sex/gender outsiders*], it seems, are perceived as legitimate targets which can be openly attacked. This is an attitude which draws strength from the example set by all the major social institutions which continue to deny [*sex/gender outsiders*] the status of equals.[200]

It is within the political and legal environment created by the ubiquitous messages communicated by numerous political and social leaders that *sex/gender outsiders* "choose" their strategies for avoiding confrontations and verbal abuse. As lesbians, gay men, bisexuals, and transgenderists navigate the treacherous atmosphere that imperils their safety, they receive very little assistance from the government, especially at the federal level. No respite from harassment or attack is found in the equality or anti-discrimination principles of Title VII and the Equal Protection Clause for *sex/gender outsiders*. These legal principles identify certain attributes that require special protection from discrimination,[201] but gender identity and affectional orientation/preference are not among them. When the very reason for discrimination is gender identity or affectional orientation/preference, the equality and anti-discrimination principles are deemed non-applicable or rendered silent through judicial interpretation.

Thus, protection for *sex/gender outsiders* from fighting words may come cloaked not in Queensbury's Rules for fair fighting (as both Justices Scalia and Stevens demand of the St. Paul statute) but in Wilde's rule of self-defense[202]—"shoot at sight" hate speech attackers and their cohorts with counterspeech. But one cannot underestimate the dangers associated with counter-speech. Perpetrators habitually perceive counter-speech as an "invitation" to escalated abuse, in the form of physical threat or death, as documented in the reports of *sex/gender outsiders* who have been vilified through innuendo and directly attack.[203] Under such circumstances, lesbians, gay men, bisexuals, and transgenderists can be, and are, silenced by hate speech and thereby denied full participation in society.[204] When the primary purpose of hate speech, at its most vicious, is to rend or flay the listener's soul rather than to engage in dialogue or exchange information and ideas, ferocity is a key element.

It is at the point where the speech is manifested as physical conduct that penalty-enhancement statutes, such as the one enacted by Wisconsin, become relevant. These types of statutes, as Justice Rehnquist noted in *Mitchell*, accord special recognition to crimes motivated by animosity based on a protected status viewing them more severely than crimes motivated by animosity based on an unprotected status or nothing at all.[205] While such laws might level the power imbalances that prevent neutral criminal statutes from being enforced impartially, they fail to address the underlying social conditions that produce the violence against *sex/gender outsiders* initially.[206] At most, such laws make it possible that criminal laws will be rigorously enforced against an attacker whenever lesbians, gay men, bisexuals, or transgenderists are attacked because of their gender identity or affectional orientation/preference. As Ruthann Robson accurately notes, "hate is usually not against any rule of law, . . . [and] a crime is a crime regardless of the hate."[207] It should be remembered, however, that in its analysis and validation of Wisconsin's penalty enhancement statute the Supreme Court granted the legislature the right to determine what crimes require special protection. Unlike its ruling in *R.A.V.*, the Court in *Mitchell* approved a statute in which only a class of bias-inspired conduct was protected, rather than requiring the legislature to develop a content-neutral statute. Thus, there is no guarantee that *sex/gender outsiders* will be covered by a particular penalty-enhancement statute.

NOTES

1. *Chaplinsky* at 574.
2. *Doe* (1989) at 856.
3. *Id.*
4. Biopsychology is a field of study which stipulates that the differences between sexes and among racial groups are biologically based [*Doe* (1989) at 860].
5. *Doe* (1989) at 861.
6. *Id.* at 861–862.
7. The standard for such torts is that "one who by extreme and outrageous conduct intentionally or recklessly causes severe emotional distress to another is subject to liability for such emotional distress." See: *Hustler Magazine* (1988); *Ledsiner* (1982); *Dominguez* (1981).
8. *Doe* (1989) at 862–863.
9. *Id.* at 863.
10. *Id.*
11. *Id.* at 860.
12. *Id.* at 864.
13. *Id.* at 865.
14. *Id.*

15. *Id.* at 866.

16. *Id.*

17. *Id.*

18. See: *Broadrick* at 607.

19. "Any behavior, verbal or physical, that stigmatizes or victimizes an individual on the basis of race, ethnicity, religion, sex, sexual orientation, creed, national origin, ancestry, age, marital status, handicap or Vietnam-era veteran status" [*Doe* (1989) at 856].

20. Any behavior, verbal or physical, that "(a) [i]nvolves an express or implied threat to an individual's academic efforts, employment, participation in University sponsored extra-curricular activities or personal safety; or (b) [h]as the purpose or reasonably foreseeable effect of interfering with an individual's academic efforts, employment, participation in University sponsored extra-curricular activities or personal safety; or (c) [c]reates an intimidating, hostile, or demeaning environment for educational pursuits, employment or participation in University sponsored extra-curricular activities" [*Id.* at 856].

21. *Id.* at 867.

22. Justice of the Michigan Supreme Court and professor of law at the University's Law School in the Nineteenth century.

23. Cooley (1972), as quoted in *Doe* (1989) at 869.

24. Matsuda (1989).

25. *Doe* (1989) at 869 fn.*.

26. *Id.* at 869.

27. *Id.*

28. *Id.* at 853, quoting from Lee Bollinger, *The Tolerant Society* (1986) at 78.

29. *Id.* at 868, from C. Vann Woodward, *New York Times* (22 September 1986) at B4.

30. *Id.* at 869 from Cooley (1972).

31. Matsuda (1989) at 2370–2371.

32. *Doe* (1989) at 863.

33. Matsuda (1989) at 2370–2371.

34. *Id.* at 2357.

35. *Id.*

36. *Id.* at 2358.

37. *Id.* at 2366, 2367.

38. *Id.* at 2366.

39. *Id.* at 2332.

40. *Id.* at 2359.

41. *Id.*

42. *Id.*

43. *Id.*

44. *Id.* at 2358.

45. *Id.* at 2363.

46. *Id.* at 2363, fn. 218.

47. *UWM Post* at 1165–1166.

48. *Id.* at 1166.

49. *Id.* at 1166–1167.

50. *Id.* at 1173.

51. *Chapinsky* at 571–572 (emphasis added), as quoted in *UWM Post* at 1169.

52. *UWM Post* at 1169.

53. *Id.* at 1169–1170.

54. *Cohen* at 20 [fighting words must be "directed at the person of the hearer"].

55. *Gooding* at 524 [fighting words only include those which "have a direct tendency to cause acts of violence by the person to whom, individually, the remark is addressed"].

56. *Lewis* at 132, 133 ["wantonly cursing, reviling, and using obscene or opprobrious language" has a broader sweep than the definition of fighting words].

57. *Johnson* at 2542 [fighting words refer to those that are "likely to provoke the average person to retaliation, and thereby cause a breach of the peace." Fighting words must be regarded by reasonable onlooker as a direct personal insult or an invitation to exchange fisticuffs].

58. *UWM Post* at 1170.

59. *Id.* at 1173.

60. *Id.*

61. *Id.* at 1174.

62. *Id.* at 1175.

63. *Id.*

64. *Id.*

65. *Id.* at 1177.

66. *Id.*

67. *Id.* at 1180.

68. *R.A.V.* at 2540; "Cross Burning Greets Black Family" at 1A; "Boy, 17, Is Arrested" at 3B; Terry (1992) at A16.

69. *R.A.V.* at 2541.

70. The five justices included Justice Scalia, Chief Justice Rehnquist, Justice Kennedy, Justice Souter, and Justice Thomas.

71. *R.A.V.* at 2542.

72. *Id.*

73. *Id.* at 2545.

74. *Id.* at 2550.

75. *Id.* at 2543.

76. *Id.*

77. *Id.* (quoting *Chaplinsky* at 572).

78. *R.A.V.* at 2545.

79. *Id.* at 2553, 2569.

80. Justice White filed an opinion concurring in the judgment, in which Justices Blackmun and O'Connor joined, and in which Justice Stevens joined except with regard to Part I-A. Justice Blackmun filed an opinion concurring in the judgment. Justice Stevens filed an opinion concurring in the judgment, in which Justices White and Blackmun joined in Part I.

81. *R.A.V.* at 2553 (White, J., concurring).

82. *Id.* (White, J., concurring); *Id.* at 2562 (Stevens, J., concurring).

83. *Id.* at 2545.

84. *Id.*

85. *Id.* at 2546, quoting Renton at 48 (emphasis in original).

86. *Id.*, quoting *O'Brien* at 376–377.

87. *Id.* at 2547.

88. See: *Id.* at 2556–2557 (White, J., concurring); *Id.* at 2665–2666 (Stevens, J., concurring).

89. *Id.* at 2547, 2549.

90. *Id.* at 2548.

91. *Id.*

92. *Id.*

93. *Id.* at 2549.

94. *Id.*, quoting *Burson* at 1852 (plurality).

95. *R.A.V.* at 2560 (White, J., concurring).

96. *Id.* at 2564 (Stevens, J., concurring).

97. *Id.* at 2553 (White, J., concurring).

98. *Id.*

99. *Id.* at 2553, 2558 (White, J., concurring).

100. *Id.* at 2553 (White, J., concurring).

101. *Id.* at 2554 (White, J., concurring).

102. 112 S.Ct. 1846 (1992).

103. *Burson* at 1850.

104. *R.A.V.* at 2555 (White, J., concurring).

105. *Burson* at 1865 (Stevens, J., dissenting); *R.A.V.* at 2555 fn.7 (White, J., concurring).

106. *R.A.V.* at 2554 (White, J., concurring).

107. *Id.* at 2549–2550.

108. *Burson* at 1848; *R.A.V.* at 2555 fn.8 (White, J., concurring).

109. *R.A.V.* at 2547 fn.6.

110. *Id.* at 2550 fn.8.

111. *Rust* at 212 (Brennan, J., dissenting).

112. *R.A.V.* at 2554 (White, J., concurring); *Id.* at 2564 (Stevens, J., concurring).

113. *Id.* at 2560 (White, J., concurring).

114. *Id.* at 2664 (Stevens, J., concurring).

115. *Id.* at 2554 (White, J., concurring).

116. *Id.* at 2560–2561 (Blackmun, J., concurring).

117. *Id.* at 2566 (Stevens, J., concurring).

118. *Id.* at 2545–2547.

119. *Id.* at 2546.

120. *Id.* at 2565 (Stevens, J., concurring).

121. *Id.* at 2665 (Stevens, J., concurring).

122. *Id.* at 2557 (White, J., concurring).

123. *Id.* at 2556–2557 (White, J., concurring).

124. *Id.* at 2557 (White, J., concurring).

125. *Id.* at 2546 (White, J., concurring).

126. *Miller* at 24.

127. *R.A.V.* at 2562 (Stevens, J., concurring).

128. *Id.* at 2544 fn.4.

129. *Id.* at 2557 (White, J., concurring).

130. *Id.* at 2546 (White, J., concurring).

131. *Id.* at 2557 (White, J., concurring).

132. *Id.* at 2548 (White, J., concurring).

133. *Id.* at 2546 (White, J., concurring).

134. If the Supreme Court's ruling in *Pacifica Foundation* (1975) is still valid after its ruling in *R.A.V.*, it would seem that individuals or groups who are inside the privacy of their own homes when the expressive conduct intrudes upon them might be the equivalent of a captive audience. This observation may not be accurate, however, in light of the fact that though the Joneses were inside their own home when Viktora set fire to the cross he had placed inside their yard and had nowhere to go to evade his hate message, the Court did not permit a Title VII defense of the ordinance under which Viktora was charged or seriously analyze the captive-audience principle. The *R.A.V.* Court might be indicating that the definition of a captive audience was much more confined than indicated in cases such as *Cohen* (1971), *Pacifica Foundation* (1975), *Erznoznik* (1975), or *Bethel School District No. 403* (1986).

135. *R.A.V.* at 2555 (White, J., concurring).

136. *Id.* at 2556 (White, J., concurring).

137. *Id.* at 2547 (White, J., concurring).

138. *Id.* at 2571 (Stevens, J., concurring).

139. *Id.* at 2548.

140. *Id.* at 2569–2570 (Stevens, J., concurring).

141. *Id.* at 2556–2558 (White, J., concurring); *Id.* at 2565–2566 (Stevens, J., concurring).

142. *Id.* at 2553–2554 (White, J., concurring).

143. *Id.* at 2561 (Blackmun, J., concurring).

144. *Id.* at 2542.

145. *Id.* at 2560 (Blackmun, J., concurring).

146. *Id.* at 2547.

147. *Id.* at 2554 (White, J., concurring).

148. Justice Stevens points out that "the St. Paul ordinance . . . regulates expressive activity that is wholly prescribable and does so not on the basis of viewpoint, but rather in recognition of the different harms caused by such activity." [*Id.* at 2571 (Stevens, J., concurring)].

149. *Id.* at 2569 (Stevens, J., concurring).

150. *Id.* at 2560 (White, J., concurring).

151. *Id.* at 2561 (White, J., concurring).

152. Notwithstanding the fact that all nine justices repudiated the petitioner's actions in this case, none of them embraced the civil rights position advocated by scholars such as Mari J. Mastuda. Unlike the civil rights advocates, the justices voiced their discomfort either directly (i.e., Justices Scalia and Stevens) or indirectly (i.e., Justices White and Blackmun) with condoning viewpoint-based discrimination, despite their willingness to support, within strict limits, content-based discrimination.

153. *R.A.V.* at 2548. John Sholto Douglas, 9th Marquess of Queensberry (1844–1900) was the originator (1865) of the Queensberry Rules, which govern modern boxing [Bridgwater (1953, 1968) at 897]. According to Ellmann in his biography of Oscar Wilde, "[Queensberry] was a complex [brute]. In so far as he was brutal, he practiced a rule-bound brutality. That was why at the age of 24 he had changed the nature of boxing by persuading England and America to agree to the Queensberry rules, and also by securing adoption of weight differences, so that boxers might be evenly matched. He had channelled together his belligerence and his litigiousness" [Ellmann (1984, 1988) at 381]. The Marquess of Queensberry—the father of Lord Alfred Douglas, who was a friend and lover of Oscar Wilde—was sued for libel by Wilde after publicly accusing Wilde of "posing as a sodomite." Because the jury found Queensberry not guilty of libel and that he was justified, in the public interest, in calling Wilde a sodomite, Wilde was prosecuted for (and convicted of) "indecency" under the Criminal Law Amendment Act of 1885 [See: Ellmann at 438–456].

154. *R.A.V.* at 2545.

155. *Id.* at 2547–2548.

156. *Id.* at 2550.

157. *Id.* at 2553 (White, J., concurring).

158. *Id.* at 2256 (White, J., concurring).

159. *Id.* at 2257 (White, J., concurring).

160. *Id.* at 2560–2561 (Blackmun, J., concurring).

161. *Id.* at 2561 (Blackmun, J., concurring).

162. *Id.*

163. *Id.* at 2665 (Stevens, J., concurring).

164. *Id.* at 2569 (Stevens, J., concurring).

165. *Id.* at 2561 (Blackmun, J., concurring).

166. *Id.*

167. *Id.* at 2571 (Stevens, J., concurring).

168. *Id.*

169. *Id.* at 2570 (Stevens, J., concurring).

170. *Id.*

171. *Id.* at 2548.

172. *Id.* at 2569 (Stevens, J., concurring).

173. *Id.* at 2548.

174. Wisconsin Statute, §939.645 (1)(b) (1989–1990), as quoted in *Mitchell,* 113 S.Ct. at 2197 fn.1.

175. *Mitchell* (1992) at 164, as quoted in *Mitchell* (1993) at 2197.

176. *Id.* (1993) at 2199.

177. *Id.* at 2200.

178. *Id.*

179. *Id.*

180. *Id.*

181. *Roberts* at 628, as quoted in *Mitchell* (1993) at 2199.

182. *Mitchell* (1993) at 2200–2201.

183. *Id.* at 2201.

184. *R.A.V.* at 2549.

185. *Mitchell* (1993) at 2200–2201.

186. Massaro (1991) 2345 fn.156.

187. A prime example can be found in current historical lyrics (e.g., "Watch'a Looking At?" by Audio Two, "G N'R Lies" by Guns N' Roses), as well as the monologues of talk-show hosts (e.g., Rush Limbaugh, Howard Stern), the material of popular comedians and comediennes (Andrew Dice Clay, Eddie Murphy), the rhetoric of politicians (Senator Jesse Helms, Representative William Dannemeyer), and the images in films (i.e, *Basic Instinct, Boys in the Band, Silence of the Lambs*).

188. Penelope (1992) at 110.

189. SeLegue (1991) at 935.

190. *Logan* (1985). Although *Logan* was not a "fighting words" case—indeed, it was a tort of outrage case—the court's attitude mirrors the heterocentric and heterosexist bias still voiced in judicial opinions. Cynthia Petersen warns that the effect of individuals within the *sex/gender outsider* communities attempting to appropriate derogatory language in an effort to disarm the oppressor "may be to support unwittingly those who would deny that labelling a victim [with an anti-lesbian/gay male/bisexual/transgenderist epithet] during an assault is evidence of heterosexist bias" [Petersen (1991) at 247].

191. Massaro (1991) at 254.

192. Garnets, Herek, and Levy (1993) at 586–587.

193. Kirk and Madsen (1989, 1990) at 98.

194. *Id.*

195. Ratzinger (1986) at 377–382; Navaro-Valls (1992) at 173–179.

196. Ratzinger (1986) at 380–381.

197. *Id.* at 381 (emphasis added).

198. Navaro-Valls (1992) at 176.

199. *Id.*

200. State of New York, Mario M. Cuomo, Governor (1988).

201. Indeed, an appeal to Title VII and the Equal Protection Clause could bolster a claim that selective group coverage in speech codes merely augments governmental protection of groups based on race, color, creed, religion, and sex. Equal protection jurisprudence permits neither Congress nor the states to infringe on the rights of suspect or quasi-suspect classes or to burden a fundamental right, unless such a discriminatory classification is necessary to promote a compelling government interest (in the case of a suspect class or a fundamental right) or is substantially related to the achievement of an important government objective (in the case of a quasi-suspect class).

202. When the Marquess of Queensberry confronted Oscar Wilde regarding Wilde's involvement with the Marquess' son, Lord Alfred Douglas, Wilde "asked: 'Lord Queensberry, do you seriously accuse your son and me of improper conduct?' [Queensberry] said, 'I do not say that you are it, but you look it, and you pose it, which is just as bad. If I catch you with my son together again in any public restaurant I will thrash you.' [Wilde] said, 'I do not know what Queensberry rules are, but the Oscar Wilde rule is to shoot at sight'" [Ellman (1984, 1988) at 447]. Wilde followed his rule, against his own best interests, by initiating libel proceedings against the Marquess of Queensberry after Queensberry left a card at the Albemarle Club accusing Wilde of "posing as a sodomite." The Marquess, however, violated his own rule of fair fighting through his "wanton attacks" on Wilde. For a thorough description and analysis of the interactions of Queensberry and Wilde, see Ellman (1984, 1988).

203. Herek and Berrill (1992); Kirk and Madsen (1989, 1990) at 98–106; Miles (1992); National Gay and Lesbian Task Force Policy Institute (1990).

204. See: Halley (1985); Rubenstein (1993); Editors of the *Harvard Law Review* (1989, 1990).

205. *Mitchell* (1993) at 2199.

206. See: Robson (1992) at 149–151.

207. Robson (1992) at 149.

CHAPTER 6

Conclusion

This book has argued that hate speech regulations are potentially threatening to lesbians, gay men, bisexuals, and transgenderists—especially if the restrictions do not have clearly prescribed definitions and scope. Consequently, the answer to this book's subtitle, "Can They Say That About Me?" is "Yes, they can . . . " provided the communication occurs in an open forum, within the context of political discourse, and in a time, place, and manner unlikely to cause acts of violence or to violate tort law.[1] When the spewed hate remains at the level of a "reflex reaction"—a mindless parroting of the stereotypes, caricatures, myths, or lies accepted by the dominant culture—it still defames, insults, and injures *sex/gender outsiders*; even when it reaches, or intensifies to, the level of hateful, debilitating "spirit murder," such speech cannot be prohibited, for fear of the even greater risk of repression against lesbians, gay men, bisexuals, and transgenderists. While Arlene Zarembka's observation is correct, that "[o]ppression depends as much on psychological terror against the victims as it does on physical assault,"[2] it does not follow that speech restrictions are necessarily the solution.

Words do not exist in a vacuum. They are inseparable from the tone of voice, implicit social approval, and the historical meanings etched into the words. It is true that under some circumstances counter-speech may be virtually impossible, due to the intrinsic dangers of employing it; however, it is also true that unless targeted individuals are willing to speak, it may prove impossible to realize full political and legal rights. Lesbians, gay men, bisexuals, and transgenderists can ill afford to have their silence interpreted as acquiescence by either opponents or potential allies. Nor can they allow themselves to be paralyzed by fear or a sense of helplessness. As Audre Lorde observes, "you're never really a whole person if you remain silent, because there's always that one little piece inside you that wants to be spoken out, and if you keep ignoring it, it gets madder and madder and hotter and hotter, and if you don't speak it out one day it will just up and punch you in the mouth from the inside."[3] Vigorous free expression is essential in the continuing struggle for first-class citizenship. The famous slogan "silence equals death"[4] applies to every facet of one's life as a *sex/gender outsider.* As Nan Hunter astutely recognizes, "[s]elf-identifying speech does not merely reflect or communicate one's identity; it is a major factor in constructing identity. Identity cannot exist without it. That is even more true when the distinguishing group characteristics are not visible. . . . Therefore, in the field of lesbian[,] . . . gay[, bisexual, and transgender] civil rights, expression is a component of the very identity itself."[5]

I am not condoning "open season" on *sex/gender outsiders* (for that would be tantamount to suicide), nor do I accept hate speech as political/rational discourse, as opposed to "spirit murder." What I am acknowledging is a reality: in this country lesbians, gay men, bisexuals, and transgenderists are deemed to be both expendable and legally persecutable by the status quo. As Zarembka acknowledges, "[w]e know that Gay rights symbols, as well as our very existence arouse anger and alarm (and sometimes resentment) in many heterosexuals."[6] Such emotions are fundamental to many of the legal initiatives which seek not only to silence *sex/gender outsiders* but also to strip them of all legal protections. Ultimately, however, the harms arising from hate speech may involve less risk for lesbians, gay men, bisexuals, and transgenderists than the potentially greater threat (in both kind and duration) posed by censoring speech. One need only survey the dismal record of government attempts to regulate the dissemination of ideas to understand the threat posed to *sex/gender outsiders* or any group disfavored by the majority. Nowhere is this better exemplified than in the campaign to censor the expression of lesbians, gay men, bisexuals, and transgenderists who seek explicitly to celebrate, or critically examine societal attitudes toward, their gender identity or affectional orientation/preference in their art. Frohnmayer's "obscenity oath," Senator Helms' Amendment to the NEA appropriations statute, and the Williams-Coleman's proposal requiring artists to be "sensitive to the general standards of decency . . . of the American public" are costs imposed on those who reject silence and who dare to present their truth. As Minnie Bruce Pratt warns, "there is no 'free' speech [for *sex/gender outsiders*]: we pay, in money or blood, time or pain, to assert our human dignity, to assert that we are even human."[7]

Speech suppression, once condoned and implemented, is difficult to contain within neatly defined boundaries. The possibility of official thought-control—the power of the government to define "what [it] regard[s] as a suitable level of discourse within the body politic"[8]—lies beneath the surface of speech regulations. It can be, and customarily is, employed just as easily against those who believe themselves safe as it can be against the intended target. The extent of regulated speech is not (necessarily) static; it changes at the government's whim. It seems naive to assume that speech codes restricting verbal attacks on the basis of gender identity or affectional orientation/preference will not be used to curb the speech rights of lesbians, gay men, bisexuals, and transgenderists.[9] Whenever gender identity and affectional orientation/preference are at issue, government speech restrictions endorsed by lesbian, gay men, bisexuals, and transgenderists—except under the most severely limited circumstances—indubitably resemble boomerangs. As Kenneth Karst astutely perceives, "[i]t is dangerous for any subordinate group . . . to define expressive behavior outside the freedom of expression because the behavior is effective in conveying its message."[10] Laws that seek to restrict speech are generally enforced disproportionately against individuals and groups whose views challenge the *status quo* or agitate for change.[11] Institutionalized legal, political, and social ostracism is an integral part of reality in this society, one that is corroborated daily in the lives of many *sex/gender outsiders*.[12] Attempts to secure the full civil and human rights for *sex/gender outsiders* are unpopular in this society and lead to bitter fights between supporters and opponents of lesbians, gay men, bisexuals, and transgenderists. To allow the government or majority rule to dictate whose side of the issue will be voiced or orchestrate what language will be used is even more hazardous than withstanding the pain and injury inflicted by even the most vicious hate speech.

The Court's decision in *R.A.V.* would seem to agree. While one may disagree with the way the arguments are supported in *R.A.V.*, Justice Scalia's decision does effectively invalidate most hate speech regulations. Under the First Amendment, the government is given no special dispensations that permit the regulation of hate messages just because it disapproves of the content. Only hate speech that presents a clear and present danger of imminent danger *in every individual case*, according to Justice Scalia's interpretation of the "fighting words" doctrine, can be restricted under the Constitution. No hate expression falling outside the parameters of the "fighting words" doctrine may be punished under the neutrality principle articulated in *R.A.V.* Although targeted individuals might find the emotional content of hate speech offensive, Justice Scalia contends, an intellectual message is nevertheless being communicated by the speaker—albeit one of hostility.

If the verbal assaults levied against *sex/gender outsiders* or any other group are rooted in the hate speakers' sense of fear or inadequacy,[13] their hostility cannot be eradicated through censorship. Darrell Yates Rist wisely observes that "[m]ore harm is done to civil liberties by censorship than by violent, ignorant statements."[14] Counter-speech and a firm commitment to the elimination of the underlying conditions that allow animosity based on gender identity or affectional orientation/preference to thrive may well prove more expedient than censorship in the struggle to abolish expressions of hate.

Sex/gender outsiders would do well to embrace the second principle of Kwanza, *Kujichagulia.* Audre Lorde explains the essence of this principle as "self-determination—the decision to define ourselves, name ourselves, and speak for ourselves, instead of being defined and spoken for by others."[15] Lesbians, gay men, bisexuals, and transgenderists need to answer heterocentric and heterosexist invectives with non-heterocentric and non-heterosexist expressions. But this counter-speech must be part of a comprehensive educational and political strategy aimed at raising people's consciousness, dismantling prevailing stereotypes and myths, and obliterating the social conditions that perpetuate attacks of hatred based on gender identity and affectional orientation/preference.

While fighting to eliminate the discrimination and violence faced by *sex/gender outsiders,* the lesbian, gay male, bisexual, and transgendered communities might heed Robson's warning to "not let the rule of law define the violence against us—define it as not-speech, as categorized, as not the rule of law itself. In order to stop the violence against us, we must define it for ourselves and then develop our . . . strategies—both within and without the rule of law."[16] While nothing less than undermining the institutional structures that encourage and reinforce prejudice, discrimination, and violence based on gender identity and affectional orientation/preference will ultimately eradicate hate speech,[17] the solution for *sex/gender outsiders* may lie not in focusing exclusively on the verbal manifestation of the symptom but rather in identifying and then eliminating the root conditions which trigger, enflame, and perpetuate the hate speech. Hate speech restrictions will be effective only if they are methodically linked to a comprehensive program designed to eradicate hatred and discrimination. Anything less would be illusionary and dangerous.

NOTES

1. Restatement (Second) of Torts, Section 46 (1977) recognizes an independent tort of "outrageous conduct causing severe emotional distress." Outrageous conduct is defined as that which goes "beyond all possible bounds of decency, [and is] atrocious and utterly intolerable in a civilized community. . . ."

2. Zarembka at 41.

3. Lorde, "Transformation of Silence into Language and Action," at 42.

4. This slogan, first used in 1986 by individuals involved in founding ACT UP, "appear[s] from the gay activist response to the AIDS epidemic, used to remind gay people that they need to be vocal to pressure governments to provide sufficient care to themselves and their community" [Stewart (1995) at 234].

5. Hunter (1995) at 1718.

6. Zarembka at 41.

7. Pratt, "Poetry in the Time of War" (1991) at 234.

8. *Cohen* at 23–24 [holding that a person wearing a jacket that proclaimed "fuck the draft" did not violate a state statute which prohibited "maliciously and willfully disturb(ing) the peace . . . by . . . offensive conduct" (*Id.* at 16)].

9. See: Siegel (1991).

10. Karst (1990) at 139.

11. *Id.* at 142 fn.9.

12. Law (1988) at 194.

13. Karst (1990) at 139–140.

14. Rist (1990) at 482.

15. Lorde, "Transformation of Silence into Language and Action" at 43.

16. Robson (1992) at 155.

17. For example: *Hardwick* (1986); state sodomy laws; military policies on gays and lesbians; marriage laws; child custody laws.

Bibliography

ARTICLES AND BOOKS

Achtenberg, Roberta (ed.), Karen B. Moulding (ed., release 7) [under the auspices of National Lawyers Guild: Lesbian, Gay, Bisexual Rights Committee], *Sexual Orientation and the Law*. Dearfield, IL: Clark, Boardman, Callaghan, 1984, 1994.

Adams, Barry D. *The Rise of a Gay and Lesbian Movement*. Boston: Twayne Publishers, 1987.

Allen, Brent Hunter. "The First Amendment and Homosexual Expression: The Need for an Expanded Interpretation." *Vanderbilt Law Review* 47 (1994): 1073-1106.

Arriola, Elvia Rosales. "Sexual Identity and the Constitution: Homosexual Persons as a Discrete and Insular Minority." *Women's Rights Law Reporter* 10 (1988): 143-176.

Badgett, M.V. Lee. "Employment and Sexual Orientation: Disclosure and Discrimination in the Workplace," in Alan L. Ellis and Ellen D.B. Riggle (eds.), *Sexual Identity on the Job: Issues and Services*. Binghamton, NY: Harrington Park Press, 1996, 29-52.

Baer, Ruth. *Equality Under the Fourteenth Amendment: Reclaiming the Fourteenth Amendment*. Ithaca, NY: Cornell University Press, 1983.

Bagnall, Robert G., Patrick C. Gallagher, and Loni L. Goldstein. "Burdens on Gay Litigants and Bias in the Court System: Homosexual Panic, Child Custody, and Anonymous Parties." *Harvard Civil Rights-Civil Liberties Law Review* 19 (1984): 497-559.

Bailey, J. Michael and Richard C. Pillard, "A Genetic Study of Male Sexual Orientation." *Archives of General Psychiatry* 48 (1991): 1089.

Barrett, Ellen M., Rev. "Legal Homophobia and the Christian Church." *Hastings Law Journal* 30 (1979): 1019-1027.

Barrett, Martha Barron. *Invisible Lives: The Truth About Millions of Women-Loving Women*. New York: Perennial Library, 1990.

Baruch, Chad. "Dangerous Liaisons: Campus Racial Harassment Policies, the First Amendment, and the Efficacy of Suppression." *Whittier Law Review* 11 (1990): 697-721.

Battaglia, Jack. "Regulation of Hate Speech by Educational Institutions: A Proposed Policy." *Santa Clara Law Review* 31 (1991): 345-392.

Bell, Derrick. *And We Are Not Saved*. New York: Basic Books, 1987.

_____. *Faces at the Bottom of the Well*. New York: Basic Books, 1992.

Bem, Sandra Lipsitz. *The Lens of Gender: Transforming the Debate on Sexual Inequality*. New Haven, CT: Yale University Press, 1993.

_____. "The Measurement of Psychological Androgyny." *Journal of Consulting and Clinical Psychology* 42 (1974): 155-162.

Bernstein, Bobbi. "Power, Prejudice, and the Right to Speak: Litigating 'Outness' Under the Equal Protection Clause." *Stanford Law Review* 47 (1995): 269-293.

Berrill, Kevin T. "Anti-Gay Violence and Victimization in the United States." *Journal of Interpersonal Violence* 5 (1990): 274-294.

_____. "Primary and Secondary Victimization in Anti-Gay Hate Crimes." *Journal of Interpersonal Violence* 5 (1990): 401-413.

Black, Hugo L. "The Bill of Rights." *New York University Law Review* 35 (1960): 865-881.

Blumenfeld, Warren J. and Diane Raymond. *Looking at Gay and Lesbian Life*. Boston: Beacon Press, 1988.

Bork, Robert H. "Neutral Principles and Some First Amendment Problems." *Indiana Law Journal* 47 (1971): 1-35.

Bornstein, Kate. *Gender Outlaw: On Men, Women, and the Rest of Us*. New York: Vintage, 1994.

Boswell, John. *Christianity, Social Tolerance, and Homosexuality*. Chicago: University of Chicago Press, 1980.

"Boy, 17, Is Arrested in Cross Burnings; St. Paul Family Expresses Relief." *Minneapolis Star Tribune* 24 June 1990, 3B.

Bradley, Martha Sonntag. *Kidnapped from That Land: The Government Raids on the Short Creek Polygamists*. Salt Lake City, UT: University of Utah Press, 1993.

"*Brief Amicus Curiae* of James E. Andrews as Stated Clerk of the General Assembly of the Presbyterian Church (U.S.A.) in Support of Respondents: *Romer v. Evans*," filed 19 June 1995 in the Office of the Clerk, Supreme Court of the United States, Docket No. 94-1039.

"Brief for Petitioners: *Romer v. Evans*," filed 21 June 1995 in the Office of the Clerk, Supreme Court of the United States, Docket No. 94-1039.

"The Brief of *Amicus Curiae* of the Concerned Women for America, Inc.: *Romer v. Evans*." *Amici Curiae Brief: Romer v. Evans*, filed 21 June 1995 in the Office of the Clerk, Supreme Court of the United States, Docket No. 94-1039.

Bridgewater (editor-in-chief). *Columbia Viking Desk Encyclopedia: Volume Two*. New York: Viking Press, 1953, 1968.

Brown, Mildred L. and Chloe Ann Rounsley. *True Selves: Understanding Transsexualism: For Families, Friends, Coworkers, and Helping Professionals*. San Francisco: Jossey-Bass, 1996.

Browne, Kingsley R. "Title VII as Censorship: Hostile-Environment Harassment and the First Amendment." *Ohio State Law Journal* 52 (1991): 481-550.

Brownstein, Alan E. "Regulating Hate Speech at Public Universities: Are First Amendment Values Functionally Incompatible with Equal Protection Principles?" *Buffalo Law Review* 39 (1991): 1-52.

Brownworth. "An Unreported Crisis," *The Advocate* 5 November 1991.

Buchanan, G. Sidney. "Same-Sex Marriage: The Linchpin Issue." *University of Dayton Law Review* 10 (1985): 541-573.

Bull, Chris and John Gallagher. *Perfect Enemies: The Religious Right, the Gay Movement, and the Politics of the 1990s*. New York: Crown Publishers, 1996.

Bullough, Vern L. and Bonnie Bullough. *Cross Dressing, Sex, and Gender*. Philadelphia: University of Pennsylvania Press, 1993.

Byrne, J. Peter. "Racial Insults and Free Speech Within the University." *Georgetown Law Journal* 79 (1991): 399-443.

Cammermeyer, Margarethe. "Statement." U.S. Senate, Committee on Armed Services, 103d Congress, 1st Session, Senate Hearing 103-845, "Policy Concerning Homosexuality in the Armed Forces" (Washington, D.C.: Government Printing Office, 1993): 646-654.

Card, Claudia. *Lesbian Choices*. New York: Columbia University Press, 1995.

Carrington, Paul. "A Senate of Five: An Essay on Sexuality and Law." *Georgia Law Review* 23 (1989): 859-910.

Chafee, Zechariah, Jr. *Free Speech in the United States*. Cambridge: Harvard University Press, 1941.

Channing, William E. "Slavery (1836)," in William E. Channing, *The Works of William E. Channing* (1882; reprint, New York: Burt Franklin, 1970): 688-743.

Chase, Mary Anne C. "Disaggregating Gender from Sex and Sexual Orientation: The Effeminate Man in the Law and Feminist Jurisprudence." *Yale Law Journal* 105 (1995): 1-105.

Chew, Wayne. "Title VII Rights of Homosexuals." *Golden Gate University Law Review* 10 (1980): 53-59.

Childester, David. *Patterns of Power: Religion and Politics in American Culture.* Englewood Cliff, NJ: Prentice-Hall, 1988.

Choper, J.H. "Defining 'Religion' in the First Amendment." *University of Illinois Law Review* 3 (1982): 579–613.

Clausen, Jan. *Beyond Gay or Straight: Understanding Sexual Orientation.* Philadelphia, PA: Chelsea House Publishers, 1997.

Cohn-Sherbok, Dan. *The Crucified Jew: Twenty Centuries of Christian Anti-Semitism.* London: Fount, 1992.

Colker, Ruth. *Hybrid: Bisexuals, Multiracials, and Other Misfits Under American Law.* New York: New York University Press, 1996.

Comstock, Gary David. "Appendix C: The Police as Perpetrators of Anti-Gay/Lesbian Violence," in Gary David Comstock, *Violence Against Lesbians and Gay Men.* New York: Columbia University Press, 1991: 152-162.

_____. "Victims of Anti-Gay/Lesbian Violence" *Journal of Interpersonal Violence* 4 (1989): 101-106.

_____. *Violence Against Lesbians and Gay Men.* New York: Columbia University Press, 1991.

"Constitutional Limits on Anti-Gay-Rights Initiatives." *Harvard Law Review* 106 (1993): 1910-1309.

"The Constitutional Status of Sexual Orientation: Homosexuality as a Suspect Classification." *Harvard Law Review* 98 (1985): 1285-1309.

Cooley, Thomas McIntyre. *A Treatise on the Constitutional Limitations.* 8th ed. Boston: Little, Brown, & Co., 1927.

Cory, Donald Webster (pseud.). *The Homosexual in America.* New York: Greenberg, 1951.

Cossman, Brenda, Shannon Bell, Lise Gotell, and Becki L. Ross. *Bad Attitude/s on Trial: Pornography, Feminism, and the Butler Decision.* Toronto: University of Toronto Press, 1997.

Coward. "Activists Frustrated by Unused Hate Crime Stats." *Washington Blade* 23 (31 July 1992): 1.

Crittenden, S.H., Jr. "Report of the Board Appointed to Prepare and Submit Recommendations to the Secretary of the Navy for the Revision of Policies, Procedures, and Directives Dealing with Homosexuals." 21 December 1956–15 March 1957; unpublished report, released 1977 in discovery request for *Berg* (1978), referenced Shilts (1993): 281–283.

"Cross Burning Greets Black Family on St. Paul's East Side." *Minneapolis Star Tribune* 22 June 1990, 1A.

Cruz, David B. "Piety and Prejudice: Free Exercise Exemption From Laws Prohibiting Sexual Orientation Discrimination." *N.Y.U. Law Review* 69 (1994): 1176-1237.

D'Amato, Anthony. "Harmful Speech and the Culture of Indeterminacy." *William and Mary Law Review* 32 (1991): 329-351.

Dannemeyer, William. *Shadow in the Land: Homosexuality in America*. San Francisco: Ignatius Press, 1989.

Dannemeyer, William E. "Testimony Before the Subcommittee on Postsecondary Education Concerning Federal Funding for the Arts." Subcommittee on Postsecondary Education, Congress, Session, Hearing, Washington, D.C.: Government Printing Office, 1990.

D'Emilio, John. *Sexual Politics, Sexual Communities: The Making of a Homosexual Minority in the United States, 1940-1970*. Chicago: University of Chicago Press, 1983.

D'Emilio, John, and Estelle B. Freedman. *Intimate Matters: A History of Sexuality in America*. New York: Harper & Row 1988.

d'Garcia, Edward. *Girls Lean Back Everywhere: The Law of Obscenity and the Assault of Genius*. New York: Random House, 1992.

Debo, Angie. *A History of the Indians of the United States*. Norman, OK: Oklahoma University Press, 1970.

Deikman, Arthur J. *The Wrong Way Home: Uncovering Patterns of Cult Behavior in American Society*. Boston: Beacon Press, 1990.

Delgado, Richard. "Campus Antiracism Rules: Constitutional Narratives in Collision." *Northwestern University Law Review* 85 (1991): 343-387.

_____. "Words That Wound: A Tort Action for Racial Insults, Epithets, and Name-Calling." *Harvard Civil Rights-Civil Liberties Law Review* 17 (1982): 133-181.

Deloria, Vine Jr. *Custer Died for Your Sins: An Indian Manifesto*. New York: MacMillian, 1970; Norman, OK: Oklahoma University Press, 1988.

Docter, Richard F. *Transvestites and Transsexuals: Toward a Theory of Cross-Gender Behavior*. New York: Plenum Press, 1988.

Dollimore, Jonathan. *Sexual Dissidence: Augustine to Wilde, Freud to Foucault*. Oxford: Clarendon Press, 1991.

Douglas, James. "I Sit and Look Out: Employment Discrimination against Homosexuals and the New Law of Unjust Dismissal." *Washington University Journal of Urban and Contemporary Law* 33 (1988): 73-136.

Duberman, Martin B. *Stonewall*. New York: Dutton, 1993.

Ducat, Craig R. *Constitutional Interpretations: Rights of the Individual Volume II*. Minneapolis/St. Paul: West, 1974, 1996.

Dyer, Kate (ed.). *Gays in Uniform: The Pentagon's Secret Reports*. Boston: Alyson Publications, 1990.

Editors of the *Harvard Law Review*, *Sexual Orientation and the Law*. Cambridge, MA: Harvard University Press, 1989, 1990.

Edsall, Thomas Byrne and Mary D. Edsall. *Chain Reaction: The Impact of Race, Rights, and Taxes on American Politics*. New York: Norton, 1991.

Ekins, Richard and David King (eds.). *Blending Genders: Social Aspects of Cross-Dressing and Sex-Changing*. New York: Routledge, 1996.

Ellis, Allen L. and Ellen D.B. Riggle (eds.). *Sexual Identity on the Job*. New York: Harrington Park Press, 1996.

Ellman, Richard. *Oscar Wilde*. New York: Vintage Books, 1984, 1988.

Ellsworth, Maria S. *Mormon Odyssey: The Story of Ida Hunt Uldall, Plural Wife*. Chicago: University of Chicago Press, 1992.

Emerson, Thomas. *System of Freedom of Expression*. New York: Vintage Books, 1970.

Emerson, Thomas. "The Formulation of Legal Doctrine in General," in Bosmajian (ed.), *The Principles and Practice of Freedom of Speech* (2d ed.). Lanham, Md: University Press of America, 1983. pp. 303-315.

_____. "Toward a General Theory of the First Amendment" *Yale Law Review* 72 (1963): 877-956.

Eskridge, William N., Jr. *The Case for Same-Sex Marriage: From Sexual Liberty to Civilized Commitment*. New York: Free Press, 1996.

Ettner, Randi. *Confessions of a Gender Defender: A Psychologist's Reflections on Life Among the Transgendered*. Evanston, IL: Chicago Spectrum Press, 1996.

Ezorsky, Gertrude. *Racism and Justice: The Case for Affirmative Action*. Ithaca, NY: Cornell University Press, 1991.

Faderman, Lillian. *Odd Girls and Twilight Lovers: A History of Lesbian Life in Twentieth-Century America*. New York: Penguin, 1991.

Feinberg, Leslie. *Transgender Liberation: A Movement Whose Time Has Come*. New York: World View Forum, 1992.

_____. *TRANSgender Warriors: Making History From Joan of Arc to RuPaul*. Boston: Beacon Press, 1996.

Fernandez, Joseph M. "Recent Developments: Bringing Hate Crimes Into Focus—The Hate Crime Statistics Act of 1990, Pub. L. No. 101–275." *Harvard Civil Rights-Civil Liberties Law Review* 26 (1991): 261-293.

Forer, Lois G. *Unequal Protection: Women, Children, and the Elderly in Court*. New York: W.W. Norton & Co., 1991.

Fried, Charles. "The New First Amendment Jurisprudence: A Threat to Liberty." *University of Chicago Law Review* 59 (1992): 225-253.

Gager, John A. *The Origins of Anti-Semitism: Attitudes Toward Judaism in Pagan and Christian Antiquity*. New York: Oxford University Press, 1983.

Gale, Mary Ellen. "Reimagining the First Amendment: Racist Speech and Equal Liberty." *St. John's Law Review* 65 (1991): 119-185.

Gallagher, Joseph (ed.). *Homosexuality and the Magisterium: Documents From the Vatican and the U.S. Bishops, 1975-1985*. Mt. Rainier, MD: New Ways Ministry, 1986.

Gallo, Jon J. "The Consenting Adult Homosexual and the Law: An Emperical Study of Enforcement and Administration in Los Angeles County." *U.C.L.A. Law Review* 13 (1966): 643-797.

Garnets, Linda, Gregory M. Herek, and Barry Levy. "Violence and Victimization of Lesbians and Gay Men: Mental Health Consequences," in Linda D. Garnets & Douglas C. Kimmel (eds.), *Psychological Perspectives on Lesbian and Gay Male Experiences*. New York: Columbia University Press, 1993: 579–597.

George, Sue. *Women and Bisexuality*. London: Scarlet Press, 1993.

Gerety, Tom. "Redefining Property." *Harvard Civil Rights-Civil Liberties Law Review* 12 (1977): 233-296.

Glueck, Grace. "Art on the Firing Line." *New York Times* 9 July 1989, §2 (Arts and Leisure), 1, col.3.

Goldstein, Ann B. "History, Homosexuality, and Political Values: Searching for the Hidden Determinants of *Bowers v. Hardwick*." *Yale Law Journal* 97 (1988): 1073-1103.

Goldstein, Leslie F. "Limits of the First Amendment: Verbal Terrorism on College Campuses." Paper presented at the Annual Meeting of the Midwest Political Science Association Meeting (April 1992).

Goldstein, Robert J. *Political Repression in the Modern America*. Cambridge, MA: Schenkman Pub. Co., 1978.

Gomez, José. "The Public Expression of Lesbian/Gay Personhood as Protected Speech." *Journal of Law and Inequality* 1 (1983): 121–153.

Gramick, Jeannine and Pat Furey (eds.). *The Vatican and Homosexuality: Reactions to the "Letter to the Bishops of the Catholic Church on the Pastoral Care of Homosexual Persons."* New York: Crossroad, 1988.

Green, Richard. *Sexual Science and the Law*. Cambridge, MA: Harvard University Press, 1992.

Greenwalt, Kent. "How Empty is the Idea of Equality." *Columbia Law Review* 83 (1983): 1167-1185.

_____. "Insults and Epithets: Are They Protected Speech." *Rutgers Law Review* 42 (1990): 287-307.

Gressman, Eugene. "Bicentennializing Freedom of Expression." *Seton Hall Law Review* 20 (1990): 378-417.

Grey, Thomas. "Civil Rights v. Civil Liberties: The Case of Discriminatory Verbal Harassment." *Social Philosophy & Policy*. (Spring 1991): 87-107.

Gunther, Gerald. *Constitutional Law: Cases and Materials* (10th ed.). Mineola, NY: Foundation Press, 1937, 1980.

_____. "Learned Hand and the Origins of Modern First Amendment Doctrine: Some Fragments of History." *Stanford Law Review* 27 (1975): 719-773.

Hacker, Andrew. *Two Nations, Black and White: Separate, Hostile, Unequal*. New York: Scribner, 1992.

Halley, Janet L. "The Politics of the Closet: Towards Equal Protection for Gay, Lesbian, and Bisexual Identity." *UCLA Law Review* 36 (1985): 915-976.

_____. "Reasoning About Sodomy: Act And Identity In And After *Bowers v. Hardwick.*" *Virginia Law Review* 79 (1993): 1721-1780.

_____. "Sexual Orientation and the Politics of Biology: A Critique of the Argument from Immutability." *Stanford Law Review* 46 (1994): 503-568.

Hammer, Dean H., Stella Hu, Victoria L. Magnuson, Nan Hu, and Angela M.L. Pattatucci. "A Linkage Between DNA Markers on the X Chromosome and Male Sexual Orientation." *Science* 261 (1993): 321-327.

Hansen, Klaus J. *Mormonism and the American Experience.* Chicago: University of Chicago Press, 1981.

Harry, J. "Derivative Deviance: The Cases of Extortion, Fag-Bashing, and the Shakedown of Gay Men." *Criminology* 19 (1982): 546–564.

Harvey, J.F. "Homosexuality." *The New Catholic Encyclopedia* (1967): 116.

Hayes, John Charles. "The Tradition of Prejudice Versus the Principle of Equality: Homosexuals and Heightened Equal Protection Scrutiny After *Bowers v. Hardwick,*" *Boston College Law Review* 31 (1990): 375-475.

Heatherly, Gail. "Gay and Lesbian Rights: Employment Discrimination." *Annual Survey of American Law* 4 (1986): 901-912.

Heger, Heinz. *The Men With the Pink Triangle: The True, Life-and-Death Story of Homosexuals in the Nazi Death Camps* (Revised Ed.). Boston: Alyson, 1980, 1994.

Hein, S.M. "Discussion of Banning Words: A Comment on Words that Wound." *Harvard Civil Rights-Civil Liberties Law Review* 18 (1983): 585-592.

Hentoff, Nat. " 'Speech Codes' and Free Speech," in Patricia Aufderheide (ed.), *Beyond P.C.: Toward a Politics of Understanding.* St. Paul, MN: Greywolf Press, 1992).

Herdt, Gilbert (ed.). *Third Sex, Third Gender: Beyond Sexual Dimorphism in Culture and History.* New York: Zone Books, 1993.

Herek, Gregory M. "Hate Crimes Against Lesbians and Gay Men: Issues for Research and Policy." *American Psychologist* 44 (1989): 948–955.

_____. "Stigma, Prejudice, and Violence Against Lesbian and Gay Men," in J. Gorsiorek and J. Weinrich (eds.), *Homosexuality: Social, Psychological, and Biological Issues.* 2d ed. Newbury Park, CA: Sage, 1991: 60-80.

Herek, Gregory M. and Kevin T. Berrill (eds.). *Hate Crimes: Confronting Violence Against Lesbians and Gay Men.* Newbury Park, CA: Sage, 1992.

Herscher. "S.F. Again Tops U.S. in Reports of Gay Bashing." *San Francisco Chronicle,* 7 June 1990.

Hunter, James Davison. *Culture Wars: The Struggle to Define America.* New York: Basic Books, 1991.

Hunter, Nan D. "Identity, Speech, and Equality." *Virginia Law Review* 79 (1995): 1695-1719.

_____. "Life After Hardwick." *Harvard Civil Rights-Civil Liberties Law Review* 27 (1992): 531-534.

Hunter, Nan D., Sherryl E. Michaelson, and Thomas B. Stoddard, *The Rights of Lesbians and Gay Men: The Basic ACLU Guide to a Gay Person's Rights* (3d ed.). Carbondale, IL: Southern Illinois University Press, 1992, "Appendix A: Criminal Statutes Relating to Consensual Homosexual Acts Between Adults," 148-175.

Hutchins, Loraine and Lani Kaahumanu (eds.). *Bi Any Other Name: Bisexual People Speak Out.* Boston: Alyson, 1991.

Ide, Arthur Frederick. *Gomorrah & the Rise of Homophobia.* Las Colinas, TX: The Liberal Press, 1985.

Jaimes, M. Annette. *The State of Native America: Genocide, Colonization, and Resistance.* Boston: South End Press, 1992.

Jaynes, Gerald David and Robin M. Williams, Jr. (eds.). *A Common Destiny: Blacks and American Society.* Washington, DC: National Academy Press, 1989.

Jeffrey, Christina F. "Political Correctness, Academic Freedom and the First Amendment." Paper delivered at the Annual Meeting of the Political Science Association (August 1992).

Karst, Kenneth. "Boundaries and Reason: Freedom of Expression and the Subordination of Groups." *University of Illinois Law Review* 1990 (1990): 95-149.

_____. "Equality as a Central Principle in the First Amendment." *University of Chicago Law Review* 43 (1975): 20-68.

_____. "The Supreme Court 1976 Term, Forward: Equal Citizenship Under the Fourteenth Amendment." *Harvard Law Review* 91 (1977): 1-68.

Katz, Jonathan Ned. *Gay American History: Lesbians and Gay Men in the U.S.A.* New York: Meridan, 1976, 1992.

_____. *Gay/Lesbian Almanac: A New Documentary.* New York: Carroll & Graf Publishers, 1983.

Keen, Lisa. "D.C. Likened to Sodom and Gomorrah." *The Washington Blade* 7 August 1992: 1, 17.

Kirk, Marshall and Hunter Madsen. *After the Ball: How America Will Conquer its Fear and Hatred of Gays in the 90s.* New York: Plume, 1989, 1990.

Koepke, Jens B. "The University of California Hate Speech Policy: A Good Heart in Ill-fitting Garb." *Hastings Comm/Ent Law Journal* 12 (1990): 599-625.

Kogan, Terry. "Legislative Violence Against Lesbians and Gay Men." *Utah Law Review* 1994 (1994): 209-245.

Kohler, Mark. "History, Homosexuals, and Homophobia: The Judicial intolerance of *Bowers v. Hardwick*." *Connecticut Law Review* 19 (1986): 129-142.

Koppelman, Andrew. "The Miscegenation Analogy: Sodomy Law as Sex Discrimination." *Yale Law Review* 98 (1988): 145-164.

192   Bibliography

_____. "Why Discrimination Against Lesbians and Gay Men is Sex Discrimination." *New York University Law Review* 69 (1994): 197-287.

Kozma, Scott. "*Baehr v. Lewin* and the Same-Sex Marriage: The Continued Struggle for Social, Political, and Human Legitimacy." *Williamette Law Review* 30 (1994): 891–916.

Lange, Ellen N. "Notes: Racist Speech on Campus: A Title VII Solution to a First Amendment Problem." *Southern California Law Review*, 64 (1990): 105-134.

Langmuir, Gavin I. *History, Religion, and Antisemitism.* Berkeley: University of California Press, 1990.

_____. *Toward a Definition of Antisemitism.* Berkeley: University of California Press, 1990.

Law, Sylvia. "Homosexuality and the Social Meaning of Gender." *Wisconsin Law Review* 1988 (1988): 187-235.

Lawrence, Charles, III. "If He Hollers Let Him Go: Regulating Racist Speech on Campus." *Duke Law Journal* 1990 (1990): 431-483.

LeMarche and Rubenstein, William B. "The Love That Dare Not Speak: Censoring Gay Expression." *The Nation,* 5 November 1990: 542-546.

Lerner, Gerda. *The Creation of Patriarchy.* New York: Oxford University Press, 1986.

LeVay, Simon. "A Difference in Hypothalamic Structure Between Heterosexual and Homosexual Men." *Science* 253 (1991): 1034-1037.

Leyland, Winston (ed.). *Gay Roots: An Anthology of Gay History, Sex, Politics, and Culture.* San Francisco: Gay Sunshine Press, 1993.

Linzer, Peter. "White Liberal Looks at Racist Speech." *St. John's Law Review* 65 (1991): 187-244.

Littleton, Christine. "Women's Experience and the Problem of Transition: Perspective on Male Battering of Women." *University of Chicago Legal Forum* 1989 (1989): 23-57.

Lorde, Audre. "Age, Race, Class, and Sex: Women Defining Difference," in Audre Lorde, *Sister Outsider: Essays and Speeches.* Trumansburg, NY: Crossing Press, 1984: 114-123.

Lorde, Audre. *Sister Outsider: Essays and Speeches.* New York: Norton, 1984.

_____. "Transformation of Silence into Language and Action," in Audre Lorde, *Sister Outsider: Essays and Speeches.* Trumansburg, NY: Crossing Press, 1992.

_____. "To the Poet Who Happens to be Black and the Black Who Happens to be a Poet." *Callallo* 14 (1991): 39.

Mackenzie, Gordene Olga. *Transgender Nation.* Bowling Green, OH: Bowling Green State University Popular Press, 1994.

MacKinnon, Catherine A. "Reflections on Sex Equality under Law." *Yale Law Journal* 100 (1991): 1281-1328.

MacKinnon, Catherine A. *Sexual Harassment of Working Women: A Case of Sex Discrimination.* New Haven: Yale University Press, 1979.

Magnuson, Roger. "Civil Rights and Sexual Deviance: The Public Policy Implications of the Gay Rights Movement." *Hamline Journal of Public Law and Policy* 9 (1989): 217-235.

Massaro, Toni M. "Equality and Freedom of Expression: The Hate Speech Dilemma." *William and Mary Law Review* 32 (1991): 211-265.

Matsuda, Mari J. "Public Response to Racist Speech: Considering the Victim's Story." *Michigan Law Review* 87 (1989): 2320-2381.

Matsuda, Mari J., Charles R. Lawrence III, Richard Delgado, and Kimberle Williams Crenshaw. *Words That Wound: Critical Race Theory, Assaultive Speech, and the First Amendment.* Boulder, CO: Westview Press, 1993.

Matthessen, Peter. *In the Spirit of Crazy Horse.* New York: Viking, 1980, 1983.

McDaniels, Michael A. "Preservice Adjustment of Homosexual and Heterosexual Military Accessions: Implications for Security Clearance Suitability," in Kate Dyer (ed.), *Gay in Uniforms: The Pentagon's Secret Report.* Boston: Alyson, 1990: 113–123.

McKay, Robert B. "The Preference for Freedom." *New York University Law Review* 34 (1959): 1182-1227.

McGowan, David F. and Ragesh K. Tangri. "A Libertarian Critique of University Restrictions of Offensive Speech." *California Law Review* 79 (1991): 825-910.

Meiklejohn, Alexander. "The First Amendment is Absolute." *Supreme Court Review* 1961 (1961): 245.

Meiklejohn, Alexander. *Political Freedom.* New York: Oxford University Press, 1965.

Messerschmidt, Jim. *The Trial of Leon Peltier.* Boston: South End Press, 1983.

Miles. "The Fabulous Fight Back: On the Streets After Dark to Confront Gay Bashers." *Out/Look* 17 (Summer 1992): 54.

Mill, John Stewart. *On Liberty: A Norton Critical Edition,* edited by David Spitz. New York: W.W. Norton, 1975.

Miller, Neil. *Out of the Past: Gay and Lesbian History From 1869 to the Present.* New York: Random House, 1995.

Minow, Martha. *Making All the Difference: Inclusion, Exclusion, and American Law.* Ithaca, NY: Cornell University Press, 1990.

Minow, Martha. "Speaking and Writing Against Hate." *Cardozo Law Review* 11 (July/August 1990): 1393-1408.

Mohr, Richard. *Gays/Justice: A Study of Ethics, Society, and Law.* New York: Columbia University Press, 1988.

Moore, Arthur J. "Gay Rights and the Churches: Social Pluralism and Christian Order." *Christianity and Crisis* 46 (1986): 127-130.

Moore, R.I. *The Formation of a Persecuting Society: Power and Deviance in Western Europe 950-1250.* Oxford: Basil Blackwell, 1987.

National Gay and Lesbian Task Force. "Activist Alert." 2 July 1992.

National Gay and Lesbian Task Force. *Anti-Gay Violence, Victimization, and Defamation in 1987*. Washington, DC: National Lesbian and Gay Task Force, 1988.

National Gay and Lesbian Task Force Policy Institute. *Anti-Gay/Lesbians Violence, Victimization and Defamation* [Annual Report]. Washington, DC: National Gay and Lesbian Task Force, 1989.

_____. *Anti-Gay Violence, Victimization, and Defamation in 1989*. Washington, DC: National Lesbian and Gay Task Force, 1990.

National Museum & Archive of Lesbian and Gay History. *The Gay Almanac: The Most Comprehensive Reference Source of Its Kind*. New York: Berkeley Books, 1996.

_____. *The Lesbian Almanac: The Most Comprehensive Reference Source of Its Kind*. New York: Berkeley Books, 1996.

Nava, Michael and Robert Dawidoff. *Created Equal: Why Gay Rights Matter in America*. New York: St. Martin's Press, 1994.

Navaro-Valls, Joaqui. "Doctrinal Congregation/Revised Text: Responding to Legislative Proposals on Discrimination Against Homosexuals." *Origins: CNS Documentary Service* 22 (6 August 1992): 172–177.

Neisen, Joseph H. "Heterosexism or Homophobia: The Power of the Language We Use." *Outlook: National Gay and Lesbian Quarterly* (1990): 36.

Niblock, John F. "Anti-Gay Initiatives: A Call for Heightened Judicial Scrutiny." *UCLA Law Review* 41 (1993): 153-198.

Norgren, Jill and Sewrena Nanda. *American Cultural Pluralism and Law* (2d ed.). Westport, CT: Praeger, 1996.

Penelope, Julia. "The Lesbian New-rotics: Bogus or Breakthrough," in Julia Penelope, *Call Me Lesbian: Lesbian Lives, Lesbian Theory*. Freedom, CA: Crossing Press, 1992.

People for the American Way. *Climate of Hate: A State by State Report on Anti-Gay Activity*. Washington, D.C.: People for the American Way, 1993.

Peterson, Cynthia. "A Queer Response to Bashing: Legislating Against Hate." *Queen's Law Journal* 16 (1991): 237-260.

"The Petitioners' Religious *Amici Curiae Brief: Romer v. Evans*," filed 21 June 1995 in the Office of the Clerk, Supreme Court of the United States, Docket No. 94-1039.

Pharr, Suzanne. *Homophobia: A Weapon of Sexism*. Inverness, CA: Chardon Press, 1988.

Poliakov, Leon. *The History of Anti-Semitism: Volumes I-III*, trans. Richard Howard, Natalie Gerardi, and Miriam Kochan. New York: Vanguard Press, 1965-1975.

_____. *The History of Anti-Semitism: Volumes IV*, trans. George Klin. Oxford: Oxford University Press, 1985.

Polikoff, Nancy. "This Child Does Have Two Mothers: Redefining Parenthood to Meet the Needs of Children in Lesbian-Mother and Other Nontraditional Families." *Georgetown Law Review* 78 (1990): 459-575.

Posner, Richard. *The Problems of Jurisprudence.* Cambridge, MA: Harvard University Press, 1990.

_____. *Sex and Reason.* Cambridge, MA: Harvard University Press, 1992.

Pratt, Minnie Bruce. *Crime Against Nature.* Ithaca, NY: Firebrand Books, 1990.

_____. "Poetry in the Time of War," in Minnie Bruce Pratt, *Rebellion: Essays 1980–1991.* Ithaca, NY: Firebrand Books, 1991: 227-246.

_____. *Rebellion: Essays 1980–1991.* Ithaca, NY: Firebrand Books, 1991.

_____. *S/He.* Ithaca, NY: Firestone Books, 1995.

Rabban, David M. "The First Amendment in Its Forgotten Years." *Yale Law Review* 90 (1981): 514-597.

Ratzinger, Cardinal Joseph (Perfect). "Doctrinal Congregation's Letter to Bishops: The Pastoral Care of Homosexual Persons." *Origins: CNS Documentary Service* 16 (13 November 1986): 377–382.

Reing, Timothy W. "Comment: Sin, Stigma, & Society: A Critique of Morality and Values in Democratic Law and Policy." *Buffalo Law Review* 38 (1990): 859-901.

"Religion and Morality Legislation: A Reexamination of Establishment Clause Analysis." *N.Y.U. Law Review* 59 (1984): 301-409.

Renteln, Alison Dundes. "Culture and Culpability: A Study of Contrasts," in Alison Dundes Renteln and Alan Dundes (eds.), *Folk Law: Essays in the Theory and Practice of Lex Non Scripta (Volume II).* New York: Garland, 1994: 863-880.

"The Respondents' Religious *Amici Curiae Brief: Romer v. Evans,*" filed 21 June 1995 in the Office of the Clerk, Supreme Court of the United States, Docket No. 94–1039.

"Responding to Legislative Proposals on Discrimination Against Homosexuals." *Origins: CNS Documentary Service* 22 (6 August 1992): 173-179.

Rich, Adrienne. "Compulsory Heterosexuality and Lesbian Existence." *Signs* 5 (1980): 631-660.

Richards, David A.J. *Conscience and the Constitution: History, Theory, and Law of the Reconstruction Amendments.* Princeton, NJ: Princeton University Press, 1993.

Richards, David A.J. "Constitutional Legitimacy and Constitutional Privacy." *New York University Law Review* 61 (1986): 800-862.

_____. "Constitutional Privacy and Homosexual Love." *New York University Review of Law and Social Change* 14 (1986): 895-905.

_____. "Free Speech and Obscenity Law: Toward a Moral Theory of the First Amendment." *University of Pennsylvania Law Review* 123 (1974): 45-91.

_____. *Foundations of American Constitutionalism*. New York: Oxford University Press 1989.

_____. "Sexual Preference as a Suspect (Religious) Classification: An Alternative Perspective on the Constitutionality of Anti-Lesbian/Gay Initiatives." *Ohio State Law Journal* 55 (1994): 491–553.

_____. *Toleration and the Constitution*. New York: Oxford University Press 1986.

Rist, Darrell Yates. "Homosexuals and Human Rights." *The Nation* 9 April 1990: 482-484.

Rivera, Rhonda. "Our Straight-Laced Judges: The Legal Position of Homosexual Persons in the United States." *Hastings Law Journal* 30 (1979): 799-955.

_____. "Recent Developments in Sexual Preference Law." *Drake Law Review* 30 (1981): 311–346.

Robson, Ruthann. *Gay Men, Lesbians, and the Law*. Philadelphia, PA: Chelsea House Publishers, 1997.

_____. *Lesbian (Out)Law: Survival Under the Rule of Law*. Ithaca, NY: Firebrand Books, 1992.

Rosenberg, David. "Racist Speech, the First Amendment, and Public Universities: Taking a Stand on Neutrality." *Cornell Law Review* 76 (1991): 549-588.

Rubenfeld, Jed. "The Right of Privacy." *Harvard Law Review* 102 (1989): 737-807.

Rubenstein, William B. (ed.). *Lesbians, Gay Men, and the Law*. New York: New Press, 1993.

Salmons, David B. "Toward a Fuller Understanding of Religious Exercise: Recognizing the Identity-Generative and Expressive Nature of Religious Devotion." *University of Chicago Law Review* 62 (1995): 1243–1274.

Sarbin, Theodore R. and Kenneth E. Karols. "Non-Conforming Sexual Orientations and Military Suitability," in Kate Dyer (ed.), *Gay in Uniforms: The Pentagon's Secret Report*. Boston: Alyson, 1990: 5-97.

Scanlon, Thomas. "A Theory of Freedom of Expression." *Philosophy & Public Affairs* 1 (1972): 204-226.

Schacter, Jane S. "The Gay Civil Rights Debate in the States: Decoding the Discourse of Equivalents." *Harvard Civil Rights-Civil Liberties Law Review* 29 (1994): 283-317.

Schneider, Carl. "State-Interest Analysis in Fourteenth Amendment 'Privacy' Law: An Essay on the Constitutionalization of Social Issues." *Law & Contemporary Problems* 51 (1988): 79-122.

Schneyer, Kenneth L. "Avoiding the Personal Pronoun: The Rhetoric of Display and Camouflage in the Law of Sexual Orientation." *Rutgers Law Review* 46 (1994): 1313–1394.

Schwartz, Deborah R. "A First Amendment Justification for Regulating Racist Speech on Campus." *Case Western Reserve Law Review* 40 (1989/1990): 733-779.

"Securing Freedom From Harassment Without Reducing Freedom of Speech: *Doe v. University of Michigan* (721 F.Supp. 852)." *Iowa Law Review* 76 (1991): 383-403.

Selcraig, Bruce. "Reverend Wildmon's War on the Arts," *New York Times Magazine* 2 September 1990: 22–25, 43, 52-53.

SeLegue, Sean M. "Campus Anti-Slur Regulations: Speakers, Victims, and the First Amendment." *California Law Review* 79 (1991): 919-970.

Seper, Cardinal Franjo (Perfect). "The Vatican Declaration on Sexual Ethics." *Origins: CNS Documentary Service* 5 (22 January 1976): 485-494.

Shank, S. Adele, "Sticks and Stones: Homosexual Soclicitations and the Fighting Words Doctrine." *Ohio State Law Journal* 41 (1980): 553-574.

Shilts, Randy. *And the Band Played On: Politics, People, and the Aids Epidemic.* New York: St. Martin's Press, 1987.

_____. *Conduct Unbecoming: Gays and Lesbians in the U.S. Military.* New York: St. Martin's Press, 1993.

Siegel, Paul. "Lesbian and Gay Rights as a Free Speech Issue: A Review of Relevant Caselaw." *Journal of Homosexuality* 21 (1991): 203-259.

Smolla, Rodney A. *Free Speech in an Open Society.* New York: Vintage Books, 1992.

Smolla, Rodney A. "Rethinking First Amendment Assumptions About Racist and Sexist Speech." *Washington & Lee Law Review* 47 (1990): 171-211.

Snitow, Ann. "A Gender Diary," in Marianne Hirsch and Evelyn Fox Keller (eds.), *Conflicts in Feminism.* New York: Routledge, 1990.

Sr. Mary Elizabeth. *Legal Aspects of Transsexualism.* San Juan Capistrano, CA: J2CP Information Service 1988.

Sr. Mary Elizabeth. "Transsexual Civil Rights," in *Transsexualism: A Collection of Articles, Editorials, and Letters.* Wayland, MA: IFGE (1988).

Stetson, Dorothy McBride. *Women's Rights in the U.S.A.: Policy Debates amd Gender Roles.* Pacific Grove, CA: Brooks/Cole Publishing, 1991.

Stewart, William. *Cassell's Queer Companion: A Dictionary of Lesbian and Gay Life and Culture.* London: Cassell, 1995.

Storr, Robert. "Art, Censorship, and the First Amendment." *Art Journal* 50 (1991): 12-28.

"Student Discriminatory Harassment." *Journal of College and University Law* 16 (1989): 311-324.

Terry, Don. "Rights Advocates Uncertain about Ruling's Impact." *New York Times* 23 June 1992, A16.

Thomas, Kendall. "Beyond the Privacy Principle." *Columbia Law Review* 92 (1992): 1431-1516.

_____. "The Eclipse of Reason: A Rhetorical Reading of *Bowers v. Hardwick*." *Virginia Law Review* 79 (1993): 1805-1832.

Tong, Rosemary. *Women, Sex, and the Law.* Totowa, NJ: Rowman & Allanheld, 1984.

Tribe, Lawrence. *American Constitutional Law*. Minolta, NY: Foundations Press, 1978.

_____. *Constitutional Choices*. Cambridge: Harvard University Press, 1985.

Valdes, Francisco. "Queers, Sissies, Dykes, and Tomboys: Deconstructing the Conflationn of 'Sex,' 'Gender,' and 'Sexual Orientation' in Euro-American Law and Society." *California Law Review* 83 (1995): 1-377.

Webster's II New Riverside Desk Reference. Boston: Houghton Mifflin Co., 1992.

Weinberg, Martin S., Collin J. Williams, & Douglas W. Pryor. *Dual Attraction: Understanding Bisexuality*. New York: Cornell University Press, 1994.

Wells, Merle W. *Anti-Mormonism in Idaho, 1872-1892*. Provo, UT: Brigham Young University Press, 1978.

Wells-Petry, Melissa, Major. *Exclusion: Homosexuals and the Right to Serve*. Washington, D.C.: Regnery Gateway, 1993.

Western, Peter. "The Empty Idea of Equality." *Harvard Law Review* 95 (1982): 537-596.

Wilkinson, J. Harvie III and G. Edward White. "Constitutional Protection for Personal Lifestyles." *Cornell Law Review* 62 (1977): 563-625.

Williams, Patricia. "Spirit-Murdering the Messenger: The Discourse of Finger pointing as the Law's Response to Racism." *Miami Law Review* 42 (1985): 127-157.

Wise, Donna. "Case Note: Challenging Sexual Preference Discrimination in Private Employment." *Ohio State Law Journal* 41 (1980): 501-531.

Wishman, Vera. *Queer by Choice: Lesbians, Gay Men, and the Politics of Identity*. New York: Routledge, 1996.

Wittig, Montique. *The Straight Mind and Other Essays*. Boston: Beacon Press, 1992.

Wolfson, Evan. "Civil Rights, Human Rights, Gay Rights: Minorities and the Humanity of the Different." *Harvard Journal of Law and Public Policy* 14 (1991): 21-39.

_____. "Free Speech Theory and Hateful Words." *University of Cincinnati Law Review* 60 (1991): 1-42.

Wolgast, Elizabeth. *Equality and the Rights of Women*. Ithaca, NY: Cornell University Press, 1980.

Young, Iris Marion. *Justice and the Politics of Difference*. Princeton, NJ: Princeton University Press, 1990.

Zarembka, Arlene. "Decision Bodes Ill for Bias Laws." *The Washington Blade* 19 September 1992.

Zawadsky, John. "Note: Right to Marry Deemed Fundamental Right." *Wisconsin Law Review* 1979 (1979): 682-705.

Zingo, Martha T. and Kevin E. Early. "Perspective Shades Perception: Equal Protection Theory," in Martha T. Zingo and Kevin E. Early, *Nameless Persons: Legal Discrimination Against Non-Marital Children in the United States*. Westport, CT: Praeger, 1994: 111-139.

BILLS, LEGISLATIVE DEBATES, POLICIES, AND STATUTES

"Act of March 3, 1887," Chapter 397, 24 Stat. 635 (repealed 1909), 24 Stat. 641 (repealed 1978).

"Anti-Polygamy Act," Chapter 126 §3, 12 Stat. 501 (1862), (repealed 1978).

Briggs-Initiative: California Proposition 6, §3(b)(2) (1978).

"Civil Rights Act of 1964: Title VII," Public Law No. 88-352, Title VII, 78 Stat. 241, 253-266 (codified as amended as 42 U.S.C. §§2000e-2000e-17 (1982 & Supp.V 1987).

Colorado's Amendment 2: Colorado Constitution, Art. II, §30b (1992).

Committee of the Judiciary. *Anti-Gay Violence: Hearing Before the Subcommittee on Criminal Justice of the Committee on the Judiciary, House of Representatives.* Washington, DC: Government Printing Office, 1986: Serial No. 132.

_____. *Police Misconduct: Hearing Before the Subcommittee on Criminal Justice of the Committee on the Judiciary.* Washington, DC: Government Printing Office, 1983: Serial No. 98-50.

"The Defense of Marriage Act (DOMA)," P.L.104-664, (1997).

Department of Commerce. U.S. Bureau of Census. *Statistical Abstract of the United States*, 112th. "U.S. Census Figures: Population by State." Washington, DC: Government Printing Office, 1991.

"Don't Ask, Don't Tell." "National Defense Authorization Act for Fiscal Year 1994." P.L.103-160, (Subtitle G Sec.571 §654(b)(1)(A)&(B)), 107 Stat. 1547 (§571), 10 U.S.C. §654(b), November 30, 1993.

"Failed Attempts to Amend Title VII to Include Affectional Orientation/Preference: H.R. Report No. 238," 92nd Congress, 1st Session, pp. 4–5, reprinted in 1972 *U.S. Code Congressional and Administrative News* 2137, 2140–2141 (1972); "Civil Rights Amendments Act of 1979: Hearings on H.R. 2074 Before the Subcommittee on Employment Opportunities of the House Committee on Education and Labor" 96th Congress, 2d Session, Washington, DC: Government Printing Office, 1979: pp. 6–7; "Civil Rights Amendments Act of 1981: Hearings on H.R. 1454 Before the Subcommittee on Employment Opportunities of the House Committee on Education and Labor" 97th Congress, 2d Session, Washington, DC: Government Printing Office, 1982: pp. 1-2.

Federal Policy for Personnel Procedures: 5 U.S.C. §2302(b)(10)(1988).

Georgia Annotated Code §16-6-2(a)-(b) (Michie 1984).

"Hate Crimes Statistics Act of 1990." Public Law No. 101-275, 1990 U.S.C.C.A. (104 Statute) 140, 28 U.S.C. §534, §2 (a) 1-3; as amended by Public Law No. 103-322, 1994 U.S.C.C.A. (108 Statute) 2131, Title 38 U.S.C. §320926.

Helms AIDS Education Amendment: Pub. L. 100-202, §514(a), 101 Stat. 1329-289 (1988).

"Helms Amendment," "Department of Interior and Related Agencies Appropria-
    tion Act, 1990, Title II—Related Agencies, Department of Health and
    Human Services, Commission of Fine Arts," Pub. L. 101-121 [H.R.
    2788] §3040(a), 103 Stat. 741 (1989).
"Helms Amendment 1251," 136 *Congressional Record* S1169 (daily ed., 8 Febru-
    ary 1990).
Restatement (Second) of Torts §45 (1965).
"St. Paul Bias-Motivated Crime Ordinance." St. Paul, MN, Legis. Code, §292.02
    (1990).
State of New York, Mario M. Cuomo, Governor. *Governor's Task Force on Bias-
    Related Violence, Final Report* (Douglas H. White, chair), March 1988,
    as quoted in Gary David Comstock, *Violence Against Lesbians and Gay
    Men.* New York: Columbia University Press, 1991: 118.
Subcommittee on Postsecondary Education, Committee on Education and Labor,
    House of Representatives. *Hearing on the Reauthorization on the Na-
    tional Endowment for the Arts* [Volume 1, Serial #101-76 (5 March
    1990); Volume 2, Serial #101-77 (21 March 1990); Volume 3, Serial
    #101-77 (4 April and 2 May 1990)]. Washington, D.C.: Government
    Printing Office, 1990.
Subcommittee on Postsecondary Education, Committee on Education and Labor,
    House of Representatives. *Hearing on the Rights of Artists and Scholars
    to Freedom of Expression and the Right of Taxpayers to Determine the
    Use of Public Funds.* Washington, D.C.: Government Printing Office,
    1990.
U.S. Senate, 104th Congress, "Defense of Marriage Act," *Congressional Record*
    S10100–10125 (10 September 1996).

INTERNET AND MISCELLANEOUS

American Family Association. "Homosexuality in America: Exposing the
    Myths." (Tupelo, MS: American Family Association, undated) in *Ameri-
    can Family Association* [http://www.afa.net/toc0.htm].
"Before Stonewall: The Making of a Gay and Lesbian Community" (a documen-
    tary). Distributed by Video Finders, 4401 Sunset Blvd., Los Angeles, CA
    90027.
Buchanan, Pat. "Address" at Republican National Convention, 17 August 1992,
    Houston, Texas.
Pavola, Curt (Co-Director of Lavander Action in Olympia, Washington). "Lan-
    guage About Love and Sexuality," in *Queer Resource Directory*
    [http://qrd.tcp.com/qrd/culture/language.about.love.and.sexuality].
Summersgill, Bob (comp.). "U.S. Legal Issues About Sex," in *Queer Resource Di-
    rectory* [http://qrd.tcp.com/qrd/law].

LEGAL CASES

Abrams v. United States, 250 U.S. 616 (1919).

Acanfora v. Board of Education, 491 F.2d 498 (4th Cir. 1974).

Adarand Constructors, Inc. v. Pena, 115 S.Ct. 2097 (1995) (Ginsberg, J., dissenting).

Adderley v. Florida, 385 U.S. 39 (1966).

Alaska Gay Coalition v. Sullivan, 578 P.2d 951 (Alaska, 1978).

American Booksellers Association, Inc. v. Hudnut, 771 F.2d 323 (7th Cir. 1985), *aff'd mem.*, 475 U.S. 1001 (1986).

Ashton v. Kentucky, 384 U.S. 195, 200 (1966).

Baehr v. Lewin, No. 91-1394-05 (Haw. Ct. App. Sept. 3, 1991), *rev'd on other grounds*, 852 P.2d 44 (Haw. 1993).

Baker v. Wade, 553 F.Supp. 1121 (N.D. Tex. 1983), *rev'd*, 743 F.2d 236 (5th Cir. 1984), *aff'd on reh. en banc*, 769 F.2d 289 (5th Cir. 1985), *cert. denied*, 106 S.Ct. 3337 (1986).

Barbour v. Department of Social Services, 198 Mich. App. 183, 497 N.W.2d 216 (1993).

Barclay v. Florida, 463 U.S. 939 (1983) (plurality opinion).

Barnes v. Costle, 561 F.2d 983 (D.C. Cir. 1977).

Baskerville v. Culligan International Co., 50 F.3d 428 (7th Cir. 1995).

Bates v. Little Rock, 361 U.S. 516 (1960).

Beauharnais v. Illinois, 343 U.S. 250 (1952).

Bella Lewitzky Dance Foundation v. Frohnmayer, 754 F.Supp. 774 (1991).

Ben-Shalom v. Marsh, 703 F.Supp. 1372, (E.d. Wis. 1989), *rev'd*, 881 F.2d 454 (7th Cir. 1989), *cert. denied sub nom.*, *Ben-Shalom v. Stone*, 110 U.S. 1296 (1990).

Ben-Shalom v. Secretary of State, 489 F.Supp. 964, 975 (E.D. Wis., 1980), *aff'd on other grounds*, 826 F.2d (7th Cir., 1987).

Berg v. Claytor, (591 F.2d 849 (D.C. Cir. 1978).

Bethel School District No. 403 v. Fraser, 478 U.S. 675 (1986).

Blum v. Gulf Oil Corp., 597 F.2d 936 (5th Cir. 1979).

Blum v. Yaretsky, 457 U.S. 991 (1982).

Bolling v. Sharpe, 347 U.S. 495 (1954).

Bowen v. Gillard, 483 U.S. 587 (1987).

Bowers v. Hardwick, 478 U.S. 186 (1986).

Brandenburg v.Ohio, 395 U.S. 444 (1965).

Broadrick v. Oaklahoma, 413 U.S. 601 (1973).

Brown v. Board of Education, 347 U.S. 483 (1954).

Buchanan v. Batchelor, 308 F.Supp. 729 (N.D. Tex. 1970), 401 U.S. 989 (1971).

Buckley v. Valeo, 424 U.S. 1 (1976).

Burson v. Freeman, 112 S.Ct. 1846 (1992).

Burton v. Wilmington Parking Authority, 365 US 715 (1961).

Cantwell v. Connecticut, 310 U.S. 296 (1940).

Carey v. Population Services International, 431 U.S. 678 (1977).

Cariddi v. Kansas City Chiefs Football Club, Inc., 568 F.2d 87 (8th Cir. 1977).

Chaplinsky v. New Hampshire, 315 U.S. 568 (1942).

Childers v. Dallas Police Department, 513 F. Supp. 134 (N.D. Tex. 1981), *aff'd*, 669 F.2d 732 (5th Cir. 1982) (*mem.*).

Church of the Holy Trinity v. United States, 143 U.S. 457 (1892).

City of Cleburne v. Cleburne Living Center, 473 U.S. 432 (1985).

City of Dallas v. England, 846 S.W.2d 957 (Tex. Ct. App. 1993).

City of New Orleans v. Duke, 427 US 297 (1976).

The Civil Rights Cases, 109 US 3 (1883) (Harlan, J., dissenting).

Cleveland Board of Education v. LaFleur, 414 U.S. 632 (1974).

Coates v. City of Cincinnati, 402 U.S. 611 (1971).

Cohen v. California, 403 U.S. 15 (1971).

Collins v. Smith, 447 F.Supp. 676, (N.D. Ill.), *aff'd*, 578 F.2d 1197 (7th Cir.), *cert. denied*, 439 U.S. 916 (1978).

Commonwealth v. Doucette, 462 N.E.2d 1084 (Mass. 1984).

Commonwealth v. Sefranka, 382 Mass. 108, 414 N.E.2d 602 (1980).

Commonwealth v. Wasson, 842 S.W.2d 487 (Ky. 1992).

Communist Party of the United States v. Control Board, 387 U.S. 1 (1961).

Connick v. Myers, 461 U.S. 138 (1983).

County of Allegheny v. A.C.L.U., Greater Pittsburgh Chapter, 492 U.S. 573 (1989).

Cox v. New Hampshire, 312 U.S. 569 (1941).

Craig v. Boren, 473 U.S. 190 (1976).

Craig v. Y&Y Snacks, Inc., 721 F.2d 77 (3d Cir. 1983).

Croson v. City of Richmond, 488 U.S. 469 (1989).

Davis v. Beason, 133 U.S. 333 (1890).

Dawson v. Delaware, 112 S.Ct. 1093 (1992).

Debs v. United States, 249 U.S. 211 (1919).

Dennis v. United States, 341 U.S. 494 (1951).

DeSantis v. Pacific Telephone and Telegraph Co., 608 F.2d 327 (9th Cir. 1979).

DeShaney v. Winnegago County Department of Social Services, 489 U.S. 189, 197 (1989).

Dillon v. Frank, 1992 U.S. App, LEXIS 766, 58 Emp. Prac. Dec. (CCH) 41332 (6th Cir. 1992).

Doe v. Bolton, 410 U.S. 179 (1973).

Doe v. Commonwealth's Attorney, 403 F. Supp. 1199 (E.D. Va. 1975, *summarily aff'd without opinion*, 425 U.S. 901 (1976).

Doe v. University of Michigan, 721 F.Supp. 852 (E.D. Mich. 1989).

Dominguez v. Stone, 638 P.2d 113 423 (N.M. Ct. App. 1981).

Dronenburg v. Zech, 741 F.2d 1388 (D.C. Cir. 1984).

Dunn v. Blumstein, 405 U.S. 330 (1972).

Eisenstadt v. Baird, 405 U.S. 438 (1972).

Elrod v. Burns, 427 U.S. 347 (1976).

Enslin v. North Carolina, 214 S.E.2d 318 (N.C. Ct. App. 1975), *aff'd*, 425 U.S. 903 (1976).

Equality Foundation of Greater Cincinnati, Inc. v. City of Cincinnati, 860 F.Supp. 417 (S.D. Ohio 1994), *rev'd*, 1995 U.S. App. LEXIS 10462 (6th Cir. 1995).

Erznoznik v. City of Jacksonville, 422 U.S. 205 (1975).

Evans v. Romer, 854 .2d 1270 (Colo. 1993) (*en banc*), *cert. denied*, 114 S. Ct. 419 (1993); *Romer v. Evans*, 882 P.2d 1334 (Colo. 1994), *affirmed*, U.S. Supreme Court, Docket No. 94–1039 (20 May 1994).

Fagg v. United States, 34 M.J. 179 (CMA 1992).

FCC V. Pacifica Foundation, 438 U.S. 726 (1975).

Feiner v. New York, 340 U.S. 315 (1951).

Firefighters Institute for Racial Equality v. City of St. Louis, 549 F.2d 506 (8th Cir. 1977).

Flower v. United States, 407 U.S. 197 (1972).

Forsyth County, Georgia v. Nationalist Movement, 112 S.Ct. 2395 (1992).

Fox v. Sierra Development Corporation, 876 F.Supp. 1169 (D. Nev. 1995).

Fricke v. Lynch, 491 F. Supp. 381 (D.R.I. 1980).

Frohwerk v. United States, 249 U.S. 204 (1919).

Frontiero v. Richardson, 411 U.S. 677 (1973).

F.S. Royster Guano Co. v. Virginia, 253 US 412 (1920).

Garcia v. Elf Atochem North America, 28 F.3d 446 (5th Cir. 1994).

Gay Activists Alliance v. Washington Metropolitan Area Transit Authority, 48 U.S.L.W. 2053 (D.D.C. 1979).

Gay Alliance of Students v. Matthews, 544 F.2d 162 (4th Cir. 1976).

Gay & Lesbian Students Ass'n v. Gohn, 850 F.2d 361 (8th Cir. 1988).

Gay Lib v. University of Missouri, 558 F.2d 848 (8th Cir. 1977), *cert. denied sub nom. Ratchford v. Gay Lib*, 434 U.S. 1080 (1988).

Gay Student Organization, University of New Hampshire v. Bonner, 509 F.2d 652 (1st Cir. 1974).

Gay Student Services v. Texas A&M University, 612 F.2d 160 (5th Cir.), *cert denied*, 449 U.S. 1034 (1980),

Gertz v. Robert Welch, Inc., 418 U.S. 323 (1974).

Gish v. Board of Education, 145 N.J. Super. Ct. 96, 366 A.2d 1337 (1976), *cert. denied*, 434 U.S. 879 (1977).

Gitlow v. New York, 268 U.S. 652 (1925).

Gooding v. Wilson, 405 U.S. 518 (1972).

Greer v. Spock, 424 U.S. 828 (1976).

Griggs v. Duke Power Co., 401 U.S. 424 (1971).

Griswold v. Connecticut, 381 U.S. 479 (1965).

Gulf, Colorado, & Santa Fe Railway Company v. Ellis, 165 US 150 (1897).

Hampton v. Mow Sun Wong, 426 U.S. 88 (1976).

Harper v. Virginia Board of Education, 383 U.S. 663 (1966).

Harris v. McRae, 448 U.S. 297 (1980).

Hatheway v. Secretary of the Army, 641 F.2d 1376 (9th Cir., 1981).

Hayes v. Missouri, 120 U.S. 68 (1887).

Henson v. Dundee, 682 F.2d 897 (11th Cir. 1982).

Hernandez v. Texas, 347 U.S. 475 (1954).

Hess v. Indiana, 414 U.S. 105 (1975).

High Tech Gays v. Defense Industrial Security Clearance Office, 668 F.Supp. 1361 (N.D. Cal. 1987), *rev'd*, 895 F.2d 563 (9th Cir. 1990), *rehearing en banc denied*, 909 F.2d 375 (9th Cir. 1990).

Hill v. INS, 714 F.2d 1470 (9th Cir. 1983).

Hirabayashi v. United States, 320 U.S. 81 (1945).

Holloway v. Arthur Andersen & Co., 566 F.2d 659 (9th Cir. 1977).

Hopkins v. Baltimore Gas and Electric Co., 77 F.3d 745 (4th Cir. 1996), *cert. denied*, 117 S.Ct. 70 (1996).

Horn v. Duke Homes, Inc., Division of Winsor Mobile Homes, 755 F.2d 599 (7th Cir. 1985).

Hustler Magazine, Inc. v. Falwell, 485 U.S. 46 (1988).

Inman v. City of Miami, 197 So.2d 50 (1951), *cert. denied*, 201 U.S. 1048 (1968).

In re J.S. & C, 129 N.J. Super. Ct. 486, 324 A.2d 90 (1974).

Jantz v. Muci, 759 F.Supp. 1543 (D. Kan. 1991).

Jetts v. Dallas Independent School District, 491 U.S. 701 (1989).

Jones v. Alfred H. Mayer Co., 392 US 409 (1968).

Kirpatrick v. Seligman & Latz, 337 N.W.2d 1047 (5th Cir. 1981).

Konigberg v. State Bar of California, 366 U.S. 36 (1961).

Korematsu v. United States, 322 U.S. 214 (1944).

Kottenman v. Grevenberg, 233 La. 328, 96 So.2d 601 (1957).

Kramer v. Union Free School District, 395 U.S. 621 (1969).

Late Corporation of the Church of Jesus Christ of Latter-Day Saints v. United States, 136 U.S. 1 (1890).

Ledsinger v. Burmeister, 114 Mich. App. 12, 318 N.W.2d 558 (1982).

Lesbian/Gay Freedom Day Committee v. INS, 541 F. Supp. 569 (N.D. Cal. 1982), *vacated in part*, 741 F. 2d 1470 (9th Cir. 1983).

Lewis v. City of New Orleans, 415 U.S. 130 (1974).

Lindsley v. Natural Carbonic Gas Co., 220 U.S. 61 (1911).

Logan v. Sears, Roebuck & Co., 466 So.2d 121 (Ala. 1985).

Logan v. Zimmerman Brush Co., 455 U.S. 442 (1982).

Lovell v. Griffin, 303 U.S. 444 (1938).

Loving v. Virginia, 388 U.S. 1 (1967).

Lyng v. Castello, 477 U.S. 635 (1986).

Mahone v. Waddle, 564 F.2d 1081, 1028–1029 (3d Cir. 1977), *cert. denied* 348 U.S. 904 (1978).

Martin v. Wilks, 490 U.S. 755 (1989).

Massachusetts Board of Retirement v. Murgia, 427 U.S. 307 (1976).

Masses Publishing Co. v. Patten, 244 Fed. 535 (S.D. N.Y. 1917).

Mathews v. Lucas, 427 U.S. 495 (1976).

Maynard v. Hill, 125 U.S. 190 (1888).

McConnell v. Anderson, 451 F.2d 193 (8th Cir. 1971).

McDonald v. Board of Elections, 394 U.S. 802 (1969).

McGinnis v. Royster, 410 U.S. 263 (1973).

McGowen v. Maryland, 366 U.S. 420 (1961).

McKeey v. City of Rockwall, Texas, 877 F.2d 409 (5th Cir. 1989).

McLaughlin v. Florida, 379 U.S. 184 (1964).

McLaurin v. Oklahoma State Regents for Higher Education, 388 U.S. 637 (1949).

McWilliams v. Fairfax County Board of Supervisors, 72 F.3d 1191, 1195 (4th Cir. 1996), *cert. denied*, 1996 WL 324733 (1996).

Meinhold v. U.S. Dept. of State, 808 F.Supp. 1455 (C.D. Cal. 1993).

Memorial Hospital v. Maricopa County, 415 U.S. 250 (1974).

Meritor Savings Bank v. Vinson, 477 U.S. 57 (1986).

Michigan Organization for Human Rights v. Kelley, No. 88-815820 CZ (Mich. Cir. Ct., Wayne Cty. July 9, 1990) (no appeal taken) [summarized at 1990 *Lesbian/Gay Law Notes 53*].

Miller v. Bank of America, 600 F.2d 211 (9th Cir. 1979).

Miller v. California, 414 U.S. 881 (1973), *reh'g denied*, 413 U.S. 15 (1973).

Mills v. Shepherd, 445 F.Supp 1231 (W.D. N.C. 1975).

Moose Lodge No. 107 v. Irvis, 407 US 163 (1965).

Morales v. State of Texas, (Austin Dis. Ct. 10 Dec. 1990) [reported at 1991 *Lesbian/Gay Law Notes 1*].

Morton v. Macy, 417 F.2d 1161 (D.C. Cir. 1969).

Moseley v. Esposito, Civ. Action No. 89–6897–1, slip opinion (Georgia Superior Court, 6 September 1989).

National Gay Task Force v. Board of Education, 729 F.2d 1270 (10th Cir. 1984), *aff'd mem.*, 470 U.S. 903 (1985).

National Socialist Party v. Skokie, 434 U.S. 43 (1977).

Near v. Minnesota, 283 U.S. 697 (1931).

New York v. Ferber, 458 U.S. 747 (1982).

New York County Board of Ancient Hiberians v. Dinkins, et al., 814 F. Supp. 358 (1993).

New York Times v. Sullivan, 376 U.S. 254 (1964).

Nogueras v. University of Puerto Rico, 1995 U.S. Dist. LEXIS 8958 (D. P.R. June 13, 1995).

Olleman v. Evans, 750 F.2d 970 (D.C. Cir. 1984), *cert. denied* 471 U.S. 1127 (1985).

Olmstead v. United States, 227 U.S. 438 (1928).

Oncale v. Sundowner Offshore Services, Inc., 83 F.3d 118 (5th Cir. 1996), *petition for cert. filed* 65 U.S.L.W. 3432 (U.S. Dec. 16, 1996) (No.96-568).

One Eleven Wines and Liquors, Inc. v. Division of Alcoholic Beverage Control, 50 N.J. 329, 235 A.2d 12 (1967).

Ortiz v. Bank of America, 547 F.Supp. 550 (E.D. Cal. 1982).

Osburne v. Ohio, 24, 495 U.S. 103 (1990).

Paddock Bar, Inc. v. Division of Alcoholic Beverage Control, 46 N.J. Super. 405, 134 A.2d 779 (1957).

Padula v. Webster, 822 F.2d 97 (D.C. Cir. 1987).

Palimore v. Sidoti, 466 U.S. 429 (1984).

Palko v. Connecticut, 302 U.S. 319 (1937).

Paris Adult Theatre I v. Slaton, 413 U.S. 49 (1973).

Patterson v. McLean Credit Union, 491 U.S. 164 (1989).

People v. Baldwin, 112 Cal. Rptr. 290 (Ct. App., 1974).

People v. Brashier (1992).

People v. Onofre, 51 N.Y.2d 476, 434 N.Y.S.2d 947, 415 N.E.2d 936 (1980), *cert. denied*, 451 U.S. 987 (1981).

People v. Rodriquez, 63 Cal. App.3d Supp. 1, 133 Cal. Rptr. 765 (1976).

People v. Steven S., 31 Cal. Rptr.2d 644 (Cal. Ct. App. 1994).

People v. Uplinger, (58 N.Y.2d 936, 447 N.E.2d 62, 460 N.Y.S.2d 514 (1983), *cert. dismissed*, 467 U.S. 246 (1984).

Personnel Administrator of Massachusetts v. Feeney, 442 U.S. 256 (1979).

Petition of Nemetz, 485 F.Supp. 470 (E.D. Va. 1980), *rev'd sub nom.*, *Nemetz v. INS*, 647 F.2d 432 (4th Cir. 1981).

Phillips v. Martin-Marietta Corp., 400 U.S. 542 (1971).

Phillips v. Michigan Department of Corrections, 731 F.Supp. 792, 794 (W.D. Mich. 1990), *aff'd*, 932 F.2d 969 (6th Cir. 1991).

Planned Parenthood of Southeastern Pennsylvania v. Casey, 505 U.S. 833 (1992).

Plessy v. Ferguson, 163 U.S. 537 (1896).

Plyler v. Doe, 457 U.S. 202 (1982).

Police Dept. v. Mosley, 408 U.S. 92 (1972).

Price Waterhouse v. Hopkins, 490 U.S. 228 (1989).

Pritchett v. Sizeler Real Estate Management Co., 1995 U.S. Dist. LEXIS 5565 (E.D. La. April 25, 1995).

Procunier v. Martinez, 416 U.S. 396 (1974).

Pruitt v. Weinberger, 659 F.Supp. 625 (C.D. Cal. 1987), *appeal denied, Cheny v. Pruitt*, 963 F.2d 1160 (9th Cir. 1992).

Pryor v. Municipal Court, 25 Cal.3d 238, 254, 599 P.2d 636, 645, 158 Cal. Rptr. 330, 339 (1979).

Quick v. Donaldson Co., 90 F.3d 1372 (8th Cir. 1990).

R.A.V. v. City of St. Paul, 112 S.Ct. 2538 (1992).

Ratchford v. Gay Lib, 434 U.S. 1080 (1978).

Reagan v. Time, Inc., 468 U.S. 641 (1984).

Renton v. Playtime Theatres, 475 U.S. 41 (1986).

Reynolds v. United States, 98 U.S. 145 (1878).

Rich v. Secretary of the Army, 516 F.Supp. 621 (1981).

Risinger v. Ohio Bureau of Worker's Compensation, 883 F.2d 475 (6th Cir. 1989).

Roberts v. United States Jaycees, 468 U.S. 609 (1984).

Roe v. Wade, 410 U.S. 113 (1973).

Romer v. Evans, 64 LW 4353 (1996).

Roth v. United States, 354 U.S. 476 (1957).

Rowland v. Mad River Local School District, 730 F.2d 444 (6th Cir. 1984), *cert denied*, 470 U.S. 1009, *reh'g denied*, 105 S. Ct. 2127 (1985).

Runyon v. McCrary, 427 U.S. 160 (1976).

Rust v. Sullivan, 500 U.S. 173 (1991).

Ryczek v. Guest Services, Inc., 877 F.Supp. 754 (D.D.C. 1995).

Saal v. Middendorf, 427 F.Supp.192 (11th Cir. 1980); *rev'd sub nom., Beller v. Middendorf*, 632 F.2d 788 (9th Cir. 1980).

Saint Francis College v. Al-Khazraji, 481 U.S. 604 (1987).

San Antonio Independent School District v. Rodriguez, 411 U.S. 1 (1973).

Saulpaugh v. Monroe Community Hospital, 4 F.3d 134 (2d Cir. 1993), *cert. denied* 114 S.Ct. 1189 (1994).

Schenck v. United States, 429 U.S. 47 (1919).

Schick v. State, 570 N.E.2d 918 (Ind. Ct. App. 1991).

Schneider v. State, 308 U.S. 147 (1939).

Schochet v. State, 580 A.D. (Ma. App. 1990).

Scott v. Macy (II), 402 F.2d (D.C. Cir. 1968).

Shaare Tefila Congregation v. Cobb, 481 U.S. 615 (1987).

Shahar v. Bowers, 58 FEP (BNA) 668 (N.D. GA., 1992).

Shahar v. Bowers, 836 F. Supp. 859 (N.D. Ga. 1993), *appeal pending*.

Shapiro v. Thompson, 394 U.S. 618 (1969).

Silva v. Municipal Court, 40 Cal. App.3d 733, 115 Cal. Rptr. 479 (1974).

Singer v. United States Civil Service Commission, 530 F.2d 247 (9th Cir. 1976), *vacated and remanded*, 429 U.S. 1035 (1977).

Skinner v. Oklahoma, 316 U.S. 535 (1942).

Smith v. Collins, 436 U.S. 916 (1978), *cert. denied.*

Smith v. Goguen, 415 U.S. 566 (1974).

Smith v. Liberty Mutual Insurance Co., 395 F.Supp. 1098 (N.D. Ga. 1975), *aff'd* 569 F.2d 325 (5th Cir. 1978).

Sommers v. Budget Marketing, Inc., 667 F.2d 748, 750 (8th Cir. 1982) (*per curiam*).

Speiser v. Randall, 357 U.S. 513 (1958).

Stanley v. Georgia, 394 U.S. 557 (1969).

State v. Bonanno, 245 La. 1117, 163 S.2d 72 (1964).

State v. Linsey, 310 So.2d 89 (La. 1975).

State v. Saunders, 75 N.J. 200, 381 A.2d 333 (1977).

State v. Stokes, 274 N.C. 409, 163 S.E.2d 770 (1968).

State v. Talley, 858 P.2d 217 (Wash. 1993).

State v. Vawter et al., 642 A.2d 349 (N.J. 1994).

State ex. rel. Grant v. Brown, 39 Ohio St. 2d 112, 313 N.E.2d 847 (1974) (*per curium*), *appeal dismissed and cert. denied sub nom. Duggan v. Brown*, 420 U.S. 916 (1975).

State of Michigan v. Schmidt, (Mi. 1996).

State of Missouri v. Thornton, 532 S.W.2d 37 (Mo. Ct. App. 1975).

State of Ohio v. Phipps, 389 N.E.2d 1128 (1979).

Steffan v. Cheney, 720 F.2d 74 (D.C. Cir. 1990), *rev'd*, 780 F.Supp. 1 (DDC 1991), *rev'd sub. nom. Steffan v. Aspin*, 8 F.3d 57 (DC Cir. 1993), *vacated and district court's judgment aff'd sub. nom., Steffan v. Perry*, 41 F.3d 677 (D.C. Cir. 1994) (*en banc*).

Steward v. United States, 364 A.2d 1205 (D.C. 1976).

Strailey v. Happy Times Nursery School, Inc., see *DeSantis* (1979).

Street v. New York, 394 U.S. 576 (1969).

Supre v. Ricketts, 92 F.2d 958 (10th Cir. 1986).

Terminiello v. Chicago, 337 U.S. 1 (1949).

Texas v. Johnson, 109 S.Ct. 2533 (1989).

Thomas v. Collins, 323 U.S. 516 (1945).

Thornburgh v. American College of Obstetricians and Gynecologists, 476 U.S. 747 (1986).

Time, Inc. v. Hill, 385 U.S. 374 (1967).

Tinker v. Des Moines Independent Community School District, 393 U.S. 503 (1969).

Torcaso v. Watkins, 367 U.S. 488 (1961).

Toward a Gayer Bicentennial Committee v. Rhode Island Bicentennial Foundation, 417 F. Supp. 632 (D.R.I. 1976).

Trimble v. Gordon, 430 U.S. 762 (1977).

Turner v. Safley, 482 U.S. 78 (1987).

Ulane v. Eastern Airlines, Inc., 742 F.2d 1081 (7th Cir. 1984), *cert. denied*, 471 U.S. 1017 (1985).

United States v. Carolene Products Co., 304 U.S. 144 (1938).

United States v. Coffeeville Consolidated School District, 513 F.2d 244 (5th Cir. 1975).

United States v. Kauten, 33 F.2d 703 (2d Cir. 1943).

United States v. MacIntosh, 283 U.S. 605 (1931).

United States v. O'Brien, 391 U.S. 367 (1968).

United States v. Schwimmer, 279 U.S. 644 (1929), *overruled, Giroward v. United States*, 328 U.S. 61 (1946).

United States v. Seeger, 380 U.S. 163 (1965).

U.S. Railroad Retirement Board v. Fritz, 449 U.S. 166 (1980).

UWM Post v. University of Wisconsin, 774 F.Supp. 1163 (E.D. Wis. 1991).

Valdes v. Lumbermen's Mutual Casualty Company, (The Kemper Group), 507 F.Supp. 10 (S.D. Fla. 1980).

Valentine v. Chrestensen, 316 U.S. 52 (1942).

Vallerga v. Department of Alcoholic Beverage Control, 53 Cal.2d 313, 347 P.2d 909 (1959).

Vandeventer v. Wabash National Corporation, 867 F. Supp. 790 (N.D. Ind. 1994).

Village of Skokie v. National Socialist Party of America, 366 N.E.2d 347 (1st Dir. 1977).

Virginia State Board of Pharmacy v. Virginia Citizens Consumer Council, 425 U.S. 748 (1976).

Voyles v. Ralph K. Davies Medical Center, 403 F.Supp. 456 (N.D. Cal. 1975), *aff'd* without published opinion, 570 F.2d 354 (9th Cir. 1978).

Walker v. City of Birmingham, 388 U.S. 307 (1967).

Wallace v. Jaffree, 472 U.S. 38 (1985).

Wards Cove Packing Co. v. Antonio, 490 U.S. 642 (1989).

Washington v. Davis, 426 U.S. 229 (1976).

Watkins v. United States, 847 F.2d 1329 (9th Cir. 1988), *withdrawn*, 875 F.2d 699 (9th Cir. 1989), *cert. denied*, 498 U.S. 957 (1990).

Watson v. Fort Worth Bank & Trust, 487 U.S. 977 (1988).

Weber v. Aetna Casualty & Surety Co., 406 U.S. 164 (1972).

Weinberger v. Wiesenfeld, 420 U.S. 636 (1975).

Weiss v. United States, 595 F.Supp. 1050 (5th Cir. 1984).

Welsh v. United States, 398 U.S. 333 (1970).

West Virginia State Board of Education v. Barnette, 319 U.S. 624 (1934).

Whitney v. California, 274 U.S. 357 (1927).

Widmar v. Vincent, 454 U.S. 263 (1981).

Williams v. Saxbe, 413 F.Supp. 654 (D.D.C. 1976).

Williamson v. A.G. Edwards & Sons, Inc., 876 F.2d 69 (8th Cir. 1989), *cert. denied*, 110 S.Ct. 1158 (1990).

Wisconsin v. Mitchell, 169 Wis.2d 153, 164 (1992), 113 S.Ct. 2194 (1993).

Woodley v. Maynard, 430 U.S. 705 (1977).

Woodward v. Moore, 451 F.Supp. 346 (D.D.C. 1978), *aff'd sub nom. Woodward v. United States*, 871 F.2d 1068 (Fed. Cir. 1989), *cert. denied*, 494 U.S. 1003 (1990).

Wrightson v. Pizza Hut of America, Inc., 99 F.3d 138 (4th Cir. 1996).

Yates v. United States, 354 U.S. 298 (1957).

Zablocki v. Redtail, 434 U.S. 374 (1978).

Zippes v. TWA, Inc., 445 U.S. 385 (1982).

Index

as subordinated by sodomy laws,
109–10, 112–13; as suspect classi-
fication, 81; suspect classification
status denied by Supreme Court,
60–61
Georgia, sodomy law in, 110–17
Gertz v. Robert Welch, Inc., 24
Gitlow v. New York, 18–19
Glad Day Bookstore (Boston), 39
Gomez, José, 42
Gooding v. Wilson, 19, 22, 107–8,
146
Greater Cincinnati Gay Society,
39–40
Greenwalt, Kent, 31, 32, 51–52
Grey, Thomas, 31, 32
Griggs v. Duke Power Co., 65
Guía Gay, 39
Gunther, Gerald, 21

Halley, Janet, 116
Hall, Radcliff, 39
Hardwick, Bowers v., 7, 58–60,
74, 82, 94 n.174, 109, 110–17,
166
Hate Crimes Statistics Act of 1990,
6–7, 103, 122–27, 135 n.141,
166
Hate speech: accommodationists on,
6, 30–32; civil libertarians on, 6,
23–27; civil rights adherents on, 6,
27–30; definition of, 1; directed at
sex/gender outsiders, 144, 164–65,
180; and fighting words doctrine,
139–41, 143, 146–48, 150–61,
179–80; and First Amendment,
1–2, 6–7; and Fourteenth Amendment, 1–2, 6–7, 29, 30, 157; and
homosexuality, 164–65; restrictions on, 1–2, 6–7, 27–30, 139–68,
157, 178–80; state court decisions
regarding, 139–49; Supreme Court
decisions regarding, 19–20, 24,
149–68; and Title VII, 1–2, 6–7,
148–49, 156–57, 159

Hellman, Lillian, 39
Helms Amendment to Interior De-
partment Appropriations Act, 13
n.22, 36–37, 117–21, 166, 178
Helms, Jesse, 36–37, 117, 119–20,
121, 178
Herek, Gregory, 123
Hess v. Indiana, 22
Heterocentrism, 107, 113, 114, 122,
124, 180
Heterosexism, 107, 113, 114, 122,
124, 136 n.142, 164–65, 180
Heterosexuality: expression of,
37–38, 42; and right to privacy,
111; as societal norm, 5, 51, 68,
107, 113, 114, 122, 124; and Supreme Court, 112
*Holloway v. Arthur Anderson and
Co.*, 64–65
Holmes, Oliver Wendell, 22, 26; on
First Amendment, 17–18
Homophobia, 107, 113, 124, 136
n.142, 141, 144–45, 164–65
Homosexuality: Catholic church on,
4, 165–66; Equal Employment Opportunity Commission (EEOC) on,
64; expression of, 37–38, 42; as
form of dissent, 38; in Hate
Crimes Statistics Act, 125; and
hate speech, 164–65;
homosexual-advance defense, 15
n.33; and Judeo-Christian tradition, 73; Motion Picture Code ban
on references to, 39; and right to
privacy, 111; and sexual harassment, 68–69; and sodomy laws,
108–17; and solicitation laws,
103–8; and speech codes, 141,
144–45; as subject to legal discrimination, 55–59. *See also* Affectional orientation/preference;
Gender identity; *Sex/gender outsiders*
Hughes, Holly, 120, 121
Hunter, James, 75–76

About the Author

MARTHA T. ZINGO is an Associate Professor of Political Science at Oakland University. Among her earlier publications is the co-authored *Nameless Persons* (Praeger, 1994).

ISBN 0-275-95249-5

90000>

EAN

9 780275 952495

HARDCOVER BAR CODE